Demography and Religion in India

For my family

Demography and Religion in India

Sriya Iyer

OXFORD
UNIVERSITY PRESS

OXFORD
UNIVERSITY PRESS

YMCA Library Building, Jai Singh Road, New Delhi 110 001

Oxford University Press is a department of the University of Oxford. It furthers the
University's objective of excellence in research, scholarship, and education
by publishing worldwide in

Oxford   New York

Auckland   Bangkok   Buenos Aires   Cape Town   Chennai
Dar es Salaam   Delhi   Hong Kong   Istanbul   Karachi   Kolkata
Kuala Lumpur   Madrid   Melbourne   Mexico City   Mumbai   Nairobi
São Paulo   Shanghai   Singapore   Taipei   Tokyo   Toronto

with an associated company in Berlin

Oxford is a registered trade mark of Oxford University Press
in the UK and in certain other countries

Published in India
By Oxford University Press, New Delhi

© Oxford University Press 2002

ISBN 019 5660 48 X

Typeset in Giovanni Book
by Eleven Arts, Keshav Puram, Delhi 110035
Printed in India by Rashtriya Printers, Delhi 110032
Published by Manzar Khan, Oxford University Press
YMCA Library Building, Jai Singh Road, New Delhi 110 001

Acknowledgements

This book which describes the influence of religion on demographic decisions made by women and men in south India would not have been possible without the support of several extraordinary individuals.

The first is Srilata Iyer, my mother, who traversed the Deccan patiently and enthusiastically in order to conduct my fieldwork with me. A universal problem with survey data is that it is difficult to induce people to reveal their private choices to a researcher. Economists routinely distinguish between agents' 'stated preferences' and their 'revealed preferences'. Anthropologists often comment on the difficulties of approaching a rural society as an outsider in order to understand the manner in which these communities make choices about aspects of their lives. It is even more difficult for a young urban woman to persuade predominantly rural women to reveal their views on extremely sensitive issues such as their sexuality or religious beliefs that form the core of their personal lives. Therefore, in order to allay their inherent suspicions of one 'young enough to be my granddaughter' as one elderly woman remarked, my mother accompanied me to interview the women in Ramanagaram. Identifying with an Indian woman, who was a wife and mother like themselves and who was putting herself through some inconvenience to help her daughter always struck a chord of empathy with the women. Moreover, as many as 40 per cent of the women interviewed remarked that they thoroughly approved of my work being thus chaperoned. In this context Devamma from village C, asked pointedly, 'Amma (mother), I definitely approve of you coming here to help your daughter with her work, but I have a question. You sent her all alone, unchaperoned, across the seas and far away from you to study in England; yet within our own country, you chose to come with her to Ramanagaram. Why?'.

Srilata Iyer's support is linked with the exceptionally kind and calm counsel of my father, S. R. Iyer, who provided crucial comments on several chapters, who made access to Ramanagaram possible for me and without whose support I would never have ventured 'across the seas and far away' to Cambridge.

In Karnataka, I thank Sucharita and S. Ranganathan, for their home away from home at the Indian Institute of Science in Bangalore. The late Professor M.N. Srinivas first suggested that I undertake my fieldwork in Ramanagaram, and looked over my questionnaire. The staff of the Ramanagaram branch of the SBI helped with statistical data and local information. I thank Syed Shahabuddin and Iqbal Banu particularly for making us feel so very welcome. This study would not have been possible without the co-operation of the 201 brave Hindu, Muslim, and Christian women of Ramanagaram *taluk*, who put up with all the ninety-three questions so willingly, and so readily took me into their hearts and homes.

At Cambridge, I thank Sheilagh Ogilvie, my doctoral supervisor, whose guidance and friendship have been invaluable. Partha Dasgupta, and Michael Lipton provided detailed comments on the original dissertation and much encouragement thereafter. For helpful discussions and comments on different aspects of this research, I thank Shaun Bond, Vani Borooah, Raj Chandavarkar, Jean Drèze, Jeremy Edwards, Geoff Harcourt, Andrew Harvey, Jane Humphries, Colin Rowat, Robert Rowthorn, Paul Seabright, Melvyn Weeks, and participants at the session on religion and fertility at the 2001 meetings of the Population Association of America in Washington, D.C.

Soumya and Mukund Rajan, Keshav Desiraju, Usha Rajaram, and the Kathir Velus provided affectionate encouragement, as did the Fellows of St Catharine's College. The Centre for History and Economics at King's College, Cambridge first sparked my interest in religion and demography by providing me with a grant in 1993–4 to undertake research in Indià. Subsequently, my doctoral dissertation was supported by a Lloyds Research Studentship from Newnham College (1995–8), a Cambridge Commonwealth Trust Scholarship (1995–8), and a Population Council Social Science Research Fellowship (1998–9). The additional research undertaken for this book is supported by a British Academy Post-doctoral Fellowship. All of these grants are very gratefully acknowledged. Kavita Iyengar and Shreemoyee Patra of Oxford University Press have been patient and helpful in bringing this book to publication.

Last, but by no means least, I thank my husband Chander Kathir Velu, for his constant support and inspiration.

Contents

Tables

Tables xi

ILLUSTRATIONS

chapter one

Introduction

> Those who move neither forward nor backward are not
> men of the Word, nor refiners of essence.
> Poor craftsman, misunderstanding the Word, they are those
> who spin useless thread for themselves.[1]

The conflict between the sacred and the secular has always rested at the heart of India's chequered history. The former defines the role for ideology, religious beliefs and their expression, value systems, and their influence on a society. The latter follows the impulse toward economic betterment and is mirrored particularly in the competitive nature of India's political process.[2] For most in the Indian subcontinent, deep spirituality coexists with competition, and both factors routinely govern day-to-day living. Religion is linked intimately with the economics of survival.

However, where these two factors are interlinked to generate divisions along religious lines, the outcome has been manifest in the resurgence of what is termed 'communalism', which has been largely, though not entirely, a feature of the post-colonial period. Communalism is defined as a phenomenon which uses religion not merely as a set of beliefs or ethical values but as a means to establish the identity of a social community, to attain economic and political ends. This has sometimes involved authoritative postures which seek to impose cohesion and

[1] Le Mee, 1975: Rg Veda verse X.71.9: 147.

[2] It is recognized that political competition is also often about religion, a factor that is evident in India and in other countries characterized by religious pluralism.

uniformity over diverse members of a religious community in the process of identity-formation, coupled with antagonistic attitudes towards members of rival religious groups in the quest for economic 'rents'. Though communal conflict in India has taken place between Hindus and Sikhs, and Hindus and Christians, it is mainly Hindu–Muslim conflict which has recurred the most over the decades.

In the process of identity-formation and the common quest for issues which emphasize difference between religions, disciplines which are often thought unrelated to religion are routinely brought in as part of the armoury in the confrontations (verbal and otherwise) over seats in educational institutions, government jobs, or political office. A major issue, which has been the subject of many different claims and counter-claims, is fertility, and demographic and economic differences have been shown to have exacerbated communal conflicts in the past (Iyer, 1994). In a country of such a large population as India, where some members of virtually all of the main religious communities can claim to be a party to high fertility, it seems, at the outset, absurd to stress fertility differentials by religion. However, many political leaders (and others) have made statements about the fertility behaviour or demographic experiences of members of other religions. Most of these statements have been pure rhetoric and rabble-rousing, at best, or blatant untruths, at worst.[3] In fact, there has not been very much academic or scientific work which has dealt specifically or explicitly with the existence or causes of demographic differentials by religion in India.[4] This issue has not been dealt with in detail by the Indian Census, which only in 1995 made public demographic information by religion, but which mainly restricts itself to state and district level comparisons.

The demographic information made available by the Indian Census of 1981, 1991, and 2001 suggests that Muslims have higher fertility than Hindus, that this may outweigh differences in mortality, and that without controlling for the effect of any other factor which might affect fertility,

---

[3]For an example, M.V. Ramamurthy writes, 'Muslims are by and large emotional and aggressive. Often in communal troubles they take the initiative though ultimately they are the worse sufferers. The Muslims, have not, till now, taken up the family planning programme with zeal and hence their population is growing at a higher rate than that of the Hindus. ... At this rate their population may become considerable in relation to the total population of our country. This is creating alarm in the minds of Hindus.' This extract is taken from the foreword to a book (originally in the Telugu language and now translated into English) by Subbamma, 1988: vi.

[4]Some exceptions are Shariff, 1993; Jeffery and Jeffery, 1997; Moulasha and Rama Rao, 1999; Jeffery and Jeffery, 2000.

TABLE 1.1: ALL-INDIA AGE-SPECIFIC FERTILITY RATES BY RELIGIOUS GROUPS, 1999

| Religion | \multicolumn{7}{c}{Age in completed years} | TFR |
	15–19	20–4	25–9	30–4	35–9	40–4	45–9	15–49
Hindu	0.06	0.27	0.24	0.14	0.08	0.03	0.02	4.2
Muslim	0.09	0.34	0.30	0.21	0.15	0.04	0.03	5.8
Christian	0.04	0.17	0.12	0.07	0.03	–	–	2.1
Others	0.02	0.23	0.26	0.14	0.07	0.03	0.03	3.9

Source: Shariff, 1999: Appendix A.8.5, p. 331.

such differences will persist, mainly because the process of demographic transition has started earlier for Hindus than for Muslims (Goyal, 1990). Data provided by the NCAER (National Council of Applied Economic Research) (see Table 1.1) on age-specific fertility rates by religious groups in India also suggests that age-specific fertility varies between Hindus and Muslims in India today (Shariff, 1999).

The data suggest that the all-India total fertility rate (TFR) for Muslims is considerably higher than for Hindus. Age-specific fertility rates also indicate that Muslim women are bearing a larger number of children at earlier ages than are Hindu and Christian women. However, the Census information and the data provided by the NCAER's Human Development Report consider mean levels in fertility only, and with the exception of the woman's age, do not control for the effect of other socio-economic influences on fertility.

The present study is an attempt to redress this deficiency. It adopts a two-pronged approach to studying the determinants of fertility in the context of religion. On the one hand, the study is a theoretical discussion of religion and fertility in the context of population policy in particular and development policy more widely. On the other hand, it also adopts a micro-demographic approach to studying the determinants of fertility in a small cluster of communities in south India (which have witnessed communal conflicts in the past), and combines this approach with economic and econometric analysis. This study does not, and cannot, claim to be representative of the behaviour of all of India's population. However, it does hope to capture the behaviour and demographic decision-making of some Hindu, Muslim, and Christian women in rural Karnataka, and suggests a framework for analysing issues of religion and population. Further, by integrating the discussion of economic factors such as income, with social and historical factors such as consanguinity, and the change in social norms occasioned by 'ideational change', it hopes to illustrate the necessity for such a multi-pronged approach to the study of fertility determinants in India. Finally, this study seeks to provide an account of the interplay between the economic, demographic, and religious factors which influence, in India, women's age at first marriage, their contraceptive adoption, and their fertility. In so doing, this study also hopes to assess the possible implications for state-level population policies in India, which may need to take into account differences in nuptiality, contraceptive adoption, and fertility across religious groups.

Religion performs many roles in a society. First, it can be a powerful means of expressing unfulfilled aspirations. Religion may also function as a means to construct an identity and as a tool of dissent. Historically, religion in India has long been used as a tool of dissent. For example, the *Bhakti* movement in the late fifteenth and early sixteenth centuries mobilized popular support against the emphasis on rituals and the dogmatic finality characteristic of Hinduism and Islam at the time. If we examine the history of communalism in India, we find that communal incidents are not unique to post-Independent years, but are evident as early as the eighteenth century and in the colonial period as well (Bayly, 1983; Pandey, 1990). The historical roots of communalism illustrate that organized caste hierarchies, the ability of religion to aid in identity-formation, and the fact that economic success depended on rent-seeking *vis-à-vis* the colonial state were the three factors which initially contributed to the rise of communalism. In particular, the origins of communalism as we see it today have been linked to 'predatory commercialization' due to imperfect markets in land and labour which developed in the colonial period (Bagchi, 1991: 193–218).

Coming to the twentieth century, communal organizations, which numbered less than a dozen in 1951, today number more than 500 with many millions enrolled as members. Whereas only 61 districts in 1961 were affected by communal riots, this rose to 250 out of a total of 350 districts in all of India by 1987 (*India Today*, 15 June 1987: 38). Compared with the earlier decades, the 1980s and the 1990s have witnessed a new phase of communal confrontation, characterized by great loss of life and property, detailed planning, and a particular concentration in industrial or commercial centres. Moreover, in the late 1980s, there has been an exacerbation of military postures around two major issues: first, the disputed mosque in Ayodhya, and second, Muslim personal law, centred around the Shah Bano case.[5] Thus, in the 1980s and 1990s, and most

---

[5]On 23 April 1985, the Supreme Court of India upheld an order granting maintenance to a Muslim woman, Shah Bano of Indore, from her divorced husband under Section 125

recently following the demolition of the Babri Masjid mosque on 6 December 1992, be it in Punjab, Assam, Bhiwandi, Telangana, Hyderabad, Meerut, Surat, or Ahmedabad, communal confrontations have left no corner of India untouched.[6] In the 1990s, and the disputed mosque at Ayodhya is a case in point, religion has come to be used not merely as the reflection of personal ideology but also as a theological weapon to highlight the insecurity of the poor or inequality between classes, or for 'rent-seeking' purposes due to group competition, which enables religious groups to gain legitimacy both in the eyes of the masses and in the eyes of the state. Perhaps this is the consequence of recognizing that in the specific context of India's caste and social structure, group mobility is essential for individual mobility.[7] This is because in such a variegated country as India, both under the colonial and the post-colonial state, control of the legislative process has been essential for economic gain; religious affiliation provides a unified way of reducing the transactions costs of forming rent-seeking groups.[8]

One way of strengthening the group may be greater fertility; this is

---

of the Criminal Procedure Code (Cr. PC). The Muslim orthodoxy reacted virulently, claiming that the court had interfered with the Koranic interpretations of Muslim personal law. The then Rajiv Gandhi government issued the Muslim Women (Protection of Rights on Divorce) Act in 1986, which legislated that Muslims were to be kept out of the purview of section 125 of the Cr. PC. This was soon followed by the government placating Hindu communalists by granting permission to open the disputed Babri Masjid at Ayodhya for Hindu worship and to perform *shilanyas* (foundation-laying ceremonies) on the disputed site for construction of a temple to Rama in October 1989, just prior to the general elections. Both injudicious concessions, motivated primarily by political considerations, resulted in widespread communal riots thereafter.

[6]Pandey, 1991; Sarkar, 1981; Chandra, 1984; Engineer, 1984b; Engineer, 1986; Engineer, 1991; Engineer, 1993b; Engineer, 1994; Vanaik, 1991; Balagopal, 1992.

[7]For example, one Muslim woman interviewed in the present study mentioned that the main community rivalry in Ramanagaram town was between the Gowdas and the Muslims, and this was especially marked at election time. These are the two relatively prosperous communities in the town, which very often fought for seats to the local panchayat, the municipality, and the state legislature. In Ramanagaram, the local committees of the political parties both mobilized residents for political activities and helped them to obtain benefits under slum improvement and welfare programmes.

[8]For more on transactions costs and rent-seeking, see Stigler, 1993: 258–73. It is recognized also that while rent-seeking to some extent explains why people seek religious affiliation, this does not explain entirely India's few, but large, movements of socio-religious protest conversion to Buddhism, Christianity, or Islam, where converts sought to escape the dogmatic finality of the caste system and avoid ascriptive rent-paying. Rent-seeking also does not explain why a majority of religionists stay on for many consecutive generations in the religion of their ancestors' affiliation. I am grateful to Michael Lipton for alerting me to these considerations.

the 'minority group consciousness' hypothesis for explaining high fertility among some ethnic or religious groups, which will be discussed further in Chapter 3. Another way may be to gain mass support by suggesting that for any one group, members of other religious groups might soon come to outnumber the group due to their high fertility, different marriage practices, or low contraceptive use. Much of this debate, however, at least among religious or political leaders, has masked the fact that there may be real demographic differences between members of different religious groups in India, but differences which have more to do with socio-economic disparities than with the content of different religious beliefs *per se*. Consequently, it is necessary to examine from an academic perspective if this has any consequences for fertility decisions. In order to do so, the present study examines the role of religion, compared to other factors, in influencing three major aspects of demographic behaviour—nuptiality, contraceptive use, and fertility in India. This examination is considered valuable in order to understand the relationship more widely between the economic, religious, and cultural determinants of fertility and their consequence for economic and social policies in India.

THE THEORETICAL FRAMEWORK

Following Bongaarts (1978: 105–32), the proximate and nonproximate determinants of fertility are distinguished. The factors are then identified which, in Indian society in the 1990s, might theoretically influence both fertility itself and two of the proximate determinants (the age at first marriage and the decision to use contraception). In modelling the determinants of nuptiality, contraceptive choice, and fertility, certain socio-economic variables are taken into account which are postulated in the theoretical literature to exert an influence on these demographic decisions, such as education, income, age, and access to infrastructure. However, as we are particularly interested in Hindu–Muslim demographics, the main focus is on the role of religion. Religion is conceptualized as affecting demography in two ways: first, through its philosophical content (or 'particularized theology'), and second, in terms of 'characteristics' or socio-economic differences between members of different religious groups (Chamie, 1977: 365–82).

The analysis undertaken is presented at two levels—first, a macro-level perspective that examines issues of religion and the proximate determinants of fertility in a theoretical framework; and second, a micro-level perspective that then tests these postulates on an empirical dataset obtained by a detailed anthropological study of a region of south India. The issues raised in the theoretical discussion are compared and contrasted throughout with the findings from the empirical case-study of Ramanagaram *taluk* (a cluster of villages grouped together for the purpose of revenue collection) to highlight the relationships between religion and reproduction in India today.

In order to study these issues empirically, micro-level fieldwork was conducted and primary data collected in a cluster of communities in the south Indian state of Karnataka.[9] The communities were Ramanagaram town and five villages in the taluk of Ramanagaram in southern Karnataka. The core of the fieldwork consisted of detailed interviews of a sample of 201 rural Hindu, Muslim, and Christian women. The interviews involved ninety-three questions administered from a carefully designed questionnaire, which collected information about the respondent's personal characteristics, the structure of her household, the decisions made by her and her husband on contraception and reproduction, and the importance of religion to the respondent and her family.

Chapter 2 provides an overview of religion, economic development, and population policy in India. Chapter 3 presents a theoretical discussion of the relationship between religion and demography. Chapter 4 discusses the anthropological study—information about Ramanagaram taluk, the data set, and the sampling methodology. Chapter 5 presents the 'census' information on the 201 women interviewed. Chapters 6–8 present the main theoretical findings of the research on religion and the proximate determinants of fertility and relate them to the results from the main empirical analysis of the data, which was undertaken both quantitatively and qualitatively. The quantitative component involved testing models of marriage age, contraceptive choice, and fertility decisions using multiple regression analysis with ordinary least squares (OLS), and logistic regression (LOGIT) techniques. The aim was to investigate whether there were any differences across religions in marriage, fertility, and the decision to use contraception, even after controlling for various economic, social, and biological factors. The qualitative component of the analysis focused on women's descriptions of their religious observance, their opinions on their families, and their views about contraception. This was done in order to provide ethnographic evidence to substantiate and to give interpretative depth to the quantitative findings. Chapter 9 puts

[9] I undertook my fieldwork in a region studied in previous decades both by the Mysore Population Study, and by Caldwell, Reddy and Caldwell, enabling me to make comparisons with these two studies. See *UN*, 1961; Caldwell, Reddy and Caldwell, 1983: 343–61.

forward the major conclusions of the present study, and suggests a possible reorientation of India's population policy in light of the theoretical discussion and empirical findings.

OVERVIEW OF THE KEY FINDINGS

In India, as in the Ramanagaram sample, Muslim marriage age is higher than Hindu marriage age, Muslim contraceptive use is lower than Hindu contraceptive use, and Muslim fertility is, on average, one child higher than Hindu fertility. For example, the 1995 National Family Health Survey (NHFS) found that the mean age at first marriage is approximately 17 years for Hindus, 16 years for Muslims and over 20 years for Christians in all of India (International Institute of Population Sciences (IIPS), 1995). There are approximately 42 per cent of Hindu couples currently using contraception compared with 29 per cent of Muslims and 34 per cent of Christians. The survey also showed that the number of children surviving is on average 2.6 for Hindus, 3.1 for Muslims, and 2.7 for Christians in all of India. Most studies of fertility differences in India stop with such comparisons between average values. The analysis undertaken in the present study decomposes the potential influence of religion into two effects (as discussed in Chapter 3). First, this study considers the 'pure religion effect' which deals with women's beliefs about their religion and its influence on reproductive decisions; the influence of priests and women's consequent religious practice. Secondly, this study examines the 'characteristics effect', that is, the extent to which religious differences in fertility are dependent on variations in other socio-economic factors, and their consequent impact on fertility. The analysis concludes that neither the 'pure religion effect' nor the 'characteristics effect' differs significantly between Hindus and Muslims as regards their marriage age (as discussed in Chapter 6) or their decision to use contraception (as discussed in Chapter 7). However, there are differences between Hindus and Muslims in the effect on their fertility of some socio-economic characteristics such as education, access to fuel infrastructure, and son-preference (as discussed in Chapter 8). There are also differences in the effect of religion between Hindus and Christians, and between Muslims and Christians. Furthermore, education has a different effect on contraceptive practice for Christians than it does for the other two religious groups.

The study therefore concludes that Hindu–Muslim differences in fertility outcomes are the result of differences between these two groups in characteristics such as female education, and the manner in which these characteristics affect demographic outcomes. However, the most important conclusion from the findings is that different socio-economic characteristics affect religious groups in India in different ways. This has important implications for population policy in particular and for development policy more widely.

OMITTED EFFECTS OF RELIGION ON FERTILITY AND SPECIAL FEATURES OF THE SAMPLE AREA

The conclusions derived from the present study do need to be qualified by acknowledging that there may exist other effects of religion on fertility which this study does not attempt to address, and certain characteristics of Ramanagaram *taluk* and the sample which are particular to this part of India.

In addition to the 'pure religion effect' and the 'characteristics effect', there are five other ways in which religion might affect fertility or its proximate determinants, but which are not dealt with explicitly in the present study, either because some information is extremely sensitive and is therefore difficult to uncover in fieldwork, or because the data was collected in five villages and the town of Ramanagaram, all of which lie in close proximity, and may therefore be too homogeneous to test certain hypotheses (as discussed here and in Chapter 4).

First, there are ecological effects. Competition between Hindus and Muslims in a multi-faith area might lead both Hindus and Muslims to have higher fertility, marry earlier, or use contraception less than in villages which contain members of one religious group only. This could not be tested explicitly for the Ramanagaram data set because the Christians and Muslims resided only in Ramanagaram town and villages B and C, but not at all in villages A, D, and E.

The second way in which religion might influence fertility is through 'variability effects'. That is, Hindus, Muslims, and Christians could differ significantly not only in the mean values of demographic variables but also in the distributional features of these variables. This possibility is examined in Chapter 5.

Religion may also affect fertility through its effects on other proximate determinants, for example, through influencing length of breastfeeding, duration of couple separation during the fertile period because of divorce or migration, or willingness to resort to abortion. The mean levels of these variables and their distributions might also affect the fertility of couples. The present study does not deal with these issues because such information is very sensitive and attempts to collect it through fieldwork are notoriously difficult.

There may also be differences in society's treatment of Hindus and Muslims that cause a varied acquisition of socio-economic and other characteristics. This possibility is extremely difficult (if not impossible) to quantify and must, therefore, be left unanalysed in a study such as the present one.

Finally, the empirical component of this study does not consider the impact of infant and child mortality as a proximate determinant because this factor did not vary perceptibly between Hindus and Muslims in Ramanagaram, as shown in Table 1.2. The mean distribution of infant and child deaths did not vary significantly between Hindus and Muslims in the Ramanagaram sample. The sample of Christians was too small (N=14) to make comparisons with the other two religious groups meaningful, given that none of the Christian women interviewed reported any child deaths.

It is possible that the higher level of education for Christian women relative to the Hindu and Muslim women accounts for the lack of child deaths reported among them. This may also explain in part the lower fertility of the Christians (as discussed in Chapter 8). However, such a conclusion is largely speculative, as the number of Christians interviewed is very small relative to the number of Hindus and Muslims. The small number of child deaths reported for all three religious groups may also reflect the positive role being played by the maternal and child healthcare programme in the state of Karnataka.

It is also necessary to understand that the role of infant and child mortality in an analysis of religion and fertility is very complex, a factor that is evident clearly when we look at the all-India data (see Table 1.3). The data show that not only is infant mortality across the Indian states lower for the Christians than for the Hindus, it is also much lower for the Muslims than for the Hindus. Moreover, this difference is also apparent for under-5 mortality, where the performance of the Muslims is distinctly superior to that of the Hindus. The differences in infant and child mortality between Muslims and Hindus is even more marked among women who are married more recently. More detailed state-level

TABLE 1.2: INFANT AND CHILD DEATHS, RAMANAGARAM SAMPLE (1996)

Reported infant and child deaths	All women	Hindus	Muslims	Christians
Mean	0.16	0.15	0.21	0.00
Standard deviation	0.03	0.04	0.06	0.00

TABLE 1.3: ALL-INDIA INFANT AND CHILD MORTALITY BY RELIGION, 1999

Religion	Infant mortality by marital duration of ever-married women				Under-5 mortality by marital duration of ever-married women			
	0–9	10–19	20+	All	0–9	10–19	20+	All
Hindu	69	79	99	86	88	110	139	119
Muslim	52	65	93	75	69	97	136	110
Christian	32	56	88	61	36	67	103	71
Others	83	79	82	81	92	114	112	109

Source: Shariff, 1999: Appendix A.8.6, p. 333.

evidence from India has also shown that there is little difference between Hindus and Muslims with respect to child mortality (Drèze and Sen, 1995). The most pronounced difference in all of India is not between Hindus on the one hand and Muslims on the other. Rather, it is between Hindus and Muslims in the north Indian states compared with their counterparts in south India. This suggests that region may matter more than religion in explaining fertility differentials in India.[10] This also suggests that the interrelationships between religion and fertility are complex, and may need to be explored independently of changes in infant and child mortality.

As discussed in Chapter 4, the sample of women analysed was selected from the population in Ramanagaram taluk in Bangalore rural district in southern Karnataka. There are some features of this district which are unique and which may qualify some of the conclusions of the present study. First, as discussed in Chapter 4, the villages covered in the sample are really peri-urban. Both here and in the urban areas, one could possibly expect more homogeneous fertility-related behaviour than in other parts of rural India. As shown in Chapter 4, the villages also have much higher male–female ratios and different age structures as compared to that in some other parts of India. As discussed in Chapter 5, the Muslims who live in Ramanagaram are better off and more urbanized as compared to some Muslim communities in other parts of India. As explained in Chapter 4, the sample was chosen specifically to examine whether religion exercised an impact on fertility even at a relatively high socio-economic level, and in areas where poverty did not compound demographic differences. However, it must be acknowledged that the conclusions which emerge from studying religious differentials in fertility

[10]Sopher, 1980; Drèze and Sen, 1995; Agnihotri, 2000: 354.

in the Ramanagaram sample may not be applicable universally to more typically rural, demographically structured, and poorer populations.

After taking into account these caveats, this study nevertheless hopes to serve two purposes. First, it seeks to identify the determinants of two proximate influences on fertility (nuptiality and contraceptive choice) and of fertility outcomes in India. Second, it attempts to assess the implications of taking into account religious differences in marriage age, contraceptive choice, and fertility for the formulation of state population policies in India, as well as in other countries characterized by religious pluralism. In doing so, this study hopes also to present a realistic account of the demographic decision-making of the women of Ramanagaram taluk, who have so generously shared their views and their experiences.

Section one

Religion and Reproduction

chapter two

Preaching, Planning, and Procreation
An Overview of Religion, Economic
Development, and Population Policy
in India

> There has been a difference of a generation or so in the
> development of the Hindu and Muslim middle classes, and that
> difference continues to show itself in many directions—political,
> economic and other. It is this lag which produces a psychology
> of fear among the Muslims.
>
> —Nehru, 1946

C ommunalism in India today is a multi-faceted occurrence whose
very complexity—involving religious, historical, political, and
socio-economic roots—defies a simple cause–effect relationship.
Government policy towards communalism has been largely dissociated
from government policy towards population and economic development.
The first two sections of this chapter review first colonial and then post-
Independence development policy in the context of religion. These sections
argue that demographic and economic change in developing societies
does not need necessarily to lead to social conflict. Yet, demographic and
economic factors are translated into communal conflicts in India, because
they are shaped by the specific nature of religious and caste identities,
the hierarchical relations between social and religious groups, the
political system, and the effects of a post-colonial history that collectively
and uniquely comprise India today. It is only when viewed in this
specific socio-political context that it can be concluded that there are
two economic factors which have contributed to the resurgence of Indian
communalism. First, communalism is the product of insecurity and
inequality—between classes, regions, or religious groups. Second, it is
fuelled by rent-seeking amongst rival factions, which are all claimants

on scarce resources. Driven by perceptions of demographic and economic disadvantage, that is based on an inaccurate perception of the nature and causes of demographic realities, their demands are being articulated increasingly in a religious idiom. The third section of this chapter presents an overview of India's population policy as it has evolved since the First Five-Year Plan, and provides suggestions for a possible reorientation of this policy in the context of religion. It argues that population policy in future could benefit from being reoriented by integrating sensitively religious differentials in population with more general development-related policies towards education and family planning. It focuses, in particular, on the New Population Policy of 2000 and its consequences for future economic development.

COLONIALISM AND COMMUNALISM

As an explanation for communalism, the imperialist theory of 'divide and rule' was attractive to many nationalist leaders during India's freedom movement. Nehru (1936) remarks in his autobiography that

It is interesting to trace British policy since the rising of 1857 and its relation to the communal problem. ... Fundamentally and inevitably, it has been one of preventing the Hindu and the Muslim from acting together and of playing off one community against another.

These leaders also argued that imperial powers used communal riots as a defence against the independence movement led by the Congress; however, the economic impact of colonialism that created the initial conditions for strife provided fertile ground for the policy of 'divide and rule' to succeed (Sarkar, 1981). This argument is supported by the fact that communal incidents are not unique to the colonial and post-Independence years, but were evident as early as the eighteenth century.

In the eighteenth century, there were communal riots in Ahmedabad in 1714, in Kashmir in 1719–20, in Delhi in 1729, and in Vidarbha in 1786. For the nineteenth century, historians report evidence of incidents in Benaras (1809–15), Koil (1820), Moradabad and Kashipur (1833), and Bareilly, Kanpur, and Allahabad (1837–52) (Bayly, 1983). However, communal incidents were not a regular aspect of provincial life in the nineteenth century (Indian Statutory Commission Report, 1930: 97–107). Riots were localized in East Bengal (1907), Peshawar (1910), Ayodhya (1912), Agra (1913), Shahabad (1917), and Katarpur (1918). Between 1920 and 1924, there were riots in Malegaon, Multan, Lahore, Saharanpur, Amritsar, Allahabad, Calcutta, Delhi, Gulbarga, Kohat, Lucknow, and

Nagpur. In southern and western India, there were no significant riots until 1928 when they affected Bangalore, Nasik, Surat, and Hyderabad. There were major riots in Calcutta and Bombay in 1926 and 1928. The Civil Disobedience Movement of 1942 yielded fresh outbursts of communal violence, which have been attributed by some historians to imperial forces that tried to control the struggle for independence (Sarkar, 1981). The most serious communal clashes however, were in 1946 and took place, at times repeatedly, in Ahmedabad, Calcutta, Noakhali, Bhagalpur, Dacca, Patna, Bombay, and Allahabad. While the imminent transfer of power was the proximate cause of these riots, the impact of colonialism and the hierarchical structure of castes and religious groups that created the preconditions for rent-seeking must not be overlooked.

One aspect of colonialism that economic historians of India have been particularly concerned with is the inequitable and uneven development between regions, religious groups, and economic classes that took place in the colonial period (Gopal, 1991). Colonialism came first to Bengal. A large body of affluent Hindus took advantage of the new avenues for learning implied by colonial policy. As is well known, this encouraged the spread of education, particularly in English, and allowed employment in the civil administration and other better-paying occupations in law, medicine, and education (Basu and Amin, 2000). The Hindu upper castes were quick to seize the opportunity. Education for the rest of the country, such as for populations in the north and the west which had greater proportions of upper-caste Muslims who could avail of these opportunities, came only with increased British dominance in the late nineteenth century. Nehru's observation in his autobiography about the 'generation gap' in education levels between religious groups may be attributed perhaps to this uneven pattern of regional development.

Economic historians have argued also that the gap between religious groups widened due to 'discriminating interventionism' undertaken by the colonial administration. Imperfectly competitive rural markets in land and labour and the commercialization of agriculture led to exploitation and the well-documented 'drain of wealth' (Bagchi, 1970; 1991). This was because the state collected land revenue and was the ultimate owner of all land, but it was divorced from the tiller by a multi-layered strata of landlords and other intermediaries whose rights to the proceeds of land were also legitimized, and who could therefore claim economic rents. There were also imperfect markets in labour because labourers in agriculture were paid less than their marginal product and because employment opportunities outside agriculture were restricted (Bagchi, 1991). Against this economic backdrop, the colonial state allocated

seats for public office for legislative or party membership according to
religion and caste. This served only to heighten the level of communal
awareness which fluctuated with government-sponsored withdrawal or
offering of concessions to particular religions or castes.

Thus, two aspects of the economic impact of colonialism are crucial
to understanding the subsequent nature of communal relations under
the post-colonial state: first, the greater access of the upper classes to the
benefits of education, jobs, and economic rents, and second, imperfectly
competitive rural markets in land and labour, which fostered rent-seeking
vis-à-vis the colonial state, and which simultaneously created greater
impoverishment and insecurity. When viewed against this backdrop of
uneven gains, religion acted as a tool of dissent to legitimize the concerns
of rent-seeking interest groups in their negotiations with the state. This
explains a seemingly peculiar paradox, that is, why those who had the
most to gain from colonialism economically, such as the middle classes,
were also the most 'communal' (Bagchi, 1991). The simple answer is
that group mobility was the easiest way to effect individual mobility.
Identification with ones' religious group then meant that economically
or otherwise, individual competition gave rise to group competition
that translated into communal confrontations.

COMMUNALISM IN POST-INDEPENDENCE INDIA

Post-independent India from 1947 to 1954 yields little data on riots. For
the whole of India barring Bihar and Uttar Pradesh, there were 20 incidents in 1950, 7 in 1951, 12 in 1952, and 4 in 1953. However, there
was a sudden spate of rioting between 1964 and 1970, with the average
number of incidents estimated at 1025, as against 81.5 for the preceding
fourteen years (Krishna, 1985). By 1970, 70 per cent of the basic administrative units in the country were affected by at least one incident of
religious rioting. The 1980s and 1990s have witnessed a new phase of
rioting, which have been very widespread in the states of Punjab and
Assam, in districts such as Telangana and Bhiwandi, and in towns such
as Moradabad, Meerut, Ahmedabad, and Hyderabad. Indeed, there has
been a period of comparative calm in the past nine years since the riots
that followed the destruction of the Babri Masjid mosque in Ayodhya in
December 1992. Even in this period however, there have been incidents
of violence against Christian communities in Allahabad, Gujarat, Orissa,
and Bihar (Vedantam, 1999), and most recently against Muslim communities in Ahmedabad and elsewhere in India in March 2002.

This section summarizes the economic features that have been associated most commonly with communal riots in post-Independence India, their repercussions, and successive government policy towards religious issues. It does not examine in detail the factors that have contributed to localized incidents of religious rioting. Rather, it stands back from the evidence on particular instances of communal rioting and attempts to draw out the most general features that have been common to the incidents of violence that have taken place in the 1980s and 1990s. It also attempts to assess whether there are certain economic aspects common to these occurrences that has relevance for state policy towards religion.

An examination of communal incidents across time and across regions in India shows that competition kindled communal behaviour whenever there was a perceived economic disadvantage between members of rival religious communities. It followed too upon increasing urbanization, congestion, and increased export opportunities, with a dominant role for political leaders and the police, who adopted an increasingly militant posture. A feature of many riots in recent decades has been that they have been located in commercial and industrial centres. These centres attract large migrant populations, with the poor inhabiting the more congested 'centres' of the cities, living in claustrophobic proximity and deprivation. The increasing prosperity of minority community traders and the premium on space leads to an outflow of the population to peripheral areas and a greater demand for prized real estate in the city centre. Public lands used for religious purposes or other activities then become prized real estate, with conflict for commercial purposes lying beneath the ostensible religious contention. For example, one has only to examine closely the case of the Babri Masjid in Ayodhya to establish that the land in question is prime urban property (Gopal, 1991). Moreover, congested areas are swelled further by migration that upsets the population balance in traditional centres and contributes to further unemployment and an increase in criminal activity in the form of trade in smuggled goods. This may explain one of the more worrying features of communal riots in India, namely, that they have not been spontaneous or sporadic outbursts of violent activity, but instead have been planned carefully and meticulously to inflict large-scale damage to life and property in burgeoning industrial towns (Ahmad, 1984).

Economic liberalization, at first cautious since the early 1980s and then more rapid since 1991, has increased the opportunities for exports, contributing to the prosperity of minority communities. This development benefited traders in the late 1970s, because the increased demand for crafts exports from the Organization of Petroleum Exporting Countries (OPEC) provided opportunities for profit for artisans and Muslim entrepreneurs (Hasan, 1981). The riots that took place repeatedly in Hyderabad and Moradabad in the 1980s have been attributed to this factor. This is because the increased gains to entrepreneurs succeeded in raising the social visibility of minority groups and increased the competition for markets and space. Increased economic gain soon manifested itself in an ever-widening political base, particularly among castes such as the Yadavs, Jats, Marathas, Reddys, and Patels among the Hindus, and the Quereshis, Ansaris, and other artisan castes among Muslims (Engineer, 1984b: 1134). Political visibility, combined with economic gain, altered the traditional structure of societal relations and operated to intensify the struggle for rents.

Religious identities served as one medium to unify and homogenize hierarchical communities in the competition for political and economic space. This explains one of the most important features of the riots—the covert support of the middle class in the form of finance and firearms; and the complete collapse of state authority to deal with the violence, expressed principally in the behaviour of the police. The middle class played a prominent role in the riots that took place in 1993 in Bombay, Bhiwandi, and Surat. The controversial role of the police in the riots that took place in Bhagalpur (1989), Meerut (1987), Delhi (1984), in Hashimpura and Malliana in Uttar Pradesh in May 1987 and in Gujarat in March 2002 testify to the gruesome division along religious lines of the law-enforcement agencies in selected states.

In the end, there were two main repercussions of the riots on the cities themselves. First, urban economists have noted that there has been a subtle realignment that has been taking place between areas (Engineer, 1993a). A study of Gujarat in 1993 pointed out that Hindus and Muslims were living in virtual isolation and that there was little interaction outside the workplace. There were 3500 incidents in Gujarat alone between 1989 and 1992. Since the demolition of the Babri Masjid in 1992, ghettoization is believed to be almost complete (Chandra, 1984), although we have yet to ascertain fully how these patterns of ghettoization have been affected by the Gujarat earthquake of January 2001.

A second consequence of the violence has been a clearing of economic space with displaced communities leaving both trades and areas. Newspaper reports suggest that as a fallout of the riots that took place in Bombay in 1993, 60 per cent of the workers originally from Uttar Pradesh, Tamil Nadu, and Bihar left the state of Maharashtra (Engineer, 1993b). The case of Bhiwandi in 1993 is typical—after the riots, the occupants of slums on government land were resettled outside the town, and the rich belonging to the majority community staked their claim and reaped profits by letting out the land, which the slum-dwellers had occupied previously, at much higher rental values (Rodrigues, 1986: 1050).

Finally, it must be recognized that communalism has in the past involved electoral gain and has legitimized the authoritarian structure of power that has developed as a consequence of the elitist character of Indian society. These elite groups, although a small percentage of the total population, still number a staggering 200 million people. These groups have access both to education and to income, but they have been shown in the past to provide covert consent to violence, which has been described as 'soft Hindutva'. The defining, albeit depressing characteristic about 'soft Hindutva' is that it has provided the state with a motive to encourage rent-seeking elements among both majority and minority groups.

What may we conclude about the policy of the state towards religious riots? After Independence, Nehruvian secularism was emphasized and the pattern of economic development that it engendered was based on fostering economic growth, self-reliance, economic independence, and a secular approach to religion. The cultural rights of all communities in India are protected by the Indian Constitution under Articles 25, 26, 27, and 28 that embody the right to freedom of religion. The commitment to secularism encompasses equal protection to all religions. Moreover, coupled with the freedom to pursue any set of religious beliefs comes the right to propagate the religion.

Some historians argue that the revival of communalism was rooted in the dismantling of the Nehruvian model that followed as a consequence of policy undertaken by the governments of Indira and Rajiv Gandhi. It is argued that after 1968 the Indian Muslim community supported Indira Gandhi mainly because of the anti-Muslim feelings created by the rival Jan Sangh (Puri, 1993: 2144). Moreover, the government supported non-interference in Muslim personal law. This support diminished after the emergency of 1975–7, and Muslim public opinion swung towards the Janata party. There were riots in 1975–7 in Jamshedpur, Aligarh, and Benaras. In 1980, Indira Gandhi returned to power and her electoral strategy was often accused of being exceedingly pro-Hindu. Her dismissal of the Akali government and storming of the Golden Temple in Punjab in 1984 contributed to fostering insecurity among minority groups (Puri, 1993: 2145). Her tenure in government witnessed a sharp rise in riot-affected districts from 61 in 1961 to 250 in 1986–7, out of a total of 350 districts in all of India.

In the late 1980s, the state's policy towards communalism was guided by developments surrounding two main issues: Muslim personal law, and the disputed mosque at Ayodhya. The first issue concerned both the issue of 'triple divorce' under Muslim law and a Muslim woman's right to maintenance after divorce, exemplified in the case of Shah Bano of Indore, who was granted, by the Supreme Court, maintenance from her husband after 43 years of marriage. The Muslim orthodoxy at the time reacted virulently, claiming that the court had interfered with Koranic interpretations of Muslim personal law. In response to this pressure, the Rajiv Gandhi government passed the Muslim Women (Protection of Rights on Divorce) Act which kept Muslims out of the purview of Section 125 of the Criminal Procedure Code, under whose remit the Supreme Court had delivered its judgement. Such attempts to placate Muslim orthodoxy were soon followed by attempts to pacify the Hindu communalists, by granting in October 1989, just prior to the general elections, government permission to open the disputed Babri Masjid at Ayodhya for Hindu worship, and to perform foundation-laying ceremonies on the disputed site for the construction of a temple to the Hindu god Rama.

Such injudicious concessions were directly responsible for many of the events thereafter. Widespread riots, the rise of the Bharatiya Janata Party (BJP) in the tenth Lok Sabha elections, their dominance in four north Indian states, and the emergence of an aggressive proselytizing Hinduism culminated in the demolition of the Babri Masjid on 6 December 1992. This was followed by communal riots in Bombay, Surat, Ahmedabad, Delhi, and Kanpur. One of the most worrying aspects of this aggressive brand of Hinduism was that it was centred closely on particular texts such as the *Ramayana*, religious processions such as *rath yatras*, and temple construction. The consequences of the demolition of the mosque are more serious when viewed against the background of economic reform, globalization, and outward orientation that India embarked upon in 1991.

In the 1996 general elections, the BJP emerged as the single largest party in Parliament, with 162 seats. Since then India has witnessed years of comparative calm, interspersed with communal incidents that have been sporadic, but also brutally violent. The benefits of economic liberalization are not being shared evenly, and there are still shortages of water and fuel in many parts of the country. Communal riots may not be routine any more, but the economic basis that fosters inequality and rent-seeking exists, and as long as it does so, there remains only an uneasy rest for India's minority of 200 million people.

In India, religion is linked to the economics of survival. Against a distressing backdrop of population increases and poverty, faith has served traditionally to regulate lives—as a means of quiet acceptance to cope with want, or as a dramatic expression of belief. Communalism is a perverted manifestation of faith's second role. The Indian economy's resilience in withstanding aggressive communal outbursts is laudable, but the calm threat of recurrent rioting amidst reform is retrograde.

If we analyse the demographic and economic roots of the resurgence of communalism in India, it must be viewed in the context of the hierarchical nature of the caste system that broadly encompasses all religious groups, and of religion as a means of constructing an identity and as a tool of dissent. The first section of this chapter traced the time-pattern of Hindu–Muslim rioting and colonialism, tracing the origins of communalism to the patterns of inequality that obtained under British rule. The second section then examined the way in which communalism progressed in independent India as the product of the particular sociopolitical context deriving from India's history.

This section has also examined the economic reasons underlying the phenomenon of communalism. There is no doubt that poverty-induced migration from the rural areas has led to urbanization and urban congestion which has caused a combustible cocktail of increasing unemployment and the growth of the urban informal sector, which have created fertile ground for communal conflict in the past. This suggests one area that government economic policy must target, namely, the reduction of unemployment in cities coupled with strengthening the agricultural base in the countryside. This would also involve ascertaining the reasons behind why individuals migrate, with particular focus on the migration of young children, who swell the ranks of the urban informal sector.

Another way in which agriculture might be strengthened is the provision of micro-credit facilities, particularly in rural areas. Education, particularly of women, needs to be the focus of development policy more widely. Targeting education involves not only providing for the physical facilities for schooling, but sustained monitoring of its quality. The state can also play an active role in advertising the importance of education via the mass media such as radio and television. The media may also be used to ensure that discrimination does not occur between religious groups in the access to health and family planning services.

As argued earlier, the 1980s and 1990s, which have witnessed a sustained attempt at macro-economic and financial reform, have also been years of widespread rioting, which has been somewhat exacerbated by ill-considered government policy. With the repercussions of the liberalized policy environment yet to have a significant impact on living standards, but already affecting distribution, the possibility of further unfulfilled aspirations bodes ill for sustained communal peace.

How then can the economic basis for communalism be tackled effectively? This study examines in depth one important aspect of the communalism phenomenon, in the wider context of India's development policy, that has caused considerable debate in India—demographic differentials between religious groups. Differences in fertility behaviour between religious groups may be accounted for in terms of socio-economic differences, not cultural or religious factors; yet the perception is that cultural and religious differences do lead to a demographic and thus an economic threat. Therefore, an assessment of the relationship between religion, economics, and demography needs to begin with an examination of India's population policy since 1947, in order to examine whether religious differentials in fertility have been important in India, whether they have been significant for the evolution of government policy on population, and whether they have altered significantly the process of economic development in India.

AN ASSESSMENT AND A SUGGESTED REORIENTATION OF INDIA'S POPULATION POLICY

Since 1947, India has borne witness to several remarkable demographic achievements—a sustained increase in life expectancy from 37 years in 1947 to 62 years in 2000; a decline in fertility from 6 births per woman in 1951 to just above 3 births in 1997 (GOI, 2000: 1). The infant mortality rate has been halved from 146 per 1000 live births in 1951 to 72 per 1000 live births in 1998. The couple protection rate has quadrupled from 10 per cent in 1971 to 44 per cent in 1999 (GOI, 2000: 1). Yet, despite these successes, India's population has increased in absolute terms from 361 million according to the Census report of 1961, to one billion in the Census report of 2001, depicting an annual growth rate of over 2 per cent. It is also expected that the population will stabilize eventually, but only after it has reached 1.5 billion, primarily because of 'population momentum': the age structure of the population is heavily biased towards the young and reproductively fertile age groups. This section evaluates India's population policy and suggests directions for a reorientation of such policy in the context of religion and fertility.

From the First Five-Year Plan in 1951–6 until the late 1990s, population was dealt with under the Ministry of Health and Family Welfare. In the First Five-Year Plan, family planning funds made up a mere 0.5 per cent of the allocation to the health sector. In fact, this document does seem to acknowledge that aspect of population policy that has become important in subsequent decades, viz. information, communication, and education. Over time, the primary emphasis of the national family planning programme was on the provision of contraceptive services, influenced predominantly by studies such as the Coale–Hoover studies of 1958. As it does today, the government sector dominated the provision of family planning services, and these services were mainly permanent methods of birth control. Perhaps the most difficult period for the family planning programme was when the government undertook a programme of coercive sterilization between 1975–7, which had disastrous consequences particularly for the reputation of the national family planning programme. In 1992, the government launched the Child Survival and Safe Motherhood Programme to reduce maternal and child mortality.

In 1996, the BJP government came to power in India. In their election manifesto, the BJP described a population policy which proposed to bring 'population growth close to stabilization by the year 2010', and to 'introduce disincentives which will apply to all sections of society in order to discourage large, unsustainable families'. They also pledged economic incentives such as to offer a fixed deposit to mature in 21 years to all those couples who had only a girl child or who adopted a girl under the 'Dattak Putri Yojana'. They also endeavoured to 'make family planning an integral part of our development policies to ensure widest applicability of these incentives and disincentives and provide motivation for a small family norm'. Consequently, in 1996 the government abandoned target-setting and embarked in 1997 on a Reproductive and Child Health (RCH) programme that put reproductive health back firmly on the policy agenda. This programme was focused on increasing information, communication, and education, training for health workers, and on providing some districts with interventions designed to increase access to reproductive and child health for certain groups. This new policy is superior to the one it replaced in that it focuses on the needs of clients, the quality of service provision, and groups that were previously not targeted explicitly by the programme such as adolescents and Scheduled Tribes. The policy is also important in that it envisages a decentralized level of decision-making where responsibility for the delivery of health care lies at the level of the primary health centre (PHC). However, as pointed out by some demographers, at the level of the state and the district, there was very little guidance offered to staff to make the transition towards decentralized planning (Visaria et al., 1999).

In February 2000, the Indian government announced the National

Population Policy, 2000. The new policy is both ambitious and comprehensive in scope and has clearly defined aims and objectives. The policy aims primarily to promote:

The commitment of government towards voluntary and informed choice and consent of citizens while availing of reproductive health care services ... continuation of the target-free approach in administering family planning services ... to achieve net replacement levels by 2010 (GOI, 2000: 2).

The policy has three objectives: an 'immediate' objective to address the unmet need for contraception and provide basic reproductive and child health care; a 'medium-term' objective to bring the total fertility rate to replacement levels by 2010; and a 'long-term' objective to achieve a stable population by 2045 'at a level consistent with the requirements of sustainable economic growth, social development and environmental protection' (GOI, 2000: 2).

The policy goes on to outline a series of national demographic goals for 2010, to be achieved by twelve 'strategic themes' which are to be pursued simultaneously. These strategic themes are: 'decentralised planning and programme implementation; convergence of service delivery at village levels; empowering women for improved health and nutrition; child health and survival; meeting the unmet needs for family welfare services; under-served population groups; diverse health-care providers; collaboration with and commitments from non-government organizations and the private sector; mainstreaming Indian systems of medicine and homeopathy; contraceptive technology and research on reproductive and child health; providing for the older population; and information, education and communication'. This study will not analyse in depth the manner in which the strategic themes and their related operational strategies are to be implemented. Rather, it will attempt to identify how taking religion explicitly into account might enhance some of these themes and enable the operational strategies to be realized in a more effective manner.

At the outset, it must be made clear that the role of religion in demographic decision-making is not woven explicitly into the new population policy. One of the most interesting features of the policy, however, is that it outlines the role that can be exerted by religious leaders, along with others such as political leaders, community leaders, and other opinion-makers, to promote the small family norm, 'in order to enhance its acceptance within society more widely'. The policy also states that 'the government will actively enlist their support in concrete ways'. However, beyond this statement the policy does not outline how religious leaders and others can influence popular opinion, nor does it expand upon the manner in which their support is likely to be enlisted. This study attempts to redress this deficiency. It will attempt to highlight clearly the manner in which government, both at national and state levels, can work together with religious leaders to influence demographic outcomes in India.

In order to implement the twelve strategic themes, the policy sees an important role for village *panchayats*, mainly because they have been given primary responsibility for health, welfare, and education by the 73 and 74 amendments to the constitution. This is clearly one area where religious leaders might work in tandem with local governments in order to strengthen the services provided. It is important that religious leaders work with governments at this level, particularly because 33 per cent of elected panchayat seats are reserved for women; the continuous interaction of religious leaders with elected women members of the panchayat would be particularly important for dealing with women's issues at the level of the village.

The policy also identifies as crucial more extensive involvement of the voluntary sector and the non-government sector in order to resolve the unmet need for family planning and extend coverage of services. This is where small community initiatives such as those organized by religious organizations could be useful. This is because while there is no doubt that religious organizations provide a unified forum to mobilize people, in a manner that has legitimacy both in the eyes of the masses and in the eyes of the state, the ready infrastructure that such organizations provide has not been used in the past to provide information about family planning and birth-spacing, or infant and child care. The use of religious organizations in this unconventional way would be particularly relevant to the policy's avowed aim 'to increase innovative social marketing schemes for affordable products' (GOI, 2000: 7). There are of course some religious groups that do provide guidance for women—the example of the Church in Ramanagaram taluk in southern India is particularly noteworthy in that it has provided a forum for the discussion of women's issues on Sunday afternoons, which greatly influences decision-making about fertility undertaken by Christian women in the taluk (Iyer, 2000).

Another theme that the policy specifically addresses, and which has not formed a part of Indian population policy in the past, is to target under-served population groups such as adolescents. Because adolescent marriage and pregnancy is particularly widespread in rural areas, the provision of reproductive health care for this group is essential. Religious groups and religious leaders could have a particularly important role in educating adolescent populations, as they are likely both to command a considerable amount of respect from the young, and to exert an important influence on their behaviour.

It is within the purview of the theme of 'information, education, and communication' that religious groups and leaders could have a major role to play in exerting an influence over demographic decision-making in India. Religious leaders who use local dialects and who are familiar with the local context in which couples make reproductive decisions, can be very effective if they convey messages that would increase the welfare of the family, such as information about encouraging the use of maternal and child health services. Religious leaders, for example, could also urge families to enforce strictly the Child Marriage Restraint Act of 1976. This measure alone would exert a tremendous impact on delaying the age at marriage, particularly in the rural areas, and consequently on total fertility. It is not too far-fetched to suggest that the impact of preaching about (delaying) procreation would be similar to the positive impact that religious leaders have exerted on the total literacy campaigns undertaken in India in the past.

In keeping, therefore, with the drive towards reorientation that has characterized India's policy towards population since the mid-1990s, this study suggests that differences between religious groups do need to be understood and then to be targeted explicitly within this new framework, primarily because different religious groups are in different stages of the fertility transition. It is important to understand the nature and causes of demographic differences by religion mainly because, as this study will argue, from a policy perspective it may become important to target certain policies more strongly towards certain religious groups than others. However, it is necessary first to assess which factors are important for the demographic decision-making of different religious groups in India, and that is what this study sets out to do. Taking the needs of different religious groups explicitly into account may serve then the dual purpose of exerting an impact both on the rate of growth of population and on counteracting at least one factor that contributes to the phenomenon of communalism.

chapter three

~

Religion and Reproduction
An Examination of the Impact of Religion on Demography

O Muslim, Hindu—faiths are two
But one the brimming cup you share;
And one the drinking house, and one
The wine which flows so freely there.

By mosque and temple all's divided
All is either 'mine' or 'thine'
But enmities thus forged are all
Forgotten in the House of Wine.

—*Bachchan, 1998: 163–4*

At the outset, it is important to examine the ways in which religion is hypothesized to affect demographic outcomes, particularly in terms of theological content. This chapter discusses the two hypotheses which propose certain links between religion and fertility: the 'pure religion effect' hypothesis and the 'characteristics' hypothesis.

A discussion of the impact of religion on fertility needs to be placed in the wider historical context of the role of religion in economic development. As early as 1905, Weber put forward his now-famous theory of the influence of the 'Protestant ethic' on the 'spirit of capitalism' and the rise of modern industrial society in Europe (Weber, 1992; Käsler, 1988. For a recent discussion of the Weber thesis, see also Landes, 1998: 174–81). However, discussions of religion and development soon went beyond looking at the impact of religion in terms of its effect on entrepreneurial spirit, to address broader issues such as religion's role as a fundamental factor in society's moral base, which may impose a 'social limit' on development. In this context, three main issues emerged: first, further debate on the Protestant ethic, which looked at the religious sources of thrift, hard work, saving, and investment; second, the corollary of this belief, that is, that some religions (such as Hinduism, Buddhism, and Islam) impeded economic growth; and third, either viewing religion and development as independent phenomena[1] or viewing religion as a dependent variable of development.[2]

As a variable which lies at the core of human development, fertility too may be affected by non-economic factors such as religion. Religion has two main components which may influence fertility: first, it articulates a set of normative values of a community, which will be called the 'pure religion effect'; and second, it is associated with other socio-economic traits which affect reproductive behaviour, which will be called the 'characteristics effect'.

HYPOTHESES ABOUT THE IMPACT OF RELIGION ON FERTILITY

Chamie has argued that there are three hypotheses about why one might observe fertility differentials by religion. These are briefly: the 'particularised theology' hypothesis, that the *intellectual content* of religion influences fertility irrespective of socio-economic and demographic contexts;[3] the 'characteristics' hypothesis, that fertility differentials reflect *socio-economic differences* between members of religious groups; and the 'minority group status' hypothesis, that the political and social *insecurity of minority religious groups* increases their fertility compared to the majority group. In discussing the theoretical literature on religion and fertility, this chapter will reduce Chamie's three hypotheses to two. The first is the 'pure religion effect' hypothesis on fertility, and the second is the

---

[1]For example, Taft Morris and Adelman concluded that in a sample of 55 non-communist under-developed countries, the cross-association between religion and modernization could not be attributed to interactions between religion and the socio-economic indicators (such as crude fertility rates), but rather was the outcome of complex historical processes in religious configuration and socio-economic development, spread over many centuries. See Taft Morris and Adelman, 1980: 491–501.

[2]For example, the *Sarvodaya* movement led by Buddhist monks in Sri Lanka provided a positive impetus to development. Religion and development also came into focus in Iran in the late 1970s and early 1980s. See Nash, 1980: 555–61. More generally, on the linkages between religion and development, see Wilber and Jameson, 1980: 467–79; Goulet, 1980: 481–9; Taft Morris and Adelman, 1980: 491–501.

[3]Chamie, 1977: 365–82. Chamie used the phrase 'particularised theology'. However, in keeping with other terminology from economics used in the present study, we use the term 'pure religion effect' to describe the same factor.

'characteristics' hypothesis, which reflects socio-economic differences between members of religious groups, but which treats minority group status as one more 'characteristic' of the population.

A fourth hypothesis that is relevant particularly in the context of India, is 'discrimination', that is, that different religious groups may have *differential access to services* such as health and family planning.

The 'Pure Religion Effect' Hypothesis

Real religion can exist without a definite conception of the deity but not without a distinction between the spiritual and the profane, ... religion generally refers to something external, a system of sanctions and consolations (Radhakrishnan, 1939: 21).

A 'pure religion effect' on fertility can operate in a number of ways. Religions often adopt positions on the moral acceptability of birth control and abortion. They often have norms about 'desired' family size. Religious rituals often provide for distinct roles for children (as is the case with religious roles for sons in South Asia). Religions can impose religious vows and practices of celibacy, either lifelong or outside marriage. Religions may take positions on the acceptability of contraception. And religions may encourage literacy in order to read the scriptures, which in turn may lead to indirect effects on fertility (See Weber, 1992: 97–8; Gellner, 1981. In chapter 1, Gellner discusses the effect of Islam on the spread of literacy in pastoral Arabian societies in the eleventh and twelfth centuries).

A number of empirical studies have argued that Catholics show different fertility than Protestants and that this is due to differences in the content of their religious beliefs (Mosher, Johnson and Horn, 1986: 367–79; Westoff and Ryder, 1977; Westoff, 1979; Sander, 1995). For example, Catholic norms on contraception and family size have been thought to influence fertility (Janssen and Hauser, 1981: 511–28). Similarly, it is often argued that the particular philosophical content of Islam affects demographic behaviour.[4]

Islam

'Islamic' fertility has been the subject of many theoretical and empirical writings which have discussed the normative values associated with Islam and their relation to fertility (Coulson and Hinchcliffe, 1978: 37–49; Youssef, 1978: 69–99; Qureshi, 1980: 563–75; Gellner, 1981; Obermeyer, 1992: 33–60). Philosophers and sociologists have argued that the content

[4]Youssef, 1978: 69–99; Qureshi, 1980: 563–75; Obermeyer, 1992: 33–60.

of Islam is essentially bounded by a written document, the *Koran*, and the written words of the Prophet Mohammad (Radhakrishnan, 1939; Gellner, 1981). Gellner has argued that the presentation of the written word in the *Koran* is very important in Islam and has considerable influence on human conduct and society (Gellner, 1981: 4).

The institutional requirements of Islam are specified in the *Sharia* or Islamic law, which is derived from two main sources: first, the Koran, and second, the Prophet Mohammad's interpretations of the word of God, and their application to various situations (Ragab, 1980: 513–21). These rulings are collectively termed the *Sunna*. The Koran and the Sunna were codified over several centuries along with interpretations of Islam by Muslim scholars who undertook the task of *ijtihad* or 'finding rules for novel situations', all of which collectively comprise the Sharia. However, the codification of the Sharia continued only until the eleventh century, which, according to some scholars, has subsequently robbed the Sharia of its vitality because it did not dynamically change in accordance with new situations which arose in later centuries (Ragab, 1980: 513–21; Landau, 1958: 128). The Sharia was made applicable to all Muslims in India in 1937. A majority of Muslims in India are Sunnis, as are a majority of the Muslim women interviewed in the Ramanagaram sample.[5]

Officially, Islam has no formal organization and no church, and unlike Hinduism, Islam has no concept of priesthood (Gellner, 1981: 48). According to Qureshi, 'A Muslim's duty is to God and neither to any individual nor to any church' (Qureshi, 1980: 564). However, Islam does possess a plethora of small religious groups, termed 'orders' or 'brotherhoods', some of which revolve around specific saints. There are also groups of people who dedicate their lives to the study of Islamic texts such as the Koran, or the performance of religious duties, and who occupy a position of respect among Muslims. These are the *ulema* who occupy an important place in Muslim society.[6]

How is the structure of Islam hypothesized to affect women's fertility? Many scholars have pointed out that in the Koran, 'injunctions that wives should be treated fairly and equitably, that divorce should take place only with due consideration, and that in general women's rights should be respected, abound' (Coulson and Hinchcliffe, 1978: 37–8). Islam is, however, hypothesized to affect fertility directly by its position

[5]There are, of course, other Muslim sects in India such as the Shias and the Alawites. However, there is little difference in practice between Shias, Sunnis, and Alawites in their theological attitudes towards contraception and fertility.

[6]Qureshi, 1980: 564. The *ulema* are men learned in Islamic scriptures. It must be emphasized that they are not 'priests' in the traditional sense of individuals through whom members of a religion may communicate with God.

on the moral acceptability of birth control, and by its views on marriage, polygyny, and divorce (Qureshi, 1980: 564). It is popularly believed that because Islam permits a man to take multiple wives, father large numbers of children, and unilaterally divorce his wife, this collectively encourages high fertility in Islamic populations because men do not bear equally the cost of having to rear their own offspring. This is also the view that has been repeatedly put forward by Hindu right-wing political parties in the Indian subcontinent.

Islam on marriage, polygyny, and divorce

In the Koran all Muslim males are encouraged to marry, and the universal remarriage of widowed and divorced women is highly encouraged (Youssef, 1978: 88). In most Muslim countries, the minimum female age at first marriage is 18 years, but marriages which are contracted between parties below the minimum age are still considered legally valid (Coulson and Hinchcliffe, 1978: 37–8). All sects of Islam recognize the right of 'marriage guardians' to arrange marriages for female infant wards without their prior consent. An important feature of Islamic marriage contracts is the *mahr* or the *sadaq* or dower, which is paid to the bride or her guardian, and which constitutes women's right to property. The tight control of parents and guardians over the selection of marriage partners and strict seclusion before marriage are also features of Islamic societies (Youssef, 1978: 78).

Islamic law does not require a husband to obtain permission from a court or from current wives in order to have another marriage (Coulson and Hinchcliffe, 1978: 37–8). Although the *Koran* stresses that a man is urged not to take on a second wife unless he is in a position to treat all wives equally, the law interprets this as a matter for the man's own conscience and does not recommend legal intervention in this decision. In some interpretations of Islam, Muslim men can take a second wife only with the consent of the first wife. There is also evidence that in some Islamic countries, the man does need to obtain permission from the courts, or obtain sanction from an arbitration council, before contracting a second marriage (Youssef, 1978: 41). Several scholars have also cited the empirical evidence from the Arab nations that polygyny is not widespread (Obermeyer, 1992: 33–60; Ghallab, 1984: 232–41; White, 1978: 52–68).

In India and in the Ramanagaram sample, there is little evidence of polygyny. The Census of 1961 outlined that polygyny was highest among the tribal communities of India and was practised least by Muslims. In fact, polygyny among Hindus was found to be higher than among Muslims. It was estimated that in 1931–41 in India, the number of polygynous families as a percentage of total families was 6.8 per cent for Hindus and 7.3 per cent for Muslims. This percentage fell in 1961 to 5.1 per cent for Hindus and to only 4.3 per cent for Muslims (Indian National Social Action Forum Manual, 1997, Chapter 4). This suggests that the incidence of polygyny is not significant for fertility behaviour in India. In the Ramanagaram sample, only 4 out of the 187 marriages were polygynous unions. Moreover, given the degree of female monogamy and the low degree of non-marital sexual activity within the religion, polygyny on its own may not necessarily raise fertility, as it implies that some men inevitably marry later or not at all. It may also be that the main impact of polygyny on fertility is expressed through women's roles. Thus, the extent to which Islam directly impacts on fertility by enforcing norms concerning marriage and polygyny, is strongly debated in the literature.

The issue on which scholars of Islam are more unanimous, is that Islam permits a man to divorce his wife, in some situations, unilaterally. As Coulson and Hinchcliffe argue, 'It is a fundamental principle of Islamic law that the power of divorce is in the hands of the husband, and may be exercised at will, however blameless she (the wife) may be, without having recourse to a court of law' (Coulson and Hinchcliffe, 1978: 42). Although many Muslim countries do require pronouncements of divorce to be made in a law court, an important aspect of divorce under Islamic law even today is that the power to divorce remains solely in the hands of the husband, considerably weakening the bargaining position of the wife.[7] In addition, a divorced or widowed woman retains custody of any children only for a limited period after divorce, after which custody passes normally to a male relative. The provision for unilateral divorce by the husband is an aspect of the Sharia which is particularly important in India, because in the late 1980s and early 1990s an issue which was at the forefront of the 'communalism' phenomenon was the debate over the Muslim woman's right to maintenance after divorce.

Islam on birth control and abortion

Islam has traditionally been portrayed as not permitting birth control or abortion in any situation. This may be because of a streak of fatalism, 'a strong belief in the active providence of God' (Youssef, 1978: 87), and the belief that 'Allah creates sexuality and determines procreation and

---

[7]For example, the *talaq al-bida* or 'divorce of innovation' consists of the husband pronouncing three talaqs at a time, immediately dissolving the marriage. In other forms of divorce, where the talaq may be pronounced over several months, there is a waiting period (called the *idda*), in which women are entitled to some maintenance. See Coulson and Hinchcliffe, 1978: 37–49.

barrenness' (Youssef, 1978: 87). However, scholars such as Obermeyer argue that the position of Islam on birth control and abortion depends very much on the interpretation of the different schools of Islamic jurisprudence (Obermeyer, 1992: 33–60). According to this view, Islam does permit family planning, an inference drawn from the absence of any reference to prohibition of birth control in the Koran. Obermeyer argues that Sunni and Shia positions on birth control are, in fact, derived from the writings of Al-Ghazali, a medieval Islamic theologian, who outlined many situations where birth control within Islam is permissible: including if one of the partners is afflicted with a disease which may be passed on to children; or if there is concern for the effect of too many pregnancies on the wife's health (Obermeyer, 1992: 43). She also argues that some schools of Islamic jurisprudence do permit abortion. While the Malikis school prohibits abortion outright, most other schools permit abortion up to the time when the foetus is regarded as being 'ensouled', a definition which varies to include the 40, 80, or 120 day of pregnancy, depending on the school, after which abortion is prohibited by all schools (Obermeyer, 1992).

Islam on women's status in the family, children, and son-preference

It has also been hypothesized that Islam traditionally awarded men a more prominent place than women within the family. Sons were given twice as large an inheritance as daughters and a man's testimony in court was worth twice that of a woman. Coulson and Hinchcliffe (1978: 38) argue that 'Islamic law has continued to reflect the patriarchal and patrilineal nature of a society based on the male agnatic tie. Within the scheme of family law which developed in this way, woman, whether as daughter, wife, or mother, occupied an inferior position.' Other scholars have pointed out that women in Islamic societies have been restricted to a lifestyle that guaranteed preservation of family honour and prestige, and that there is usually strict segregation of the sexes in schools and at work, and an informal separation of the sexes in all recreational activities.[8] Landes also argues that the economic implications of gender discrimination

---

[8]Youssef, 1978; Obermeyer, 1992. However, in India, the role of the Muslim woman has not always been to observe the veil and be restricted to the home. As Engineer argues, there are instances in Indian history where Muslim women who belonged to the ruling dynasties fought and led battles on the battlefield. Among them are Gul Bahisht against the Raja of Jalore in the time of Alauddin Khalji; Noorjehan (the wife of Jehangir), whose hunting exploits included killing lions and mounting elephants, and are described in the *Tuzk-i-Jahangiri*; and Chand Khatun (also called Chand Sultana), who defended the kingdom of Ahmednagar against the Mughal emperor Akbar's army. For more on this, see Engineer, 1997: 12.

in the Arab Muslim nations is serious, because it restricts the opportunities of women, and undermines the 'drive to achievement of boys and men' (Landes, 1998: 412). However, it should also be pointed out at this stage that women were restricted in many ways in Christian and Hindu societies in the past as well.

A feature of many Muslim societies, including some modern ones, which tend to increase fertility is that Muslim women gain respect and status within their own kin group and community when they marry and have children, since women derive status from motherhood even when divorced or rejected for a second wife (Youssef, 1978: 69–99). Thus, the literature seems unanimous that Islam involves low female autonomy compared with men, and that there are a number of ways in which this may encourage high fertility in Muslim societies.

Empirically, most studies which have dealt with Islam and fertility have focused on the Arab countries in North Africa and West Asia, such as Egypt, Sudan, Morocco, Algeria, Iraq, Saudi Arabia, Syria, and Yemen. Between 1950–6 and 1985–90 these nations collectively showed a total fertility rate of 6.9 children per woman and many scholars have ascribed it to religious factors and to the low status of women in this region (World Bank, 1991; Farid, 1987; Omran, 1980; Gallagher and Searle, 1983; Lutz, 1983: 15–35; Caldwell, 1986: 171–220; Nagi, 1984: 189–204).

In this section we have examined the content of Islam in general and then looked at its position on marriage and polygyny, birth control and abortion, role for children, and women's status in the family. The arguments do not appear to provide unambiguous support for the 'traditional' view of Islam and fertility (according to which Islam fosters high fertility because of polygyny and unilateral divorce). However, there seems to be some persuasive evidence that the content of the Islamic religion encourages high fertility because of low autonomy for women and son-preference. However, it is not clear whether this is any different from the effect on fertility of the content of other religions, such as Hinduism. One way of assessing the extent to which the theological content of Islam is likely to be playing a role in the social and demographic situation of Islamic societies is to compare and contrast it with the content of Hinduism.

Hinduism

Hinduism, like the curate's egg, is good only in parts. It is admirable and abhorrent, saintly and savage, beautifully wise and dangerously silly, generous beyond measure and mean beyond all example (Radhakrishnan, 1939: 338).

Hinduism is a difficult religion to analyse because of its diversity of gods, sects, philosophies, and cults. Unlike in the case of Islam, there is no one religious book which contains all the teachings of Hinduism. However, there is a large number of writings and scriptures which put forward Hindu beliefs. These include the *Vedas*, the *Upanishads*, the *Bhagavad Gita*, the *Ramayana* and the *Mahabharata*.

Philosophically, the main religious experience of Hinduism is the common quest for salvation of the human soul, in an attempt to bridge the gap between the infinite real self and the finite or empirical body. The gap is bridged when the empirical self is disciplined to tread the path of righteousness (*dharma*). Until that point, the empirical self is believed to follow a cycle of births, with life in each birth determined by the actions (*karma*) in the past birth and in the present.

However, in this common quest, Hinduism does not preach asceticism. Rather, it exhorts followers to engage in 'worldly' activities, but to do so in a detached manner. Thus, Hinduism lays out a 'code of conduct' for the individual, particularly in relation to the society in which he/she lives (Radhakrishnan, 1939: 353). In essence, this Hindu conception of a 'code of conduct' is similar to the way in which Islam prescribes a 'way of life' for its followers.

The Hindu code of conduct encapsulates the fourfold objects of life, the fourfold succession of the stages of life, and the fourfold ordering of society as follows. The fourfold objects of life (*purusartha*) are desire and enjoyment, interest, ethical living, and spiritual freedom. In order to achieve these, the individual has to progress through four stages (*aasrama*): student, householder, forest recluse, and the free suprasocial man. However, individuals are organized within society into a fourfold order (*varna*): 'the man of learning, the man of power, the man of skilled productivity and the man of service'.[9] The spirit behind this fourfold order is essentially that learning, power, skills, and service are the indispensable elements of any social order. This fourfold order is also believed to have divine sanction. For example, in the alliterative verse-poem in praise of the Hindu mother goddess Lalita, that forms a part of the *Brahmanda Purana*, the goddess is described as the 'law-giver of the form of caste and orders of life' and 'the one that fulfils the four objects of life' (Suryanarayana Murthy, 2000: 97). Thus, the goddess is meant to have sanctioned the code of conduct of social life for the ultimate spiritual

---

[9]Radhakrishnan, 1939: 351. The earliest reference to these four classes is found in the *Purusa sukta* verse in the *Rg Veda*.

well-being of her disciples (Suryanarayana Murthy, 2000: 96). Moreover, this scheme is meant to provide a framework for guidance for the individual, with an emphasis on conduct rather than belief, but strictly within a social context. Thus, while the theory of varna emphasizes the social aspects, the theory of aasrama dwells on the individual. The implications for fertility of this ordering of society and caste endogamy is that social mobility of the individual may be dependent on caste mobility, with fertility influenced by the norms of the caste, or by the restricted socio-economic opportunities of certain castes.

Hinduism on marriage, polygyny, and divorce

In a discussion of Hinduism and its impact on fertility, the 'householder' stage of life is particularly relevant. Similar to the Koranic position on marriage, Hindus are encouraged to enter married life.[10] Moreover, that marriage is important in Hinduism is indicated by the fact that Hindu gods are always depicted as being married (unlike the cases of Christianity and Islam), and that no god in the Hindu pantheon is ever depicted in a temple or other place of worship without at least one consort, which in itself may provide evidence for the sanction of polygyny.[11] However, the perfect marriage in the Hindu scriptures is the monogamous one, epitomized by the relationship between the gods Rama and Sita or Savitri and Satyavan, where both stand by each other through various trials. Polygyny was tolerated in the Hindu scriptures as well, but only in the absence of male offspring (This may be construed as an indication of son-preference, which is dealt with in a subsequent section). For example, Vyasa writes in the Mahabharata that 'A woman is supposed to have one husband, a man many wives. ... A woman may have a second husband for progeny in case of difficulty' (As quoted by Deshpande, 1978: 90). The religious epic poem Ramayana does in fact highlight the evils of polygyny (For more on this, see Radhakrishnan, 1927: 61). Polygyny became illegal for Hindus in India in 1955 with the Hindu Marriage Act legislation. Moreover, in scriptural Hinduism, the indissolubility of marriage is the ideal, but in certain circumstances, divorce is permitted. As Kautilya argues in the *Arthasastra*, 'if the husband is of bad character, or is long gone abroad, or is guilty of high treason, or is dangerous to his

[10]Radhakrishnan, 1939: 379. The Hindu scriptures outline eight different forms of marriage—*paisaca, rakshasa, asura, gandharva, arsa, daiva, prajapatya,* and *brahma.* For more on this, see Radhakrishnan, 1947: 165.

[11]For example, the *Nitimanjari* argues that 'Home is not what is made of wood and stone; but where a wife is, there is a home.' See Radhakrishnan, 1947: 149.

wife, or has become an outcast, or has lost virility, he may be abandoned by his wife' (*Arthasastra*: III.3, as quoted by Radhakrishnan, 1947: 181–2). Vyasa argues in the Mahabharata that 'A husband also can abandon a wife who is free of the husband (self-willed), acts as she pleases, who is sterile or gives birth only to daughters or whose children die young' (As quoted by Deshpande, 1978: 93).

Hinduism on birth control and abortion

Hinduism says little explicitly about limiting births. Abortion and the decision to use contraception are regarded as women's personal matters which are not within the purview of religious injunction. One explanation for this may be the notions of 'purity and pollution' which are strictly upheld in the day-to-day practice of traditional Hinduism. For example, matters pertaining to the reproductive functions of women, such as menstruation or childbirth, are viewed as making women temporarily 'impure'.[12] However, it should be noted that the reproductive functions of women are important in the context of norms about multiple partners. For example, Vyasa argues in the Mahabharata that 'Women and rivers are alike. They do not become impure by contact with men. Rivers are purified by the flow and women by menstruation' (Deshpande, 1978: 92). In scriptural Hinduism, the only reference to the control of births is indirect, in the context of norms about abstinence. For example, Vyasa argues that, 'He [the householder] should avoid intercourse with his wife when she is old or barren or ill-behaved, when her children die or when she has not yet attained maturity, when she gives birth to daughters only or has many sons' (Radhakrishnan, 1947: 189). Thus, strict notions of 'purity and pollution' may be one reason why abortion and birth control issues are not specifically addressed in the Hindu scriptures. The exceptional context in which these issues are addressed is the case of the *kumari bharya*, a woman who is pregnant but not legally married. Abortion in this case was regarded as a sin: 'A girl who has conceived or delivered (before marriage) can expiate for her sin by undergoing three-fourths of the purifactory rite for a Brahmannicide; the remaining one-fourth is supposed to have been performed after childbirth' (Deshpande, 1978: 93). In scriptural Hinduism therefore, the control of births is addressed only indirectly.

[12]This is reflected in the Hindu custom that no members of a family in which a birth has just taken place are allowed to visit a temple or to engage in auspicious religious occasions such as weddings, from a minimum of ten to a maximum of up to forty days after the birth. This is also true of deaths, though the period of mourning extends for one whole year.

Hinduism on women's status in the family, children, and son-preference

In Hinduism, the role of women in the family is considered very impo.tant. As Radhakrishnan argues, the 'general Hindu view of woman is an exalted one—it regards the woman as the helpmate of man in all his work: *sahadharmini*'. Sayana, a commentator on the *Rg Veda*, remarks that 'The wife and the husband, being the equal halves of one substance, *are equal in every respect*; both should join and take equal part in all work, religious and secular'(emphasis added) (Radhakrishnan, 1927: 61). Shakuntala, a princess from Hindu mythology, tells Dushyanta that 'when a husband and wife are carrying on smoothly, then only pleasure, prosperity and piety are possible' (Deshpande, 1978: 91). In one form, the god Shiva is androgynously depicted as half-man and half-woman, emphazing the importance of the masculine and the feminine in the Hindu faith.

As in the case of Islam, for devout Hindus establishing a household is considered a fundamental duty, and the position of the wife is regarded as being central to it. For example, 'Living beneath trees is like living at home if the wife is there, but without her even a palace is certainly a forest' (ibid.). On the position of women in the family, and the functions of the householder as a step towards spiritual growth, Hindu thought argues that 'The wife has an equal position with the husband in all domestic and religious concerns. ... Every woman has a right to marry and have a home' (Radhakrishnan, 1939: 379).

It is interesting that when compared with Islam, where the role for women was mainly to 'uphold family honour', the role for women in Hinduism is much more clearly defined to be 'equal in every respect'. However, the Hindu scriptures mainly see the woman only in relation to the man, and give her an 'equal', 'exalted position', as a 'helpmate' only within marriage and the family. For example, 'A wife should be attentive to her house, devoted to her husband, always speaking agreeably, and always attractive. A wife who appreciates her husband's qualities and cooperates with him delightfully is real wealth, while wealth is not really so' (Deshpande, 1978: 91). It is important to note that though women are not considered inferior to men in Hinduism (unlike in the case of Islam), there are few independent roles assigned to them outside the domestic sphere.

The lack of independent roles assigned to women outside the home is justified by the Hindu scriptures using notions of women's supreme 'self-sacrifice' of which they are seen as being more capable than men.

The Hindu scriptures also put forward the view that because child rearing takes up parental time, women need not be 'burdened' by having to work outside the home in order to shoulder the economic responsibilities of the family, but that the latter is to be undertaken by men: 'While man has to take to worldly pursuits (*yajñapradhanya*), woman is capable of self-control and self-denial (*tapahpradhanya*)' (Radhakrishnan, 1927: 61). It must be noted here that this essentially *religious* notion of 'women's self-sacrificing nature' is reflected, even today, in the unequal distribution of food and health-care allocations between men and women, sons and daughters, and high birth-order and low birth-order children, which many economists and others have observed in analysing intra-household resource allocation in rural households in India.[13] It is thus easy to see that as far as the content of Hinduism is concerned, women appear to be *unequally* 'equal', and that their consequent lack of autonomy may have implications for fertility.

This is reinforced by the great emphasis in Hindu philosophy on children and especially the role for surviving sons.[14] 'At the end of the (*Sraddha*) ceremony the performer asks, "Let me, O fathers, have a hero for a son!"' (Radhakrishnan, 1927: 59–60). A common Vedic blessing for newly-married Hindu women is 'May you be the mother of a hundred sons'. The *Mysore Population Study* (UN, 1961: 130) described one of the traditional Vedic blessings for married women popularly used in Karnataka 'May she bear ten sons, and make of her husband an eleventh!', which is a good example of how the 'pure religion effect' may have operated to encourage high fertility in traditional Hindu societies in the past. Moreover, the Mahabharata says, 'A daughter is a misery' (Deshpande, 1978: 96). Thus, philosophically, the emphasis of Hinduism on marriage and having children (especially sons), may provide a purely religious motive for high fertility.

Empirical evidence for the impact of the Hindu religion on fertility is scarce. The *Mysore Population Study* noted differences in fertility by religion in erstwhile Mysore state. In its in-depth study of attitudes towards family size, it concluded that Hindu religious traditions in Indian society favoured having many offspring. This study also showed that after

[13]Dasgupta, 1993a: 343–70. Although it is important to note that some evidence suggests that intra-household nutritional discrimination against women is confined to parts of north India. See Harriss, 1990.

[14]For example, 'The Hindu scriptures speak of the three debts we have to pay: to the *rishis* by Vedic study, to the gods by sacrifices, and to the ancestors by offspring.' See Radhakrishnan, 1947: 150–1.

childbirth, Hindu women spent on average, a 53–week interval away from their husbands in their parents' home, and that this was connected with Hindu religious beliefs about women's 'purity and pollution' after childbirth, while Muslim women stayed away from their husbands for an average of only 28 weeks (ibid., 132). The study argued that this may have explained higher fertility among Muslims than Hindus in Mysore state at that time (UN, 1961: 119–20; see also Chandrasekaran, 1952).

Islam and Hinduism Compared

A cursory look at the philosophical content of Islam and Hinduism suggests significant dissimilarities: a monotheistic Islam versus a poly-theistic Hinduism; an egalitarian ordering of society versus the multiple hierarchies of caste; the Islamic emphasis on a 'common creed', the Hindu experience of the 'common quest' (Radhakrishnan, 1939).

However, a more detailed look at the main tenets of Islam and Hinduism, in the specific context of religion and fertility, suggests significant similarities between the two religions. Essentially, both Hinduism and Islam view religion similarly: in Islam as a way of life, in Hinduism as an experience which prescribes a code of conduct. Second, both religions espouse a degree of fatalism and put a high value on asceticism and/or renunciation as the true path to spiritual growth. Thirdly, though in theory neither religion has a 'church' or a 'priesthood', both religions have evolved classes of people (the religious *pundits* of Hinduism and the ulema of Islam) who dedicate themselves to interpreting religious scriptures and applying them to real-life situations. More particularly, in India there is a caste system among Muslims with the same rigidity of endogamy as that found among Hindu castes. Fourth, scripturally, the position of women in these two religions is similar. In the case of Islam, though women are assigned a lower status than men, women are expected to 'uphold family honour and prestige'. In the Hindu scriptures, women have an 'exalted and equal' position, but only in the domestic sphere. Moreover, neither religion assigns an independent role for women outside the family. Fifth, both religions emphasize the importance of marriage and actively encourage it. Sixth, both religions set great store by children as a way of glorifying the family ideal, especially emphasizing the role of sons in continuing the lineage. Perhaps where the two religions do differ most is in terms of their attitude to birth control and abortion. Hinduism does not explicitly express any religious opinion (at least scripturally) for or against birth control or abortion. Indeed, Hindu concepts of 'impurity' may reduce fertility if they lead to longer sexual abstinence during menstruation and after childbirth. In contrast, various schools of Islamic thought have argued that birth control is permissible but only in restricted situations. However, this is subject to wide variation, leaving considerable room for alternative interpretations of what Islam does say on these matters at a practical level.

Finally, it must be understood, as philosophers have argued, that in countries such as India, there is a 'meeting of religions', where the Shia Muslim sect is closer to Hinduism than the Sunni sect, and Muslim sects such as the Khojas have tenets which are a mixture of Vaishnava and Shia doctrines.[15] Moreover, Sufiism is similar to the *Advaita Vedanta*, with Sufis abstaining from meat and believing in reincarnation, like orthodox Hindus.[16]

Thus, despite the theologically different points of the spectrum from which Islam and Hinduism emerge, there appear to be some significant similarities, at least in terms of their beliefs about the influence of religion on conduct, and their positions on the importance of marriage and the family. In terms of *content* alone, both religions would appear to foster high fertility, with little practical difference between the two. This is not meant to imply that the content of these two religions does not or cannot affect demographic outcomes. Rather, this suggests that any differences between Hindu fertility and Muslim fertility are more likely to be the result of different interpretations and differing degrees of adherence to religious precepts by individual Hindus or Muslims in real-life situations. It must be noted also that this is influenced by the institutions through which these religions operate: for example, in matters relating to birth control or abortion, the ulema are in a position to interpret Islam for followers, whereas in the case of Hinduism, the lack of explicit scriptural injunctions may mean that priests are not consulted on these matters. This difference in the role of religious institutions in influencing decisions about contraception was clearly evident in Ramanagaram, in an interview with the local *mullah*, who was educated in a *madrasa* in Bihar and who was personally opposed to family planning. He said clearly that he would not advocate birth control or abortion (and in fact, preached against it) to the townspeople because it was against the tenets of Islam. On the other hand, the two

[15]For example, the Khojas believe that one of their Prophets is the tenth reincarnation of Vishnu. See Radhakrishnan, 1939.

[16]Radhakrishnan describes poetically this 'meeting of religions' in Islam, which 'borrowed its idea of the Messiah from Judaism, its dogmatism and asceticism from Christianity, its philosophy from Greece, and its mysticism from India and Alexandria'. See Radhakrishnan, 1939: 339.

Hindu priests interviewed said that they were not consulted about personal matters such as birth control; and that they were usually approached by the townspeople only if a family member was suffering a grave illness.

The 'Characteristics' Hypothesis

A second, and distinct, view of how religion may affect fertility is the 'characteristics' hypothesis. This hypothesis argues that fertility differentials between populations reflect socio-economic differences between members of different religious groups (Riccio, 1979: 199–228). It is thus possible that the fertility of one religious community may differ significantly from that of another, but for reasons other than the philosophical content of religion, such as differences in income or educational levels. In addition, there are situations in which both the 'theology' and the 'characteristics' mechanisms may work in combination. For example, religion may act to discourage investment in 'child quality' if it translates into low autonomy or status for women. This is partly the 'pure religion effect' in operation, but it might work through a 'characteristics' effect as well.

One important characteristic of a religious community may be its minority group status. It is hypothesized that fertility for a minority community may be higher if it feels threatened by the majority community in political, economic or social spheres (Van Heek, 1966: 125–38; Stinner and Mader, 1975: 53–9). This is also likely if identification with a religious organization can be used for economic gain and rent-seeking activities. This is particularly relevant in countries such as India where religion has been used in the past as a means of gaining legitimacy in the eyes of the state in order to corner some portion of the gains from development. For example, at the level of local government institutions, election to political office in religiously segmented populations (such as in Ramanagaram) depends not merely on economic affluence and high social status but also on numerical preponderance. A second example is that members of particular religions may be prevented from engaging in certain occupations. Third, there may be differential access to education or types of educational system for those belonging to different religions.

Empirical evidence for the 'characteristics' hypothesis is widespread. As with the 'pure religion effect' hypothesis, this literature focuses on differences in fertility between Catholics and others, or Muslims and others. Empirical evidence for the 'pure religion effect' hypothesis is found in studies that consider the demographic experience of Catholics and

Protestants in the Unites States and Australia.[17] Other studies of Catholic–Protestant differentials have emphasized socio-economic factors in accounting for differences. These factors include education, occupation, and residence (Galloway, Hammel and Lee, 1994: 135–58; Golde, 1975). One main concern in the debates on Catholic/non-Catholic fertility in the United States in the context of the 'characteristics' hypothesis has been the increasing divergence between Catholics and non-Catholics between 1945 and the mid-1960s, followed by more rapid convergence during the 1970s.[18] Evidence for the 'characteristics' hypothesis is also to be found in studies of Islamic populations and in a number of empirical studies on countries such as the USA, Philippines, the former USSR, and Sri Lanka, which support the hypothesis that minority group consciousness is an important 'characteristic' which affects fertility.[19]

In conclusion, both the 'particularised theology' hypothesis and the 'characteristics' hypothesis suggest that differences in fertility by religion reflect the influence of organized religion on fertility. The 'pure religion effect' operates through the religion's norm-enforcing abilities and its ability to impose sanctions. However, differences in fertility by religion may merely reflect differences in the socio-economic characteristics of a religion's members. Among these characteristics, a particularly important one may be minority group consciousness. Empirical evidence for both these hypotheses has been mainly observed from (though not restricted to) fertility differentials between Catholics and non-Catholics, and those between Muslims and non-Muslims. This empirical literature has suggested that over time, as identities become less distinctive and the economy develops, there is convergence in fertility between religious communities. For example, some countries, such as Malaysia and Indonesia (and more recently Bangladesh)—all Islamic countries by political orientation—have witnessed declines in their total fertility rates. However, it should be pointed out that Malaysia and Indonesia are not

[17]There are very few studies using economics methods which explicitly consider religion in models of fertility. The few which have done so include Rosenzweig and Schultz, T.P., 1985: 992–1015; Boulier and Rosenzweig, 1978: 487–97; Sander, 1995: chapter 4. Other important studies on this issue include Miller, 1988: 65–79. Westoff and Ryder, 1977a; Mosher and Hendershot, 1984b: 671–7.

[18]Chamie, 1977: 365–82; Westoff and Jones, 1979: 209–17; Westoff and Ryder, 1977b: 431–53; Janssen and Hauser, 1981: 511–28; Mosher and Hendershot, 1984b: 671–7; Blake, 1984: 329–40. The differences in the Mosher and Hendershot analysis are probably due to the inclusion of Hispanic women who are mainly Catholic.

[19]Van Heek, 1966: 125–38; Day, 1968: 27–50; Ling, 1980: 581; Heer and Turner, 1965: 279–92; Heer, 1966: 423–44; Heer and Youssef, 1977: 155–73; Stinner and Mader, 1975: 53–9.

TABLE 3.1: SELECTED DEMOGRAPHIC INDICES BY RELIGION FOR INDIA (1995)

Religion	Total population (millions)	Sex ratio (females per 1000 males)	% of total population (1981)	% of total population (1991)[1]	% decadal growth rate (1971–81)[2]	% decadal growth rate (1981–91)[2]	Urban population	% of urban population to total population	% of total urban population
Hindu	687.6	925	82.63	82.00	24.14	22.78	164.7	24.0	76.35
Muslim	101.5	930	11.36	12.12	30.69	32.76	36.0	35.5	16.70
Christian	19.6	994	2.43	2.34	16.83	16.89	6.1	31.1	2.85
Sikh	16.3	888	1.96	1.94	26.15	25.48	3.8	23.3	1.75
Buddhist	6.3	952	0.71	0.76	22.52	35.98	2.3	36.5	1.05
Jain	3.3	946	0.48	0.40	23.17	4.42	2.4	72.7	1.09
Others	–	–	0.42	0.38	26.61	13.19	–	–	–
Religion not stated	–	–	0.01	0.05	66.88	573.46	–	–	–

Note: [1]Excludes figures for Jammu and Kashmir where the Census was not held.
[2]Excludes figures for Assam and Jammu and Kashmir.
Source: Census of India 1991, Paper 1 of 1995 on *Religion*.

wholly Muslim in terms of population, and that family planning may be more readily available in these countries, either due to the needs of the other religious populations or due to government efforts (Cleland, 1993: 345–52). This illustrates the way in which the effect of religion is heavily dependent on its being supported (or opposed or counteracted) by other institutions such as the state. This implies that though we need to consider the norm-enforcing strength of religion, we must also look towards its ability to interact with social arrangements and other institutions in society over time.

Finally, it is necessary to examine briefly trends in fertility over time by religion in India as a whole and in Karnataka state in order to see if there is empirical evidence from India supporting either the 'characteristics' hypothesis or the 'pure religion' hypothesis. In 1995, Census data on religion were published by the Government of India. These data provided statistics on selected demographic indices by religion, as shown in Table 3.1.

The data show that while the decadal growth rate of population increased for Muslims between the 1970s and 1980s, it has decreased for

Hindus and remained constant for Christians. However, the proportion of the population belonging to different religions remained almost unchanged between 1981 and 1991.

In this context, it is also useful to examine data taken from the 1991 Census on the distribution of the population by religion among the Indian states, which is shown in Table 3.2.

The data show that over the 1981–91 period, Hindu fertility has grown less than Muslim fertility in states where Hindus predominate. However,

TABLE 3.2: DISTRIBUTION OF POPULATION BY RELIGION FOR SELECTED INDIAN STATES (1981–91)

State	Hindus		Muslims		Christians	
	% of total population (1991)	% increase (1981–91)	% of total population (1991)	% increase (1981–91)	% of total population (1991)	% increase (1981–91)
Andhra Pradesh	89.14	24.74	8.91	30.66	1.83	-15.14
Bihar	82.42	22.72	14.81	29.50	0.98	13.99
Gujarat	89.48	21.12	8.73	24.05	0.44	36.96
Haryana	89.21	27.18	4.64	45.89	0.10	28.52
Himachal Pradesh	95.90	20.95	1.72	28.04	0.09	12.16
Jammu and Kashmir	32.24	–	–	–	–	–
Karnataka	85.45	20.66	11.64	25.71	1.91	11.12
Kerala	57.28	12.62	23.33	25.49	19.32	7.41
Madhya Pradesh	92.80	26.61	4.96	31.21	0.65	21.20
Maharashtra	81.12	25.29	9.67	31.40	1.12	11.26
Orissa	94.67	19.11	1.83	36.83	2.10	38.67
Punjab	34.46	12.73	1.18	42.42	1.11	21.75
Rajasthan	89.08	28.09	8.01	41.46	0.11	21.28
Tamil Nadu	88.67	15.15	5.47	21.14	5.69	13.63
Uttar Pradesh	81.74	23.11	17.33	36.54	0.14	23.04
West Bengal	74.72	21.09	23.61	36.89	0.56	19.96
India	82.41	22.78	11.67	32.76	2.32	16.89

Note: the census was not conducted in the state of Jammu and Kashmir in 1991.
Source: Census, 1991, Paper 1 of 1995 on Religion.

TABLE 3.3: DISTRIBUTION OF POPULATION BY RELIGION FOR KARNATAKA (1991)

Religion	% of total population (1981)	% of total population (1991)	% decadal increase (1971–81)	% decadal increase (1981–91)
Hindu	85.77	85.45	25.74	20.66
Muslim	11.21	11.64	33.74	25.71
Christian	2.08	1.91	26.18	11.12
Sikh	0.02	0.02	-6.28	57.80
Buddhist	0.11	0.16	198.83	72.81
Jain	0.77	0.73	29.99	14.62
Other religions	0.04	0.01	32.95	-50.97
Religion not stated	0.00	0.08	375.82	8242.03

Source: 1981 and 1991 Census of India, Paper 1 of 1995 on Religion.

other evidence shows that in states where Muslims predominate, Muslim fertility has grown less than Hindu fertility (Goyal, 1990).

It is instructive to compare these figures with those for Karnataka, shown in Table 3.3. Hindus are the majority religious community in Karnataka to an even greater extent than in India as a whole. Although the proportions of Hindus, Muslims, Sikhs, Jains, and Buddhists remained more or less constant between 1981 and 1991, there was a fall in the proportion of Christians. Compared to 1971–81, decadal growth rates have fallen for all religious communities in Karnataka, except for the Sikhs. This is consistent with the general decline in fertility figures for the state as a whole.

Finally, we can compare these figures with those for Bangalore rural district, in which Ramanagaram is located, as shown in Table 3.4. Hindus are the majority community, forming over 90 per cent of the population in the district. Minority communities such as the Muslims and the Christians form a greater proportion of the urban population than the rural population of Bangalore rural district. In particular, the Muslims make up nearly 27 per cent of the urban population, but less than 5 per cent of the rural population.

It is instructive to compare these findings with those presented by the *Mysore Population Study* conducted by the United Nations in 1961. That study found that for Mysore state as a whole, the crude birth rate was 40 per 1000, the crude death rate was 18 per 1000, and the rate of natural increase was 22 per 1000. At the time this was well above world averages, and very high in comparison with India as a whole, a fact attributable

TABLE 3.4: DISTRIBUTION OF POPULATION BY RELIGION, FOR
BANGALORE RURAL DISTRICT (1991)

Religion	Total population	% of total population	Total urban population	% of total urban population	Total rural population	% of total rural population
Hindu	1,520,520	90.88	218,281	71.97	1,302,239	95.06
Muslim	144,337	8.63	81,656	26.92	62,681	4.58
Christian	6559	0.39	2429	0.80	4130	0.30
Jain	1147	0.07	779	0.26	368	0.03
Buddhist	24	0.001	8	0.003	14	0.001
Sikh	197	0.01	85	0.03	112	0.008
Others	47	0.003	47	0.02	0	0.00
Religion not stated	365	0.022	1	0.0003	364	0.03
Total	1,673,196	100	303,286	100	1,369,908	100

Source: 1991 Census of India, Paper 1 of 1995 on Religion.

mainly to the very low death rate at the time. The total number of children ever born in the category 'towns', under which Ramanagaram was included, was 3.9. Average family size for women over age 45 years in that survey was 5.6 for women in 'towns', 6.7 for Muslims, and 5.2 for Hindus. The study attributed this difference to the shorter periods of sexual separation after childbirth between husbands and wives for Muslims compared with Hindus, and to taboos on sexual relations for prolonged periods during lactation for Hindus, and abstinence on a larger number of religious days for Hindus, which were widely observed in the local population. The study observed that 'the relatively high percentage of Muslims in the towns is a factor tending to raise the average number of children there'. The study also found that the non-backward castes showed slightly higher fertility (4.0) than the Scheduled Castes (3.3) and the backward castes (3.1) (UN, 1961: 78–121).

More recently, the NFHS calculated the total fertility rates and mean number of children ever born for women aged 40–9 years for the three years preceding the survey, and reported their results by religion (IIPS, 1995). The figures for Karnataka are shown in Table 3.5.

The differences in fertility by religion are very large. In terms of both current fertility and cohort fertility, Muslims appear to have the highest fertility of any religious group, followed by the Hindus. The difference is one child per woman, on average. More recent estimates from the

TABLE 3.5: TOTAL FERTILITY RATE AND CHILDREN EVER BORN IN KARNATAKA (1992–3)

Religion	Total fertility rate (for women aged 15-49 years)	Mean number of children ever born to women aged 40–9 years	Total wanted fertility rate
Hindu	2.73	4.57	2.10
Muslim	3.91	5.82	2.88
Christian	2.25	(3.50)	1.98
Other	(1.54)	*	(0.92)
Total	2.85	4.65	

Notes: Figures in parentheses are based on 125–249 person-years of exposure and mean based on 29–45 cases.
*indicates mean not computed as sample consisted of less than 25 cases.
Source: Compiled from the National Family Health Survey 1992–93, Karnataka, 1995: Table 5.2, p. 62 and Table 7.9, p. 126.

NCAER's Human Development Report of 1999 also suggest that the total fertility rate for ever-married Hindu women in Karnataka is 2.3 while that for ever-married Muslim women is 3.9 (Shariff, 1999). The available demographic indices for India as a whole and Karnataka in particular therefore suggest considerable differences between religious groups, especially between Hindus and Muslims.

A review of the literature suggests that it would be desirable to have more quantitative studies of the impact of Islam on fertility. This is an important area for future research and is particularly relevant for comparing the impact on fertility of Islam and of Hinduism. Modern sociological analyses of religion and fertility in the Indian context have used religion mainly as a means of categorizing the population than as an explanatory variable. Almost none have used multivariate analysis (One exception is Jeffery and Jeffery, 1997). It is partly these exogenous gaps in the existing literature—the paucity of micro-studies, of quantitative data, and of those using multivariate analysis—that has led the present study to seek to combine a multivariate analysis of religion and fertility with an anthropological exploration of the qualitative factors that affect religion and fertility in India today.

In the debate about the relationship between religion and fertility, there are four basic questions. First, should the observed higher fertility of minority communities (mainly Muslim) in India be attributed to socio-economic characteristics or to theological beliefs? Does the frequency or intensity of religious observance influence fertility? How does women's status vary across religions and is this significant for fertility? Finally, might 'convergence' between religious groups (as in the case of Catholic and non-Catholic fertility in the 1970s in the USA) take place in any society? In the present study, an attempt is made to answer these questions by examining attitudes towards religion, religious observance, and their effect on nuptiality, contraceptive choice, and fertility in the taluk of Ramanagaram in southern Karnataka.

Section two

Religion and Ramanagaram

chapter four

~~~

Ramanagaram
Mythical Origins, Present-day Realities

The town of Ramanagaram, lying on the Bangalore–Mysore highway in the south Indian state of Karnataka, is named from the hill called Ramagiri that partly surrounds the town (see Figs. 4.1 and 4.2). Popular myth explains that when the Hindu god Rama was banished from his kingdom in Ayodhya, and wandered in the forests of the Deccan for fourteen years, he chanced one day to rest on the hill of Ramagiri, so named as the 'hill of Rama'. His wife, the goddess Sita, was thirsty, and so Rama procured water for her by piercing the surrounding rocks with an arrow. The resulting pool of water was then kept within by the large boulder-like formations that may still be seen in Ramanagaram today.[1]

Ramanagaram is a bustling town of 50,437 people according to the 1991 Census. Located in Ramanagaram taluk[2] that is itself nestled between Kunigal taluk in the north-west, Chennapatna taluk in the west, and Kanakapura taluk in the east (See Figs. 4.3 and 4.4), Ramanagaram is one of the main silk towns in the sericulture belt of southern Karnataka, producing the raw silk yarn that is required for India's large and diverse silk weaving industry. The yarn is then transported to all the major weaving centres such as Kancheepuram, Dharmavaram, and Hyderabad in south India and to Varanasi in the north.

The town is watered by the river Arkavati, a tributary of the river

---

[1]This episode is narrated by Narasimaiah, 1994: chapter 1.

[2]A taluk consists of about 100–300 villages. It is served by a number of revenue inspectors. The latter is usually in charge of a *hobli*, comprising a group of 20–30 villages within a taluk.

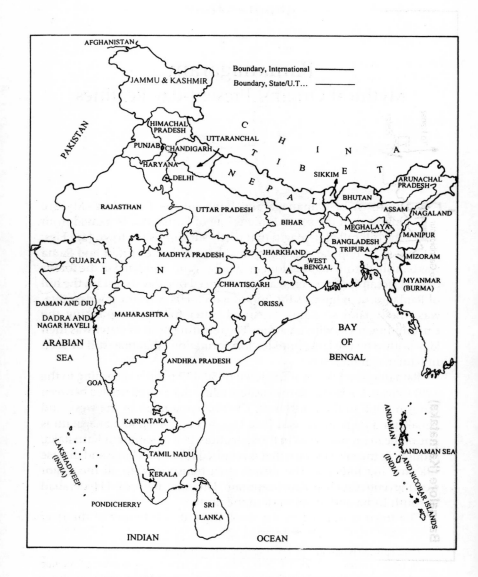

FIGURE 4.1: STATES AND UNION TERRITORIES OF INDIA

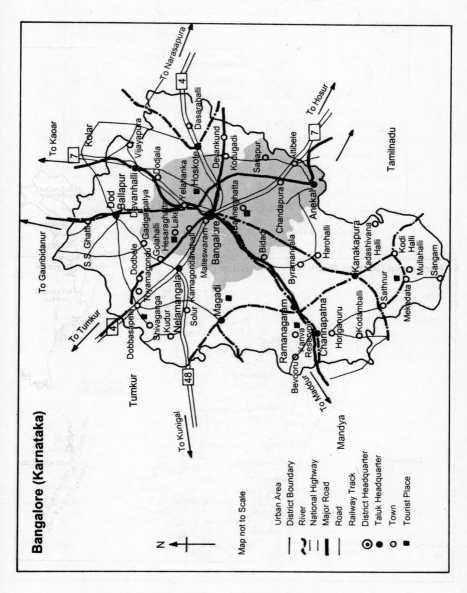

FIGURE 4.2: BANGALORE RURAL, DISTRICT, KARNATAKA

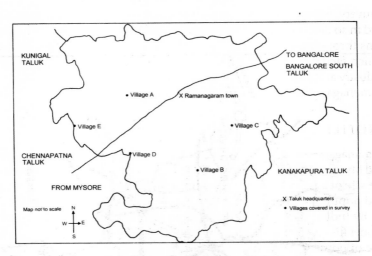

FIGURE 4.3: RAMANAGARAM TALUK, KARNATAKA

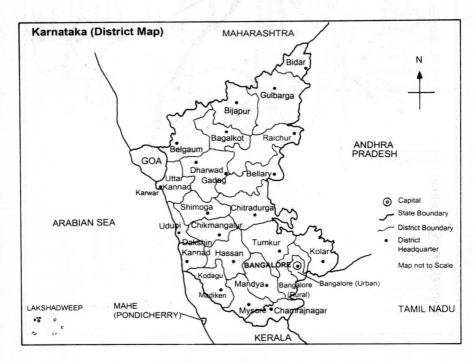

FIGURE 4.4: DISTRICTS OF KARNATAKA

Cauvery, which cuts right across the body of the taluk and the town, and in so doing parallels the Bangalore–Mysore state highway that also runs through the town (see Fig. 4.2). The river provides the soft water which facilitates the silk-reeling process and thereby sustains the silk industry at Ramanagaram. This prized natural endowment has favoured Ramanagaram's silk industry, at least until recently.

PROFILE OF A SOUTH INDIAN TOWN

Ramanagaram is situated on the state highway (SH 17) between Bangalore and Mysore, 48 kilometres from Bangalore (see Fig. 4.2).[3] Table 4.1 shows the size of Ramanagaram taluk and Ramanagaram town in terms of area and population.

By Indian standards, Ramanagaram is a medium-sized town with a moderate rate of growth of population. The annual compound growth rate of population during 1981–91 was 1.4 per cent for the town alone and 3.2 per cent including the outer growth areas.[4] The growth rate for the town alone is low compared to the 1.92 per cent for Karnataka and 2.14 per cent for India as a whole over the same period, mainly because of the substantial amount of out-migration that is continually taking place from Ramanagaram to Bangalore, and to other cities in south India and elsewhere. In 1995, mean household size in Ramanagaram was estimated to be 5.6, and nuclear families comprised some 66 per cent of

TABLE 4.1: LOCATION AND DISTRIBUTION OF HOUSEHOLDS IN
RAMANAGARAM TALUK (1991)

Ramanagaram	Area of village in hectares and of town in sq km	Number of occupied and residential houses	Number of households	Total popu-lation*	Males*	Females*
Whole taluk	630.64	38630	39057	205956	106467	99487
Rural	625.68	29559	29792	155519	80262	75257
Urban	4.96	9071	9265	50437	26205	24232

Note: *includes institutional and homeless population.
Source: 1991 Census, district/taluk primary census abstract, row 02.80.

[3]Ramanagaram is also directly on the broad-gauge railway line between Bangalore and Mysore.
[4]Government of Karnataka, 1995b, Chapter 4, section 4.5.3: 4.27.

TABLE 4.2: BREAKDOWN OF POPULATION IN RAMANAGARAM TALUK BY RELIGION, GENDER, AND RESIDENCE (1991)

Category	Demographic index	Whole taluk	Rural	Urban
Total population		205,956	155,519	50,437
Males	Numbers	106,467	80,262	26,205
	Percentage	51.69	51.61	51.95
Females	Numbers	99,489	75,257	24,232
	Percentage	48.31	48.39	48.04
Hindus	Numbers	172,745	145,942	26,803
	Males	88,964	75,089	13,875
	Females	83,781	70,853	12,928
	Percentage	83.87	93.84	53.14
Muslims	Numbers	32,101	9174	22,927
	Males	16,879	4926	11,953
	Females	15,222	4248	10,974
	Percentage	15.59	5.90	45.46
Christians	Numbers	838	218	620
	Males	455	132	323
	Females	383	86	297
	Percentage	0.41	0.14	1.23
Other religions	Numbers	277	185	87
	Males	169	115	54
	Females	103	70	33
	Percentage	0.13	0.12	0.17

Source: 1991 Census, village/town primary census abstract.

total households (Government of Karnataka, 1995a. Appendix E.1: Section 2.1–2.2: E.1.2)

The breakdown of the population in Ramanagaram taluk, by religion, residence, and gender is shown in Table 4.2.[5] The most important feature of Table 4.2 is the religious composition of the population. Hindus form 84 per cent of the population in the taluk, but only 53 per cent of the population in the town. In contrast, the Muslims form 16 per cent of the population in the taluk, but 46 per cent of the population in the town. The Christians form approximately 0.4 per cent of the population of the

---

[5]See also 1961: 56. The breakdown of the population by religion in 1961 was 70.8 per cent Hindu, 25.9 per cent Muslim, 3.0 per cent Christian, and 0.3 per cent others.

taluk and about 1.2 per cent of the population in the town. Thus, the non-Hindu communities seem to be concentrated in Ramanagaram town.

Growth and industrial development in Ramanagaram has been limited. A 1995 urban infrastructure study remarked, 'no medium- or large-scale unit has been established at Ramanagaram for almost two decades'.[6] The report identified 650 small-scale industrial units in the taluk, employing a total of 5400 persons. Of these, 300 are reported as being in the silk-producing sector (Government of Karnataka 1995a: Section 5.5). Silk-related activity is confined to the cottage and small-scale industries. The reeling and twisting units, in particular, employ a total of 3683 people, with an average of 12 persons per unit (ibid.). The level of capital employed is Rs 50,000 per firm, which is very low by national standards. The main small-scale units operated—apart from in the silk sector—in the areas of agricultural implements, chemicals, food and tobacco, glass and ceramics, repair and servicing works, leather-based units, mechanical engineering units, plastics, printing, silk, and wood-based industries.

Sericulture is the economic lifeblood of Ramanagaram taluk, and women (and to some extent children) are the mainstay of many stages in the process of silk manufacture. Also, in the models presented in later chapters, we examine whether employment in the silk industry affects women's decisions about contraception and fertility. It is therefore worthwhile to examine this industry more closely.

India is the second-largest producer of silk in the world, after China. Karnataka accounts for nearly half of national silk production. Ramanagaram is one of the chief centres in Karnataka for cocoon trading and produces the silk thread that is later woven into cloth by the nation's major weaving centres. Hindu, Muslim, and Christian women in Ramanagaram are all involved actively in different stages of the silk manufacture process. The silk manufacture process begins with mulberry growing and silkworm rearing. It progresses through marketing of the cocoons, reeling the cocoons, twisting the silk yarn, and dyeing the yarn. This yarn is later woven into cloth and finally the cloth is fashioned into garments. At every stage, women in Ramanagaram have an important role to play.

[6]The four medium-scale units are the Chamundi Textiles and Silk Mills that specializes in silk manufacture; Senapathy Whitelays Ltd. that produces electric insulation paper; Valliappa Textiles Ltd that produces cotton yarn and fabric; and Lakshman Isola Ltd. that manufactures mica paper and products. There is one KSSIDC industrial estate for small-scale industries.

The production process begins with silkworm rearing. According to the Karnataka Silk Association, there were 8206 mulberry cultivators in the taluk in 1994. Multivoltine silkworms are reared in Ramanagaram to produce mulberry silk.[7] The sericulturists first keep the silkworm eggs, obtained from the three government grainages and 28 private licensed seed producers, in circular trays with concentric circle partitions called *chandrikas* with mulberry leaves in anticipation for the worms to feed on when the larvae emerge and build their cocoons. Rearing the silkworms is a full-time activity, as the temperature and humidity levels have to be carefully controlled and the trays have to be kept safe from insects which can infect the worms with disease and result in considerable economic loss to the rearers. Therefore, the trays are arranged on wooden slats, often in the rearer's home, and are covered with netting. The women of the household have a major role to play at this stage because it is they who primarily look after the worms in the chandrikas in addition to their household duties, ensuring the requisite standards of hygiene, temperature, and humidity. This stage of the silk manufacturing process is relevant to our analysis of fertility because silkworm rearing is an income-earning occupation for women, but one which is compatible with child rearing, since it is performed in the home.

The cocoons, once formed, are taken, mainly by the women's husbands, to be marketed at the cocoon markets. By law, marketing of the cocoons may only be done in the Government Cocoon Market in Ramanagaram, by open auction method. The cocoons are then taken to the reeling units where they are first dried either in the sun or in steam, to kill the silkworm. Then the cocoons are boiled so that the sericin in the cocoon shell is softened, enabling the silk thread to be unwound in a process known as 'silk-reeling'. The devices used for silk reeling are the country *charkha*, the cottage basin, and the filature-reeling basin, though the *charkha* and the cottage basins are the most popular (Government of Karnataka, 1995a: Appendix D: Section 3.5: D.37).

The silk-reeling is done mainly by adult women and the boiling of the cocoons is mostly done by young boys and girls. Some of these women are the ones I met on my first trip to Ramanagaram, working in dingy rooms, with their hands immersed in scalding water, heated to 45°C.

[7]Silkworms are differentiated into bivoltine and multivoltine according to the number of generations the silk moth passes through during the year. The bivoltine breed produce one or two generations a year. The multivoltine race may produce up to six generations a year. Bivoltine cocoons yield 800–1500m of filament (the fibre in the cocoon shell) apiece a year, while multivoltine cocoons yield only 400m of filament apiece.

The very hot water both softens the cocoons after boiling and enables the thin thread to be extracted. Working in these darkened rooms, the women suffer from diminished eyesight, from bruised hands from keeping them continuously immersed in hot water for so many hours a day, and from asthma from the noxious fumes that emerge from the cocoon-boiling process to soften the sericin. The women need to combine threads from about 7–8 cocoons to form silk thread of the appropriate denier for twisting. There is usually a male supervisor, continuously checking the denier and quality of the reeling and the skeining/twisting into diamond formations that follows the reeling process. The twisting process involves combining several silk threads together to form skeins. The skeins are packed in 2 kg bundles called books, which are then packed in bales. The bales are eventually dyed elsewhere (non-locally) and later woven into finished silk cloth.

The main challenge that faced the Ramanagaram silk industry in the 1990s was competition from bivoltine Chinese silk, which is 30 per cent cheaper than Indian raw silk and of superior quality (ibid.: Section 5.7). Moreover, the Ramanagaram silk industry has so far proved unable to diversify into other stages of the silk manufacturing process, such as weaving or garment-making in which the greatest value added in the silk manufacturing process occurs. Other problems facing the silk industry currently are frequent power shutdowns, water shortages, and the level of environmental pollution and suffering caused by close contact with the fumes emitted during the silk manufacturing process.

Thus, the silk manufacturing process in Ramanagaram is one in which women play a vital economic role. Further, the challenges which this industry faces, both due to the lack of infrastructure and from cheaper imports of silk yarn from China, may have important repercussions on employment for women in Ramanagaram, and consequently perhaps also on their demographic decisions. However, this lack of infrastructure is not restricted to the silk sector, but is mirrored in the town more generally.

Road quality is poor in Ramanagaram, with roads that require widening, inadequate pavements, inadequate streetlighting which is not properly maintained, and shortages of buses, bus stands, and truck terminals. Only one train stops at Ramanagaram in the mornings, and one in the evenings.

In terms of power infrastructure, there is a massive shortage of electricity, which the women I interviewed continually complained about. There is only 12.5 MW of power made available to the town, with 8 to 10 hours of electricity shutdowns daily. At times, the power cuts occurred as many as fifty times a day. This particularly affected industrial equipment and the water supply.

In terms of water infrastructure and sanitation, the river Arkavati is used mainly for washing clothes, bathing, and irrigation. The northern part of the river within the city limits harbours a series of government-constructed wells to provide water to the town. There are only two water-tanks in the whole town, and there is no proper water-distribution system. Borewells are the main sources of water supply. Water is inadequate particularly in the summer, for domestic and industrial use, and especially in the poor neighbourhoods. The women interviewed complained bitterly about the lack of water infrastructure in their town. As regards sanitation, certain slum areas are severely affected by flooding in the rainy season and by the lack of adequate infrastructure, housing, and water.

As regards educational infrastructure, there are only six primary schools, few high schools, and no training colleges or professional colleges. There is only one arts college in the town. This lack of good educational infrastructure is reflected in the low mean level of education for the women interviewed in the sample (5.5 years), especially those belonging to the low and scheduled castes. Moreover, as we explore in later chapters, more years of education has been linked to lower fertility for women, higher age at marriage, and increased adoption of contraceptive techniques.

There is also an informal system of education in Ramanagaram which coexists with the formal sector. This is the *Anganwadi* or 'courtyard teacher' movement, which is part of the nationwide Integrated Child Development Services (ICDS) programme that involves several government departments whose activities are coordinated at the level of the village, the block, the district, and the state. The ICDS provides a package of services for women, children under six years of age, and adolescent girls. It includes supplementary nutrition, immunization, health check-ups, referral services, treatment of minor illnesses, nutrition and health education for adolescent girls and women in their reproductive years, and pre-school education for children from three to six years of age. The scheme also targets specifically populations from the Scheduled Castes, Scheduled Tribes, and other backward communities. The scheme has provided infrastructure and support for women and children, particularly in the rural areas. It has also empowered women to act as social organizers, something that is particularly evident in Ramanagaram taluk. As a part of this movement, educated women, who are specifically trained for the purpose in the town, conduct primary school level teaching in the courtyards of their homes (*aangan*) in the nearby villages. This system of instruction has an advantage over the six primary schools, in that mothers who cannot afford to send their children to one of the larger schools because of monetary disincentives such as the inability to pay fees, buy school uniforms, or meet other demands such as requests for donations, or because of psychic disincentives such as these schools demanding regular attendance, can instead send their children to study in the Anganwadi schools. There are altogether 205 Anganwadi teachers in Ramanagaram taluk and each school is managed by a single teacher. There are altogether 12,500 students enrolled in these schools, of which 5600 are girls. The average number of students per school is 61. The women of Ramanagaram taluk were comfortable with this system be-cause the courtyard teacher was an educated woman from their own neighbourhood, who was trustworthy, highly motivated, and with whom the mothers also consulted for information on infant and child care. The disadvantage of the Anganwadi system of education was that though the courtyard teachers were provided with some basic training at the Anganwadi centre in the town, they were not well-qualified teach-ers, and did not have the superior educational facilities of the six pri-mary schools in their courtyard classrooms. However, the Anganwadi teachers did manage to supplement the educational activities of the six schools in the town and provided an important source of primary school teaching for many of the children of the women interviewed in the Ramanagaram sample.

In terms of health infrastructure in Ramanagaram, there is only one public hospital, with fifty beds. There are only two doctors in this hospital and no specialists. There are no clinical laboratory facilities, and the private doctors are few, far between, and very costly. Catholic missionaries run the Our Lady of Lourdes Health Centre at Ramanagaram. The urban family welfare centre at Ramanagaram and the maternity hospital there are recognized as MTP (medical termination of pregnancies) centres. There are 14 chemists and druggists and 24 and 20 'pharmacists and related establishments' respectively, as defined by the municipality of Ramanagaram. The facilities in Ramanagaram for health care, though poor, are about average for an Indian town of its size. The women I interviewed recognized that the high-level health infrastructure in their town was lacking. However, there were many lower-level facilities, such as the health care provided by the Anganwadi movement. In addition to educating children, the Anganwadi teachers also educated the mothers of their neighbourhood in Oral Rehydration Therapy (ORT) procedures for their infants. These 'courtyard teachers' distributed anti-polio tablets and provided free instruction to the neighbourhood women on the benefits of breastfeeding, as well as information on infant and child care. It has been hypothesized that such low-level health care is even more important than high-level medical facilities in reducing both fertility and mortality (especially infant and child mortality) and the usefulness of having this system in Ramanagaram emerged from the interviews carried out in this study.

Reasons for Choosing Ramanagaram for Field Study

Ramanagaram was chosen for conducting fieldwork for this study for several reasons. First, this study essentially revolves around fertility and its socio-economic and religious determinants. Karnataka has seen a steady decline in fertility rates over the past decade, mainly due to the coordinated literacy and family planning programmes in the state. Yet, both in Karnataka as a whole and in Ramanagaram in particular, there is a mean difference in fertility of nearly one child on average between Hindus and Muslims. This is a significant differential and needs investigation.

However, it seemed desirable to study these fertility differentials in an area where there were not wide differences in the levels of living between the religious communities, as there are for example in the north Indian states of Uttar Pradesh or Bihar and even in the northern districts of Karnataka such as Bidar or Gulbarga, which also have significant minority populations but where poverty compounds demographic differences. The town, moreover, is moderately sized, with one major industry (silk) dominating the area. All religious communities are involved with this industry in one way or another, so there is a common point of reference for all.

As mentioned, Ramanagaram has been exposed to family planning and literacy programmes and there are some schemes operating in the area towards this end. These include the National School Health Programme and the Comprehensive School Health Programme. In fact, the first Family Planning Health Centre in Karnataka was set up in Ramanagaram in 1952, when India first started its government-sponsored National Family Planning Movement and was the first country in the world to do so. Moreover, Ramanagaram was one of the 'towns' of 10,000–25,000 population covered by the Mysore Population Study in 1961 undertaken by the United Nations.[8] Ramanagaram is therefore a good test case as one area which experienced the inception of coordinated thinking and official policy on family planning in India. It seemed important to examine if there were religious differences in fertility in an

---

[8]UN, 1961: 12. Interestingly, the field training for the Mysore Population Study was conducted in one of the villages which was surveyed in the present study as well.

environment where contraceptive technology was freely available and heavily advertised.

Bangalore rural district, in which Ramanagaram is located, is also very important for the socio-economic development of the state of Karnataka in the future, both because of its proximity to Bangalore city and because of the importance of the performance of this district for socio-economic and demographic indicators. Table 4.3 presents data on selected socio-economic and demographic characteristics of Bangalore rural district and compares these data with those for Karnataka state.

The most interesting feature of Table 4.3 is that infant mortality and under-5 mortality in Bangalore rural district is much below the levels for Karnataka state as a whole. Also, the percentage of couples protected by family planning methods in this district is much higher, and the TFR lower than that found in all of Karnataka. However, the district performs less well on economic indicators such as the percentage of people living below the poverty line (which is much higher in the district compared to all of Karnataka), and in the percentage of households using polluting sources of fuel for cooking (which is also very much higher in this district than in the rest of Karnataka state). Finally, Table 4.3 illustrates strikingly how, both in Bangalore rural district and in Karnataka state, a very high proportion of children aged 5–14 years are used for their labour, particularly in the silk-reeling industry.

The prospects of a town such as Ramanagaram being able to divert migration away from Bangalore in the next few decades is an important question, and the fact that this town (and the villages around it) and Bangalore rural district may play an important role in the socio-economic development of the state of Karnataka in future, made the choice of this area for a demographic field study more interesting.

THE DATA SET

This section outlines the data used in the study: the manner in which the sample was selected, the sample size, and the distribution of the sample between Ramanagaram and the surrounding villages. It also discusses the questionnaire that was administered to the women in the sample which is presented at the end of the book.

Methodology: Sampling Procedure, Sample Size, and Method of Interview

The sample covered Ramanagaram town and five other villages. The sampling procedure adopted was a two-stage quota sampling technique. First, the four villages to be used were identified: these will be referred to

TABLE 4.3: Socio-economic and demographic characteristics of
Bangalore rural district and Karnataka state

Index	Bangalore rural district	Karnataka state
1. *Socio-economic indices*		
GDP per capita (in Rs)	4788	5357
Population below poverty line as a proportion of total population 1993–4	38.17	33.16
Percentage of households using polluting fuel (wood, cow-dung, kerosene, and coal) for cooking 1991	96	90
Agricultural wages (in Rs)		
Male	19.32	18.80
Female	16.26	14.40
Share of earned income		
Male	0.71	0.71
Female	0.29	0.29
Adult literacy rate 1991 (%)		
Male	55.5	63.8
Female	28.1	37.5
% child labour to total child population (aged 5–14) 1991	8.58	8.80
2. *Demographic indices*		
Proportion of population		
Male	0.51	0.51
Female	0.48	0.49
Mean age at marriage (years)		
Male	26.71	26.21
Female	19.69	20.14
Difference in mean age at marriage between males and females 1991 (years)	6.41	6.07
Life expectancy at birth (years)	66.69	62.07
Child mortality under-5 (per thousand)	67	90
Infant mortality rate (per thousand)		
Male	51	74
Female	49	72
Total fertility rate (based on age-specific fertility)	3.76	3.87
Eligible couples protected by all family planning methods 1996–97	66	58

Source: Government of Karnataka, 1999, selected figures from statistical appendices, pp. 217–378.

as villages A, B, C, and D in Ramanagaram taluk (see Fig. 4.3). I chose to interview some women from both the town of Ramanagaram and the surrounding villages because the villages were intimately connected with the rural and small-scale economy of Ramanagaram. Their proximity to the town (all within a radius of 20 kilometres), coupled with their involvement in the silkworm rearing industry that sustains the silk-reeling in Ramanagaram town, made them suitable choices. In fact, many of the villagers came to the town for employment in the silk units as well. I also selected a fifth village, called village E, a bit further away on the Ramanagaram/Chennapatna taluk border. This particular village was selected because many of its inhabitants commuted daily into Ramanagaram town, where they worked in the silk-reeling units. Table 4.4 shows the size of the five villages and the number of households in each village.

Depending on the size of the town or village, I adopted a proportional sample size, with the largest sample being from Ramanagaram town itself. Within the town, households were randomly identified in each of the major neighbourhoods, from both the slum areas and the more affluent localities. However, as this study deals specifically with religion, among the households first identified within the villages/town, I eventually selected 111 Hindu households, 75 Muslim households, and 15 Christian households. The total number of households covered was 201. The Hindus who were included in the sample resided in the town and all the villages chosen, but the Muslims who were interviewed resided only in the town and three other villages. The Christians in the sample lived in the town and one other village. The number of Christian households sampled is much fewer than the number of Hindu and Muslim households, mainly because the population of Christians in the taluk is much smaller than the population of Hindus and Muslims. As in other studies based on sample data, it is acknowledged that there is always a trade-off between the depth of information collected and the number of households sampled. The sample for this study was selected in a manner which was proportional to the distribution of the population in the taluk. However, as will emerge from later chapters, the demographic differences between the Christians and the other two religious groups in Ramanagaram taluk are so very marked that the contrasts between the demographic behaviour of the three religious groups emerge even when Hindus and Muslims are compared to the very small sample of Christian households selected.

A total of 187 adult married women and 14 adult single women were interviewed for this study. It must be emphasized again that the villages covered in the sample are large by Indian standards, with unusually high male–female ratios, and are close to Ramanagaram town.

TABLE 4.4: SIZE OF VILLAGES AND DISTRIBUTION OF HOUSEHOLDS IN
RAMANAGARAM TALUK (1991)

Village/ town	Area (village in hectares, town in sq km)	Number of occupied and residential houses	Number of households	Total popu- lation*	Males*	Females*
Village A	381.95	287	289	1495	769	726
Village B	1015.56	710	712	3753	1967	1786
Village C	204.24	308	308	1756	915	841
Village D	425.17	234	234	1245	640	605
Village E	572.83	734	734	3339	1638	1701
Ramanagaram town	4.96	9071	9265	50,437	26,205	24,232

Note: *includes institutional and homeless population.
Source: Village/town primary census abstract, 1991 Census.

The villages are also associated actively with socio-economic activity in Ramanagaram town. This may imply that fertility, contraceptive use, and marriage age between Hindus and Muslims may be more homogeneous in the Ramanagaram sample than might be expected in a more purely 'rural' area of the Indian countryside. There were 14 single women who were interviewed in order to provide qualitative information about their perceptions of the decision to marry and to have children, and in order to observe whether their views were consistent with those of the married women also interviewed.

The interviews were conducted mainly on an individual basis but seven were attended by two persons (especially with the presence of elderly mothers, mothers-in-law, or young sisters, some of whom were also interviewed). Some group discussions were also conducted for two reasons. First, in order to corroborate what the individuals had said by raising the same issues which were asked in the questionnaire in a general discussion with groups of women. Second, it was important to observe the women that we had earlier interviewed in a group setting to judge the extent to which they would articulate and vocalize their beliefs among their peers. The group sizes varied from 4 to 8 depending on the locality and the religious community. Five of the women––two Hindus, two Muslims, and one Christian—were interviewed in depth and more than once, in order to carry out case studies of their lives. They all belonged to different castes and localities.

The Questionnaire

The questionnaire administered to the women was divided into five sections. Section I covered personal information regarding the respondent. This part was a mini-census which recorded all persons living in that house; their ages; primary and secondary languages spoken; religion; educational background in terms of number of years of primary, secondary, and university education, if any; and marital status including age at menarche, age at first marriage, and age at cohabitation with spouse. This section also asked questions about the husband's age, education, and occupation, and the extent of consanguinity between spouses. Details regarding the children, specifically about their ages, education, occupations, and current residence, were also covered in this section. Women were asked if their families possessed any land, and its acreage. They were then asked to list their main items of monthly expenditure and their ownership of particular items of consumer equipment.

Section II covered decision-making within the family. This section asked about rapport between family members and decision-making within the household, specifically with regard to housework, income-earning work, and spending money. This section also discussed nutrition decisions, and information concerning the value of daughters to the household. The women were asked about their married daughters' ages at marriage and unmarried daughters' proposed ages at marriage.

Section III dealt with the economic value of children in terms of costs and benefits, contributions of children to current and future income, and the direct and opportunity costs of childbearing. These questions dealt with children's hourly contributions to the time budget of the household, both in terms of helping their mothers and in performing income-earning work. Questions pertaining to old-age security motives for childbearing and son-preference were also discussed at this stage.

Section IV dealt with reproduction, contraception, and health care, including fertility decisions and attitudes towards contraception and health care. The women were asked a range of questions about their desired family size, preference for boys and girls, and for opinions about large families compared to small ones. They were also asked about their attitudes towards contraception, inter-spousal communication regarding family planning issues, the position of their religion on contraception, and the ease and frequency of health care in their town/village.

Finally, Section V involved questions pertaining to religious observance, religious beliefs, and the extent of piety in the family and in the community.

These questions were personal evaluations by the women of the importance of religion in their lives and in those of their families. There were also questions on the extent of communal interaction between religious groups in the town/village.

It also included several questions on women's status in the town/ village and the respondent's view of how variables relevant to women's well-being had changed over the past five years. These variables included, among others, the woman's assessment of the economic position of the family, the incidence of communal violence and domestic violence in the town/villages, and the status of women locally in general. Altogether ninety-three questions were asked of each woman who was interviewed. The next chapter discusses in depth the census information provided by the women through their answers.

chapter five

The 'Census' Information on the Ramanagaram Sample

This chapter discusses in depth the 'census' information provided by the 201 women interviewed in Ramanagaram through their answers to the questions in Section 1.1 of the questionnaire.

PERSONAL CHARACTERISTICS

The respondents came from five villages and the main Ramanagaram town. As is evident in Table 5.1, the minority populations are mainly concentrated in the town.

The Hindu women interviewed fell into 23 different *jatis* or sub-castes. Broadly, the four major castes within Hinduism are divided into numerous sub-castes or jatis, which are of more importance in a local setting than the major caste. The Mysore Population Study found that the number of separate Hindu caste groups in Mysore state was over a hundred, of which 14 per cent were 'scheduled', 20 per cent were 'backward', and 66 per cent were 'non-backward' castes (UN, 1961: 56–7).

TABLE 5.1: RURAL VS. URBAN RESIDENCE, RAMANAGARAM SAMPLE (1996)

Rural/Urban residence	All women	Hindus	Muslims	Christians
Ramanagaram town	124	46	64	14
Village A	8	8	0	0
Village B	24	19	4	1
Village C	17	10	7	0
Village D	10	10	0	0
Village E	18	18	0	0

The corresponding percentages for the Ramanagaram sample are 20 per cent Scheduled Castes, 35 per cent backward castes, and 45 per cent non-backward castes.

Disaggregated, the numerically strong castes in the sample were the Gowdas (24), the Scheduled Castes (21), the Brahmins (12), the Lingayats (7), and the Okkaligas (7). There were 5 Ekesus, 4 Aswajanas, 4 Bestru, 4 Kuruba, 4 Lambani, 3 Marathi, 3 Mudaliar, 2 Vishwakarmas, 2 Kumbhar, and 2 Balija. There was also one each of the Gamsettu, Ganigas, Gangemata, Gwaladuru, Maduvar, Nayak, Reddy, and Upasadu castes. The Muslims were either Sunnis (49) or Mehdavis (26). All the Christians were Protestants and of the same denomination (the Church of South India).[1] This variable is relevant to an analysis of fertility, as there may be differences in fertility by caste even among those that share the same religion.

The mean age of the women interviewed was 33.4 years for Hindu women, 36.3 years for Muslims, and 35.5 years for Christians. The mean age of the women for the entire sample as a whole was 34.7 years. In the study, the women were randomly selected, and no overt effort was made primarily to select women from particular age groups. However, as it turned out, most of the women were in the 30–40 year age decile. This is a happy coincidence because in a study of fertility, it is particularly useful to have a large sample of women who are of reproductively active age but who have more or less completed their childbearing, in order to make comparisons between groups more meaningful. Additionally, it is useful that the women completed their childbearing recently so that the factors which influenced them are more relevant to contemporary decision-making.

The women spoke a variety of languages as their primary language of communication. This reflects both the unique geographical position of Karnataka state (which shares its borders with four other Indian states) and its history of Hindu, Muslim, and British rule. Kannada, Urdu, Tamil, Marathi, English, Gujarati, Konkani, and Telugu were all reported as the primary language of communication by some women in the sample. For the 111 Hindu women interviewed, the primary language of communication was overwhelmingly Kannada. The 75 Muslim women interviewed spoke primarily in Urdu. A majority of Christian women interviewed spoke in Tamil.[2]

---

[1]This is probably because the Church of South India which is dominant in the area is Protestant in its leanings.

[2]These women spoke Tamil at home because the Christian women in this region are mainly Tamil Christian migrants from Tamil Nadu.

Apart from their primary languages of communication, the women spoke a wide variety and varying combinations of other languages. English, Hindi, Kannada, and combinations thereof were the most popular 'other' languages that the women spoke, probably because these three languages were the main medium of instruction in the schools, and the languages most popularly used in this area.

LITERACY

This variable is interesting because it is widely argued that there is an inverse relationship between fertility and literacy (See for instance, Cochrane and Farid, 1990: 144–54; Caldwell, Reddy and Caldwell, 1985: 29–53). Of the 201 women in the sample, 126 (62.7 per cent of the sample) said they could read and write in their primary language of communication. This does not, however, imply that the levels of education are very high in Ramanagaram taluk: in fact, the mean number of years of education for all 201 women was only 6.0, while that for the 187 married women was 5.5 years. Many who had been educated no further than Standard 4 (four years of primary education after two years of kindergarten) still said that they could read and write their primary language, though their knowledge of reading and writing was quite elementary. As shown in Table 5.2 among the Hindus, 49 (44 per cent) could not read, as compared with 24 of the Muslims (32 per cent) and two Christians (13.3 per cent).

In comparison with the female literacy figures for India, Karnataka state, and Bangalore rural district, in percentage terms, a much greater proportion of the women in the sample said that they were literate. However, it must be remembered that the women were only asked if they could read and write their primary language, and that if they said

TABLE 5.2: PERCENTAGE OF LITERATE POPULATION IN INDIA, KARNATAKA, BANGALORE RURAL DISTRICT, AND THE RAMANAGARAM SAMPLE

Place/Group	Male	Female	Total
India 1991*	67.3	44.3	52.2
Karnataka 1991*	64.1	39.3	32.9
Bangalore rural 1991*	52.2	32.9	42.8
Ramanagaram sample 1996	69.5	62.7	66.1
Ramanagaram Hindus	66.2	66.0	66.1
Ramanagaram Muslims	70.0	68.0	69.0
Ramanagaram Christians	92.9	86.0	89.5

Note: * Figures taken from the 1991 Census.

that they could, this was not explicitly tested. Moreover, it was my impression that many of the women may have felt embarrassed to admit that they could not read or write their primary language of communication fluently, and that even a few years of attendance in school was believed to constitute 'literacy'. However, in order to cross-check the veracity of the women's answers, they were also asked how many years of schooling they had actually had. In response to this question, and despite the optimistic percentages in Table 5.2, the mean number of years of education for the women of the Ramanagaram sample was still (as already remarked) very low at only 5.5 years for the 187 married women. Therefore, in the present study we measure women's education by the number of years of education, rather than by whether they said that they were literate. However, Table 5.2 does illustrate the interesting finding that in Ramanagaram today, women do feel that education is a 'good thing' and something to be aspired for.

In the sample as a whole, 76 women (37.8 per cent) had no education at all, 21 (10.4 per cent) had between 0 and 5 years of learning, while 69 (34.3 per cent) had between 5 and 10 years of learning. It is interesting that of the women who had been to school, 47 (23.3 per cent) had completed their Secondary School-Leaving Certificate (SSLC) Examination, equivalent to ten years of schooling after two years of kindergarten. In the fieldwork it was observed that women either had not been to school at all, or if they had, those who went up to secondary school studied till the tenth-grade level. However, after attaining this level of education, most women appeared to stop their schooling. Only 35 women (17.4 per cent) in the sample actually went on to higher education in excess of ten years of schooling.

Education levels also varied across religious groups, as is shown in Table 5.3. The Christians in the sample are the best educated in terms

TABLE 5.3: MEAN YEARS OF EDUCATION BY RELIGION FOR
RAMANAGARAM SAMPLE (1996)

Mean years of education	All women	Hindus	Muslims	Christians
Mean years of education (all women)	6.0	5.9	5.6	9.2
Mean years of primary education	3.0	2.8	3.1	4.3
Mean years of secondary education	2.6	2.6	2.3	4.1
Mean years of university education	0.4	1.4	1.1	3.3
Mean years of education (187 married women only)	5.5	5.3	5.4	9.0

of primary, secondary, and university education. They have 9.2 total mean years of education (9.0 years for married women), as opposed to 5.9 (5.3 years for married women) and 5.6 years (5.4 years for married women) for the Hindus and Muslims respectively. In fact, the Christians are also the most likely of all the religious communities to go on to higher education. These findings are similar to the 1995 National Family Health Survey (NFHS) data which show that the mean number of years of education for Hindu women in all of India was 3.5 years; it was 2.9 years for Muslims and 5.5 years for Christians. Interestingly, in the Ramanagaram sample, the Muslims had higher rates of mean primary school enrolment, but lower mean secondary school years of education than the Hindus. This may be explained by girls' education being the first casualty as the size of the family increases, or this may be because of the code of *purdah* which the Muslim families observed. The difference between the mean total years of education between Hindus and Muslims was tested at the 95 per cent confidence level and was not found to be statistically significant, which suggests that the code of purdah was not important in this respect. However, there was a statistically significant difference between Christian and Muslim mean levels of education, and between Hindu and Christian levels of education.

OCCUPATION

Of the sample of 201 women, 66.7 per cent worked outside the household. In Table 5.4, the main occupational categories, so grouped so as to be relevant to an analysis of fertility, are listed. 'Farming and allied activity' covers all those activities concerned with agriculture and agro-based processes. 'Home-related activity' deals with all those activities that are undertaken by the women from their homes and includes housework and income-earning work such as silkworm rearing. The latter are compatible with child rearing. 'Sole trader/small-scale/cottage entrepreneur' refers to instances where the woman was involved in managing and running a shop—for example, as a sweets seller or a betel-shop owner. 'Small-scale/cottage unit worker/other labourer' refers to those occupations where the women were either hourly-rate workers in a small-scale unit, such as *agarbatti* (incense-stick) workers or silk reelers, or daily-wage labourers, such as bricklaying and construction workers. 'Government department employee' refers to those women who were working in offices connected with the government, such as clerks and stenographers in the Zila Parishad Office, or women officers in the Block Development Office. 'Service-related and others' refers to occupations

TABLE 5.4: PRIMARY OCCUPATIONS OF WOMEN IN THE RAMANAGARAM SAMPLE (1996)

Employment category	All women		Hindus		Muslims		Christians	
	No.	%	No.	%	No.	%	No.	%
Home-related activity	68	33.8	31	28.0	30	40.0	7	46.7
Small-scale/cottage unit workers and other labourers	50	24.9	25	22.5	23	30.6	2	13.3
Service-related and others	49	24.4	27	24.3	17	22.7	5	33.3
Government department employee	14	7.0	10	9.0	4	5.3	0	0.0
Farming and allied activity	14	7.0	12	10.8	1	1.3	1	6.7
Sole trader and small-scale/ cottage unit entrepreneur	5	2.5	5	4.5	0	0.0	0	0.0
Unemployed	1	0.5	1	0.9	0	0.0	0	0.0
None/Not applicable	0	0.0	0	0.0	0	0.0	0	0.0
Total	201	100.0	111	100.0	75	100.0	15	100.0

connected with the service industries. These included Anganwadi workers and other school teachers, domestic servants, cooks, nurses, and tailoring class teachers. Women who were seeking jobs, but were unemployed at the time of interview come under the 'unemployed' category. Those women under the 'none/not applicable' category were those who were not employed and who were not seeking work.

For all women, home-related activities predominated, followed by work in small-scale/cottage units and service-related occupations. In later chapters, we use various measures of women's occupations based on the data from Table 5.4. Some of the women (about 20 per cent of the total) also had secondary occupations, the most popular of which was *coolie* work (bricklaying/construction work), farming, silkworm rearing, and tailoring.

HUSBAND'S CHARACTERISTICS

Information about the women's husbands sheds light on the links between the husband's characteristics and the couple's fertility. For example, it is hypothesized that greater educational attainment by the husband contributes to lower fertility for the woman.

The mean age of the husbands in the sample was 39.4 years as a whole, 37.9 years for the Hindus, 41.4 years for the Muslims, and 40.3 years for the Christians. On average, there was a difference of about 5 years between the ages of the women and those of their spouses, and this was uniform by religious group.

The mean educational level of the husband was 5.7 years of education for the whole sample, 5.5 years for the Hindu men, 5.2 years for the Muslim men, and 8.0 years for the Christians. Thus, for the sample as a whole, husbands had marginally higher mean years of education than their wives. However, if we consider all 201 women, which includes the single women, the mean years of education for women was 6.0 years. This suggests that women who had remained single went on to pursue higher education, compared with women who married, who tended to do so much less. At the 95 per cent confidence level, there was no statistically significant difference in husband's education between Hindus and Muslims and between Hindus and Christians, although there was a statistically significant difference between Muslims and Christians.

The husbands also performed a wide variety of occupations, as shown in Table 5.5. The most popular occupational categories among the husbands were farming, small-scale and cottage unit labourers and sole traders, and service-related occupations. Among these, the most popular individual occupations were 'business', coolie, factory worker, farming, silk filature, silk merchant, silkworm rearer, silk reeler, and toy maker. This reflects the dominant agricultural and small-scale economic interests of the area. There were no major differences in occupational profiles between the three religious communities, except

TABLE 5.5: PRIMARY OCCUPATIONS OF HUSBANDS IN RAMANAGARAM SAMPLE (1996)

Employment category	Total		Hindus		Muslims		Christians	
	No.	%	No.	%	No.	%	No.	%
Home-related activity	9	4.9	6	5.9	3	4.3	0	0.0
Small-scale/cottage unit workers and other labourers	41	21.9	25	24.3	16	22.9	0	0.0
Service-related and others	38	20.3	15	14.6	16	22.9	7	50.0
Government department employee	17	9.1	9	8.7	6	8.6	2	14.3
Sole trader and small-scale/ cottage unit entrepreneur	31	16.6	16	15.5	14	20.1	1	7.1
Farming and allied activity	44	23.5	30	29.1	11	15.7	3	21.4
Unemployed	7	3.7	2	1.9	4	5.7	1	7.1
Total number of ever-married men	187	100.0	103	100.0	70	100.0	14	100.0

perhaps that the Christians were in higher-status occupations on the whole.

Of all husbands in the sample, 83 per cent did not have a secondary occupation. Those husbands who did have a secondary occupation were in farming, small-scale labouring work, and home-related activity. Among the husbands there was a negative (although small) correlation between having a secondary occupation and the level of education, suggesting that those with less education more often had a secondary occupation.[3]

INCOME AND WEALTH

In this study, several questions were asked for the purpose of estimating the families' incomes. This was because direct questions on income (of the nature 'What is your total monthly income?') rarely yield reliable answers in a questionnaire survey and have to be backed up by extensive cross-checking as to their reliability. This is due to several reasons. First, respondents are usually hesitant to reveal figures pertaining to their earned income to urban interviewers who are far removed from their sphere of life (Nag, 1984). Second, there may be a tendency to understate incomes (Christensen, 1992: 124–37). There may also be a natural reticence about disclosing precise measures of economic status; this is particularly observed among the very rich and the very poor (ibid. 126). Based on these considerations, information was collected in the Ramanagaram study on five different variables which may act as proxies for income. These variables are total expenditure in rupees, *per capita* expenditure in rupees, total foodgrains expenditure in rupees, per capita foodgrains expenditure in rupees, a dummy variable for whether the family owned land or not, and an index of the number of items of consumer equipment owned by the family. This index was calculated as the sum out of a total of eight possible consumer items (transistor, bicycle, television, chair/ bench, watch, fan, cot, and scooter/moped).

Ownership of land is often deemed an important variable because there is a demand for child labour in order to work the land. In the survey, a basic question on land ownership was posed to the respondents: 'Do you own any land? If yes, is it self-owned or leased-in?' In the sample as a whole, 57 per cent said their families had no land, 43 per cent said they possessed land, 0.5 per cent said they had land but that it was part

---

[3]The correlation coefficient between education and existence of a secondary occupation was negative and took a value of –0.14.

of the joint family and undivided.[4] The land owned ranged in size from 0.5 to 18 acres. Altogether, 95 per cent of the families that had some land said that it was self-owned. Land ownership varied across religions: 55 per cent of Hindu women came from families with land, 19 per cent of Muslim families had land, while 46 per cent of Christian families owned land. The average amount of land owned per household was 1.57 acres for the Hindus, 0.38 acres for the Muslims, and 0.77 acres for the Christians. Thus the Muslims, who had a higher mean level of fertility than the Christians, also owned less land on average than the Christians. Altogether, of the 86 families that possessed some land, 95 per cent said that their land was self-owned. Among those 3 per cent of households which leased land, one was Muslim and the other two were Hindu.

Consumer Expenditure and Consumer Equipment

The women interviewed were acutely aware of the money that they spent per month, and were able to give accurate descriptions of the amount spent on food, their children, and themselves.[5] In many cases, the women reported the amount they spent in terms of the quantities of goods that they bought per month. These quantities have been multiplied by the local prices prevailing in February 1996 in the main *mandi* (market) in Ramanagaram in order to obtain estimates of the women's expenditures in rupee terms at current prices. The information on mean total and per capita monthly expenditure volunteered by the women is reported in Tables 5.6 and 5.7.

These estimates of per capita income are lower than the national per capita income figures, probably because (as discussed below) the savings and alcohol estimates do not reflect actual levels. Muslims have the largest mean total consumer expenditure, followed by the Christians and the Hindus. If we look at per capita consumer expenditure, the Christians have the highest per capita consumer expenditure, followed by the Muslims and then the Hindus. The differences between Hindus and Christians,

---

[4]The question in the questionnaire on land ownership related to ownership of land, and not to land operated.

[5]One reason why it is justified to place considerable reliance on the figures relating to women's expenditures is that the estimates provided by the women correspond very closely to one another. This is particularly true of responses given by women who belonged to the same religion and socio-economic class. Given that the interviews were conducted on an individual basis, this suggests that the women's ability to recall information relating to their expenditure was accurate, even if it might have been subject to recall bias. If recall bias was present, it seems likely that it affected all respondents similarly.

and Hindus and Muslims, were statistically significant at the 95 per cent level, but the difference between Muslims and Christians was not. These findings suggest that the Hindus had the lowest expenditure per capita compared to the Muslims and the Christians. Of all three religious communities, Christians spent the most (25 per cent of per capita expenditure) on children, perhaps reflecting a 'quantity–quality' trade-off in Christian fertility because, as we will see in Chapter 8, the Christians had the lowest fertility of all three religious groups.

Some of the women explained that they did not deliberately save money and in the event of ill-health or a daughter's wedding, would borrow money at the required time. For those who did save, I was unable

TABLE 5.6: MEAN MONTHLY TOTAL EXPENDITURE BY RELIGION, RAMANAGARAM SAMPLE (1996) (RUPEES)

Category of expenditure	All women Expenditure	%	Hindus Expenditure	%	Muslims Expenditure	%	Christians Expenditure	%
Rent	64.7	4.4	37.4	3.7	355.2	14.8	150.0	7.8
Foodgrains								
Rice	297.2	20.3	246.9	24.2	368.8	15.4	333.0	17.3
Ragi	88.6	6.1	100.5	9.8	70.6	3.0	84.3	4.4
Wheat	103.7	7.1	32.8	3.2	207.6	8.7	124.0	6.5
Pulses	5.4	0.4	6.4	0.6	3.8	0.2	5.8	0.3
Total	494.9	33.8	386.6	37.8	650.8	27.2	547.1	28.5
Other food items								
Veg fruits	36.4	2.5	27.9	2.7	50.2	2.1	32.5	1.7
Meat/fish	505.5	34.5	339.7	33.2	779.2	31.5	568.6	29.6
Milk	7.2	0.5	6.6	0.7	8.6	0.4	5.4	0.3
Total	549.1	37.5	374.2	36.6	838.0	35.0	606.5	31.5
Leisure								
Alcohol/tobacco	18.8	1.3	6.7	0.7	40.4	1.7	3.5	0.2
Cinema	9.7	0.7	11.0	1.1	11.4	0.5	12.4	0.7
Total	28.5	1.9	17.7	1.7	51.8	2.2	15.9	0.9
Children	231.7	15.8	129.7	12.7	373.5	15.6	478.6	24.9
Miscellaneous								
Soaps/saris/hair oil	96.5	6.6	76.5	7.5	125.1	5.2	125.1	6.5
Total*	1465.4	100.0	1022.1	100.0	2394.4	100.0	1923.2	100.0

Note: *Prices prevailing in the market of Ramanagaram town in February 1996.

TABLE 5.7: MEAN MONTHLY PER CAPITA EXPENDITURE BY RELIGION,
RAMANAGARAM SAMPLE (1996) (RUPEES)

Category of expenditure	All women		Hindus		Muslims		Christians	
	Expenditure	%	Expenditure	%	Expenditure	%	Expenditure	%
Rent	14.4	5.0	9.5	4.6	21.8	5.9	13.9	3.2
Foodgrains								
Rice	55.9	19.6	47.6	22.8	63.8	17.2	78.2	18.0
Ragi	18.2	6.4	22.4	10.7	12.3	3.3	17.4	4.0
Wheat	17.4	6.1	5.7	2.7	32.4	8.8	29.2	6.7
Pulses	1.1	0.4	1.2	0.6	0.7	0.2	1.9	0.4
Total	92.6	32.4	76.9	36.9	109.2	29.5	126.7	29.2
Other food items								
Veg fruits	7.4	2.6	6.2	3.0	9.0	2.4	8.0	1.9
Meat/fish	100.4	35.1	69.4	33.3	138.6	37.5	138.9	32.0
Milk	1.4	0.5	1.3	0.6	1.6	0.4	1.8	0.4
Total	109.2	38.2	76.9	36.9	149.2	40.3	148.7	34.2
Leisure								
Alcohol/tobacco	2.6	0.9	1.2	0.6	4.9	1.3	0.9	0.2
Cinema	2.1	0.7	2.2	1.1	1.6	0.4	3.1	0.7
Total	4.7	1.6	3.4	1.6	6.5	1.8	4.0	0.9
Children	43.8	15.3	24.7	11.8	59.2	16.0	108.4	25.0
Misc[1]	20.9	7.3	17.2	8.3	24.1	6.5	32.7	7.5
Total[2]	285.7	100.0	208.6	100.0	370.0	100.0	434.5	100.0

Notes: [1]Miscellaneous includes expenditure on items such as soaps, saris, hair oil etc.
[2]Prices are those prevailing in the market of Ramanagaram town in February 1996.

to determine exactly the extent of their savings, if any. Nevertheless, I was able to ask a qualitative question to establish what the women would do for extra income, which was 'What do you do about income in the event of an unforeseen occurrence such as illness?' This question had six options which the women were asked to give 'yes/no' responses to. These were: the children leave school, son/daughter sends you money from the city, use savings, borrow from neighbours, pawn jewellery, and other strategies such as someone else helps out. Using savings was not the most popular recourse. Rather, borrowing from friends and neighbours was preferred: this response was given by 38 per cent of Hindus, 25 per cent of Muslims, and 53 per cent of Christians.

The women were very happy to reveal their monthly expenditure on betel leaves and tobacco. However, they were extremely reluctant to speak of alcohol consumption either by themselves or by their husbands.

The reticence of all but a very few women about revealing their expenditure on alcohol is one drawback of the estimates of consumer expenditure derived from the responses to the questionnaire. Alcohol accounts for 0.9 per cent of total consumer expenditure per capita, which is very low compared to the scale of the alcohol problem which emerged in qualitative evidence collected during my fieldwork. Therefore, the figures in the alcohol/tobacco category of Tables 5.6 and 5.7 mainly refer to tobacco consumption, rather than to alcohol.

Cinemas were popular, as well, and an average of about Rs 10 in total or Rs 2.1 per capita was spent per month on entertainment. However, these cinema shows were attended by the Hindu and Christian women, but not at all by the Muslim women, mainly due to purdah restrictions. Women attended the cinema on average about once or twice a month. The expenditure on cinema-going is relevant to questions of fertility because messages about infant and child care were advertised at the cinema, prior to the screening of a film.

Women also allocated 7.3 per cent of their monthly expenditure per capita to miscellaneous items for themselves personally. These chiefly included clothes for themselves (usually bought once or twice a year at festival times), soap (both for clothes and for bathing), white talcum powder, coconut oil and flowers, face cream, *kohl*, and the stick-on *bindis* for Hindu women. Three products—hair oil, talcum powder, and face cream—essentially formed the core cosmetics for the Ramanagaram women.[6] My impression was that the unusual level of expenditure on these items (35.4 per cent of the total expenditure on miscellaneous items) was caused by the influence of the media, through radio, television, and billboards, in promoting these products through advertising. However, the bathing soap, hair oil, powder, and face cream were used not just by the women of the household, but also chiefly by their adult sons and a bit less frequently by elderly relatives living in the household.[7]

One reason why it is important to describe and discuss the composi-

[6]The powder was made by Ponds India Ltd. and called 'Pond's Dreamflower Talc' while the cream was rather enticingly named 'Fair And Lovely', produced by Hindustan Lever Ltd.

[7]During the interviews, the women would meet me only after they had applied their creams and powders and tidied their hair. No amount of coaxing that they should not waste their cosmetics on me seemed to deter their resolve to literally put their 'best faces forward' to strangers. If I did not inform them earlier that I was coming, this invariably meant that I would have to wait about 5–10 minutes on the doorstep while the women prepared themselves to be interviewed. Frequently, when I sought interviews with women, they would be at home oiling their daughter's hair or their own with the coconut oil.

tion of consumption expenditure in detail is that it provides qualitative evidence about women's lives in the taluk. It is important to know how much women spend on basic necessities for the household compared to expenditures on themselves or on their children. One important qualitative finding from the breakdown of consumer expenditure is that the Christians, on average, spend more on their children than do the other two religious groups. Given the enormous academic literature which has been devoted to the quantity–quality trade-off and the relationship between income and fertility, it seemed worthwhile to examine the composition of consumption expenditure in the Ramanagaram sample.

The questionnaire also posed questions concerning ownership of certain consumer durable assets: a transistor, a bicycle, a fan, a cot, a moped/scooter, a watch, a television, and a chair/bench. The number of families owning these items of consumer equipment is shown in Table 5.8.

For the sample as a whole, televisions, transistors, watches, and chairs or benches were the most popular items of consumer equipment in Ramanagaram. The ownership of a transistor or a television might indicate the extent that the family would be aware of outside influences, as well as its relative prosperity. This is related to fertility because most public information about contraception and family planning in rural areas of India is provided via the radio and television. At the 95 per cent confidence level, while the differences between Hindu and Muslim mean ownership of transistors was found to be statistically significant, the difference between Christian and Hindu, and Christian and Muslim, mean ownership of transistors was not. Televisions were also very popular in Ramanagaram, particularly within the Muslim community. One Muslim woman interviewed explained that since the Muslim women were not

TABLE 5.8: OWNERSHIP OF CONSUMER ITEM BY RELIGION,
RAMANAGARAM SAMPLE (1996)

Consumer item	All women		Hindus		Muslims		Christians	
	No.	%	No.	%	No.	%	No.	%
Transistor	103	51.2	64	57.7	27	36.0	7	46.7
Bicycle	83	41.2	47	42.3	31	41.3	5	33.3
Fan	86	42.8	39	35.1	38	50.7	9	60.0
Cot	83	41.3	35	31.5	39	52.0	6	40.0
Moped/scooter	33	16.4	21	18.9	8	10.7	4	26.7
Watch	115	57.2	64	57.7	40	53.3	11	73.3
Television	100	49.6	50	45.0	40	53.3	10	66.7
Chair/bench	124	61.7	69	62.2	42	56.0	13	86.7

allowed to go to the cinema due to the strict code of purdah their main source of entertainment was the television at home. Of the total number of households, 50 per cent had a television: 45 per cent of Hindus, 53 per cent of Muslims, and 67 per cent of Christians.

A bicycle was much prized in Ramanagaram, mainly because one of its primary uses was to carry water.[8] Because, as my fieldwork revealed, nearly twenty-seven pots were required on average per family per day, with 2.2 hours on average per person per day devoted to water collection, a bicycle considerably reduced the number of hours spent collecting water. This is relevant to an analysis of fertility, because it has been hypothesised that children may be used for water and firewood collection in areas which lack suitable infrastructure (See Dasgupta, 1993a: 343–70). Of the families in the sample, 41 per cent had a bicycle: 42 per cent of Hindus, 41 per cent of Muslims, and 33 per cent of Christians. A reason for the smaller percentage of Christian households who owned a bicycle may have been that many Christian homes possessed water taps. However, at the 95 per cent confidence level, there was no statistically significant difference between religious groups. Moreover, a greater percentage of Christians owned mopeds and scooters.

Ownership of a fan, a chair or bench, and a cot are other indicators of relative prosperity of the family. Indeed, insofar as they may be regarded as oriented toward personal comfort rather than economic necessity, they may be assessed as a measure of the ability to afford a luxury. Ownership of fans, chairs and benches indicated that the Christians were comparatively better off. However, a greater percentage of Muslims owned cots, followed by Christians and Hindus. This suggests that something other than merely income influences this aspect of consumption, since the Christians were the wealthiest group. Perhaps it is because Muslim women spend more time in the house because of the purdah restrictions, and consequently would make more continuous use of this consumer item.

In conclusion, the census information on the sample shows that Ramanagaram women are, on average, poorly educated and very often perform more than one occupation. Their husbands are, on average, slightly better educated than they are, and mainly perform only one occupation. Higher proportions of men, compared with women, perform skilled occupations. Measures of income in terms of consumer expenditure and ownership of consumer equipment show that the

---

[8]Normally, eight pots of water could be strung with rope across the body of the bicycle.

Christians in Ramanagaram are better off than Hindus and Muslims. In later chapters, these measures of education, occupation, and income are three major variables incorporated into our models of age at marriage, contraception, and fertility.

THE NATURE OF THE DEPENDENT VARIABLE: AGE AT FIRST MARRIAGE, THE DECISION TO USE CONTRACEPTION, AND CHILDREN EVER BORN

Before considering in detail the econometric analysis of the determinants of women's age at first marriage, their decision to use contraception, and their fertility, it is important to examine the characteristics of the dependent variables used in the multivariate analysis. This question will be examined first in terms of the average values and standard deviations of these three demographic characteristics, and then in terms of the distributions of these three variables in the Ramanagaram sample.

Table 5.9 shows the means and standard deviations of the woman's age at first marriage for the whole sample and for Hindus, Muslims, and Christians separately. It is evident from the table that that there was little difference in mean age at first marriage between Muslims and Christians, although there was a difference between Hindus and Muslims and between Hindus and Christians. Interestingly, the mean age at first marriage for all women in the Ramanagaram sample is lower than the prescribed legal minimum age at first marriage, which is 18 years for women in Karnataka.

TABLE 5.9: WOMAN'S AGE AT FIRST MARRIAGE, RAMANAGARAM SAMPLE (1996)

Category	Mean	Standard deviation
All women	17.27	0.28
Hindus	16.94	0.35
Muslims	17.66	0.51
Christians	17.64	0.82

Another useful way of looking at age at marriage is by examining the number of years since the woman's first marriage (see Table 5.10). The Muslims and Christians interviewed had been married longer than the Hindus. The mean number of years since first marriage differ between Hindus and Muslims and between Hindus and Christians, although not between Muslims and Christians.

An important preliminary to deciding on the appropriate method of econometric analysis of the determinants of women's age at first marriage,

TABLE 5.10: YEARS SINCE FIRST MARRIAGE, RAMANAGARAM SAMPLE (1996)

Category	Mean	Standard deviation
All women	17.59	0.82
Hindus	16.46	1.00
Muslims	19.00	1.02
Christians	18.78	1.03

is to consider the characteristics of the distribution of the dependent variable. The variable is measured in years, and is more or less normally distributed as can be seen in Table 5.11. A majority of the women interviewed were married between the ages of 11 and 25 years. Only one woman was married between the ages of 1 and 10 years; only one woman was married between the ages of 31 and 45 years. The distribution of the variable is continuous across practically all values between 11 and 30 years. It is for this reason that OLS methods are used in the econometric analysis of the models of marriage age presented in Chapter 6.

The second of our dependent variables, the one whose determinants are analysed econometrically in Chapter 7, is the decision to use contraception. In the survey, the Ramanagaram women were asked if they had ever used any method of birth control. The question was answered in the affirmative by 53 per cent of ever-married women in the whole sample, 86 per cent of Christians, 57 per cent of Hindus, and 40 per cent of Muslims, as can be seen in Table 5.12.

In the econometric analysis of the determinants of contraceptive use in Chapter 7, the dependent variable used is whether or not the woman had ever used a method of contraception, where the variable takes a value 1 if the woman had ever used a contraceptive method and 0 otherwise.

TABLE 5.11: AGE DISTRIBUTION AT FIRST MARRIAGE,
RAMANAGARAM SAMPLE (1996)

Woman's age (in years)	Frequency
0–10	1
11–15	68
16–20	86
21–25	23
26–30	4
31–35	1
36–40	0
41–45	0
More than 46	0

TABLE 5.12: WOMEN'S DECISION TO USE CONTRACEPTION,
RAMANAGARAM SAMPLE (1996)

Category	Mean	Standard deviation
All women	0.54	0.04
Hindus	0.57	0.04
Muslims	0.41	0.05
Christians	0.92	0.07

This variable follows a binomial distribution, as evident in Table 5.13. A logistic regression procedure is therefore used in Chapter 7 in order to estimate the determinants of contraceptive adoption in Ramanagaram.

Our dependent variable in the econometric analysis of fertility outcomes in Chapter 8 is the number of children ever born to a woman. The means and standard deviations for each religious group are shown in Table 5.14. The mean number of children ever born varied by religion, with the Muslims having one child more, on average, than the Hindus. The Christians had the lowest fertility of all three religious groups.

The distribution of total children ever born has the shape of a truncated continuous distribution between a minimum of 0 and a maximum of 9. As can be seen from Table 5.15, there is no heaping of this variable at 'favourite' numbers of children, and therefore there is no case to be made for defining the variable as a 'count' or 'categorical' dependent variable. The most appropriate econometric approach to use is therefore, OLS, and consequently that was the approach used to

TABLE 5.13: DISTRIBUTION OF THE DECISION TO USE CONTRACEPTION,
RAMANAGARAM SAMPLE (1996)

Whether the woman had ever used a contraceptive method	Frequency
0	86
1	100

TABLE 5.14: CHILDREN EVER BORN, RAMANAGARAM SAMPLE (1996)

Category	Mean	Standard deviation
All women	3.05	0.14
Hindus	2.66	0.16
Muslims	3.72	0.27
Christians	2.46	0.33

TABLE 5.15: DISTRIBUTION OF CHILDREN EVER BORN, RAMANAGARAM SAMPLE (1996)

Number of children ever born	Frequency
1	38
2	45
3	38
4	25
5	18
6	6
7	11
8	2
9	2
10	0
More than 10	0

estimate the determinants of the number of children ever born, as described in Chapter 8.

The means and standard deviations presented raise the following issues. First, the number of children ever born differs between Hindus, Muslims, and Christians, with the Muslims having one child more, on average, than women of the other two religious groups. However, women's age at first marriage does not differ significantly between Hindus and Muslims. The decision to use contraception differs significantly between Hindus and Muslims at the mean level, before we have controlled for other factors, and it is this which may account for the difference in fertility.

Chapters 6 through 8 discuss those variables which have been argued in the literature to act as determinants of the age at first marriage, contraceptive choice, and fertility, respectively. Each chapter then models the determinants of the dependent variable in question, in order to investigate whether it is a 'pure religion effect' or the influence of socioeconomic 'characteristics' which influences fertility and its two major proximate determinants. Ordinary Least Squares methods are used in order to estimate the determinants of the age at first marriage and the determinants of children ever born, and a LOGIT model is used to estimate the determinants of the decision to use contraception in Ramanagaram. The quantitative findings are compared and contrasted both with the qualitative findings which emerge from the statements of the women interviewed, and with data from other regions of India.

Section three

∽

Religion and the Determinants of Fertility

chapter six

The Determinants of Nuptiality
The Age at First Marriage in India

The age at first marriage is an important demographic variable that is a vital aspect of a woman's fertility decisions. Economists postulate that marriage occurs when the utility of being married exceeds the utility of staying single, taking into account the costs of finding a mate and the opportunity costs of being married (Becker, 1974b: 299–344; Becker, 1991; Sander, 1995). The possible factors, both economic and social, which may influence the woman when she contemplates the marriage decision, are elaborated in this chapter.

FACTORS INFLUENCING THE AGE AT FIRST MARRIAGE

Education

Theoretically, the educational level of the woman can influence the age at marriage in four ways.[1] First, there may exist more opportunities for the woman outside marriage if she is educated, specifically in terms of opportunities for higher education or employment outside the home. This may delay her marriage.

Second, education may enable a woman to obtain a better educated husband or one with an urban job, increasing the search time for finding a suitable partner, and delaying marriage. This clearly influenced some women in Ramanagaram, as shown by the remark of a Hindu woman, Padmabai, aged 40 years, who said, 'I want my daughter to do her B.Ed. [teacher's training degree] first, become a teacher and then only think

---

[1]See Caldwell, Reddy and Caldwell, 1983: 343–61; Shapiro, 1996: 89–103; and with particular reference to Karnataka, UN, 1961: 98–9.

of marriage—find a good educated husband, and marry only after 20. I don't save aside any jewellery for her because I am giving her an education. *Vidya* [education] is the jewel I am giving her.' This was echoed by a Muslim woman, Sofia Banu, also aged 40 years, who remarked, 'I have given my daughter an education so that she can get employment and find a good husband—it is a better investment than jewellery.'

Third, as the employment prospects of women improve if they are better educated, they are able to support themselves economically while being single and spend a greater amount of time in searching for a suitable partner—that is, they can finance a longer search-process (See Keeley, 1977: 238–50). Finally, education may also influence women's ideas about marriage, via 'learning values'.

However, the manner in which schooling is supposed to affect marriage *empirically* is not always clear-cut. In their empirical analysis of one Hindu and one Muslim caste in two villages in north India, for instance, Jeffery and Jeffery argue that women's schooling is seen more as a means to enhance a woman's prospects in the marriage market because education helps women with the discharge of 'status production' duties and in the management of household accounts (Jeffery and Jeffery, 1999: 186–92).

For Karnataka, there is evidence that education is associated with a later age at first marriage. The National Family Health Survey 1992–3 (IIPS, 1995: 50–1) showed that for the state as a whole, the median age at first marriage for women in 1993 was 6 to 7 years later among women who had completed high school than among illiterate women in all five-year age cohorts from age 20 years to age 49 years. Empirical evidence is also available from many other countries.[2] Singh found that between 1950 and 1990 there has been a rise in the age at marriage of rural women in Himachal Pradesh from less than 12 years to 19 years, and his findings suggest that this is mainly due to the rise in education in this area (Singh, 1992: 123–30). Because women's education has emerged as an important determinant of age at marriage in other studies, its effect on marriage age in Ramanagaram was also investigated.

Primary schooling in Karnataka spans five years (from Standards 1 to 5), and secondary school spans another five years (from Standards 6 to 10). At the end of the tenth year of schooling is the SSLC examination.

---

[2]There is a voluminous literature on this issue. For example, see Birdsall, 1989: 23–50; Cochrane, 1979; Carlson, 1979: 341–53; Keeley, 1977: 238–50; Summers, 1994; Appleton, 1996: 139–66; Brien and Lillard, 1994: 1167–204; Caldwell, Reddy and Caldwell, 1985: 33.

After this, girls are allowed either to read for Standards 11 and 12 in school, or the option of a two-year pre-university course. After this, there are undergraduate degrees, lasting either three or four years, followed by Master's courses, lasting two years.

In the questionnaire, the women were asked separately about their primary, secondary, and university-level education. In Chapter 5 we looked at the distribution of educational levels in the Ramanagaram sample. It may be recollected from that discussion that the mean years of education for the sample as a whole was 6.0 years. In the multiple regression models tested later in this chapter, the various measures of education used are the woman's total years of education, her primary education, her secondary education, and her university education.

The educational level of her husband is another variable which may influence a woman's age at marriage (Sander, 1995). The way in which this influence might work would be that a better educated man prefers to marry a woman who is older, whether because he wants a better educated spouse, because he believes that it is better to marry someone who is more mature, because he believes that a better educated wife will earn more, or because he believes she will cause their children to be better educated. This is Becker's theorem about 'positive assortative mating' or the 'mating of likes' (Becker, 1981: Chapter 4). A higher quality woman marries a higher quality man because she raises the productivity of a superior man and vice versa. Thus, for the market, positive assortative mating or the mating of likes is optimal when aggregate output is maximized over all marriages (For more on this see Becker, 1981: Chapter 4).

In the Ramanagaram sample, the husband's education variable was measured in a similar manner to the number of years of the woman's education. However, one could justifiably expect the education of the woman and her husband to be highly correlated with each other. This is confirmed by the fact that the correlation coefficient between wives' education and husbands' education in the Ramanagaram sample was high and positive at 0.63. This suggested the need to investigate the effect of these two variables, holding each other constant, and that was in fact done in the multivariate models estimated below.

Women's Employment

The availability of better employment opportunities for women outside the home increases the opportunity cost of women's time in marriage. Labour market participation and better pay levels may enable women to contribute to the costs of marital search for a longer period, enabling women to find more suitable grooms. This may work to increase female marriage age. In this context, there is evidence that the age at marriage for women rises markedly when women and men are employed in skilled rather than unskilled jobs (Anderson, Hill and Butler, 1987: 223–34). This variable was not included in the multivariate models estimated because a majority of the ever-married Ramanagaram women interviewed took up an occupation only after their marriage, and because full employment histories of all women before marriage were not available.

Income

A third primary influence on marriage age is income (Ermisch, 1981: 347–56). However, the manner it which it is purported to affect marriage age is complex. It is possible that income is positively associated with marriage age, in the sense that a greater income earned by a woman herself will reduce her expected gains from marriage, thereby increasing her marriage age. However, increased income earned by a man may enable him to afford the expenses of supporting a wife who is not earning an income, as well as the costs of possible children, thereby enabling him to marry earlier. A higher-income man may also be able to afford to marry a young woman who has not already received an inheritance from her parents, and who has not had a long time to save up for marriage. It is this reasoning which lies behind the claim that as a general rule in pre-industrial Europe, wealth and income were negatively associated with marriage age, with richer farmers marrying younger than poorer ones or landless people, and with the gentry and nobility marrying the youngest of all.[3]

However, the relationship between income and marriage age is even more complex than this. In some societies, at the time of their marriage, children have a claim on a proportion of the savings of parents and this takes the form of dowries.[4] Where a dowry system still operates, as in India, the ability of parents to meet dowry payments may influence the daughter's age at marriage. In south India since the 1950s, the main shift concerning marriage payments has been from bridewealth to dowry. Caldwell, Reddy and Caldwell argue that in India dowry payments 'order' a marriage market characterized by hypergamy (the practice of women marrying into wealthier families of the same caste). This is because dowry

---

[3]See Kriedte, Medick and Schlumbohm, 1981: Chapters 2 and 3 by Medick; see also Ogilvie, 1997: Chapter 8.

[4]Dowries in Karnataka (as perhaps in much of South Asia) do not typically involve land or other fixed assets. As Agarwal argues, dowries are in fact 'movable'. They usually take the form of gold jewellery, utensils, items of consumer equipment, small farm animals, and money. For more on this, see Agarwal, 1994.

serves as a compensation to the richer family for contracting the alliance (Caldwell, Reddy and Caldwell, 1983; Rao, 1993: 666–77). Thus, if parents feel that they are unable to afford the costs of a wedding (and this is quite likely if there is more than one daughter to be married), marriage for the daughter (especially if she is of lower birth order) may be delayed and hence her age at marriage higher (Epstein, 1973: 193). Naturally, this complicates the postulated relationship between income and age at marriage. In Ramanagaram, for example, wedding costs were quite high. Sakamma, aged 42 years, a Scheduled Caste woman from village C remarked, 'I want to perform a grand wedding for my daughter. I would need one *lakh* (hundred thousand rupees) to marry my daughter'.[5] Having said that, parents may also expect dowry demands to become even higher in the future and hence decide that if they can afford it, it is better to marry daughters as soon as possible.

The 'search time' required for finding a suitable partner may affect the age at first marriage (Sander, 1995). Taking a cue from option theory, *ceteris paribus*, the search time for finding a partner will be long when the option of being single is highly valued. This is important in societies such as India, where marriage, though near universal, is usually irreversible, and for the woman the cost of divorce, both social and economic, is very high. The cost of remaining unmarried is also very high. The search time is influenced by the ability to finance the 'search costs' of finding a partner. This will be influenced by the income and other characteristics of the woman and her parents (ibid.). A woman who is more highly educated and perhaps also employed may be in a position to delay marriage by being able to finance the costs of searching for a partner whom she regards as more suitable (for example, more educated). If her parents are also highly educated and in employment, they may also be able to take on the search costs of finding a more suitable partner for their daughter, thereby delaying her marriage. In societies such as India, where daughters stay at home with their parents until marriage, parents are more likely to decide how many resources to allocate to search costs and to assist in paying them.

Ideally, in order to assess the impact of income on marriage age, it would be desirable to consider the 'income of origin' for the woman prior to her marriage rather than the 'income of destination', that is, the income of the family that the woman marries into. However, given the strict codes for marriage in Ramanagaram, whereby marriages were mainly

[5]For evidence that the 'marriage squeeze' in south India has manifested itself in rising dowries, see Rao, 1993: 666–77.

arranged among families of a similar socio-economic class, it is not unrealistic to assume that the 'income of destination' is highly corre-lated with the 'income of origin' (Rao, 1993: 674). In the Ramanagaram sample, out of a total of 187 marriages, only one was an inter-caste mar-riage by choice. All the other marriages were arranged by parents and took place within the same jati.[6] Though not all jatis in Ramanagaram are economically homogeneous, the economic status of both families is usually taken into account in marriage negotiations.[7] For example, referring to the marriage negotiations for her 16 year-old daughter, which were taking place at the time of interview, Chandramma, of village A, stressed, 'We are looking very carefully. It is important for us to find a "good house" for our daughter. After all, they must be in a position to take care of her well.' Thus, we have good reasons for believing that most women married into families which belonged to a broadly simi-lar income bracket. It is also reasonable to assume that women's hus-bands' incomes as married adults were positively correlated with their own 'incomes of origin'. Other researchers have made similar assump-tions in their models of marriage and have shown them to be empiri-cally justified (Rosenzweig and Stark, 1989: 905–26). However, it must be acknowledged that the lack of information on the income-gener-ating characteristics of the women's original households is a deficiency of the Ramanagaram data set.

In the absence of any reliable source of information on women's 'incomes of origin', it was decided to rely upon the existence of at least some degree of correlation between women's 'income of origin' and their 'income of destination' and to use various measures pertaining to 'income of destination' in order to investigate possible links between income and women's age at first marriage.

Consumption measured by total expenditure was chosen as the most relevant measure of income because it was correlated with several other important income measures, it was the variable the women were best able to describe accurately and provide information on, and it has been used by other studies (Blundell, Preston and Walker, 1994; Ketkar,

---

[6]Although marriages were 'arranged' in a traditional sense, there was some degree of choice for the marriage partners in that they were consulted for their consent, after meeting with each other in the presence of other relatives.

[7]In this context, it should be noted that an economic analysis of the arranged marriage system has an intrinsic principal–agent problem, and that the standard Beckerian framework needs to be modified. This is because in the case of arranged marriages, it is the parents of women and men who undertake the search for marriage partners for their children, and who attempt to optimize that decision.

1979). In the estimates of total expenditure, the ownership of consumer durables is not included on the grounds that the latter would have probably inflated the former if included in a single measure, and is endogenous in a model of the determinants of marriage age.

Social Norms

A fourth factor that is widely theorized as influencing marriage age consists of social norms concerning marriage. Dasgupta points (1993a: 210) out the evidence in rural societies that each individual's utility is an increasing function of the average level of activity of all others (in the society). This results in an externality, with a certain pattern of behaviour being sustained even when the rationale for such behaviour may have ceased to exist. This is particularly true of social norms concerning the 'proper' time to marry, easily illustrated from statements made by women in Ramanagaram.[8] For example, Nagama, aged 36 years and a mother of four daughters, from village D, remarked, 'I will marry my daughters at 15. I know it is wrong, but I do it because it is expected, we live in a "society", though personally I want to improve them.' Another woman, Laxmiamma, aged 29 years, from village A, remarked, 'Marriage at 15 is the norm here. I feel I have suffered enough, why should I make her suffer? But, society matters too.'

Identifying changes in social norms about marriage age is difficult, because economists postulate that they are subsumed within the utility function. However, one possible way to measure changes in norms is to examine changes over time and one possible way to examine changes over time empirically is to compare the year of marriage across women. It is hypothesised that the woman's year of marriage will affect the age at marriage if there has been a general trend (most likely upwards) in norms about marriage age in the region in which she lives that is not accounted for by differences in educational attainment, income or any other variable. Thus, women who marry in more recent decades may marry at later ages.[9] This is likely to happen if there has been a change in social norms over

[8]In fact, one woman, Padmavatamma, said that it would be considered highly irresponsible if parents did not look after the matrimonial interests of offspring, especially daughters. When asked if daughters could choose partners for themselves, she said that when she was young she had had no choice but that she realized that youngsters nowadays thought otherwise. She went on to attribute youngsters' desires to choose their own partners to the influence of the cinema.

[9]This is shown clearly by Janakarajan, Olsen and Seabright, 1996. In their study of 496 marriages in two villages in Tamil Nadu in south India, they find that the female age at first marriage rose from 15.4 years in the 1950s to 18.6 years in the 1980s.

time towards a view that later marriage age is better, a view that takes hold irrespective of the individual's specific circumstances. There was mixed evidence of such 'ideational change' in the group discussions involving the Ramanagaram women. Both literate and illiterate women, older and younger women, and especially those who were still single, opined that in the 1990s, the mid-twenties was the 'appropriate' time for marriage. It is my conjecture that the women obtained this idea from the heavily advertised government-sponsored media campaigns on radio and television which spread information that marrying daughters before age 18 years was 'wrong', illegal, and not in the best health interests of daughters. The actual impact of time on marriage age is identified in a multiple regression context (as explored in the following part of this chapter).

Religious, Ethnic, and Caste Differences

The age at marriage may depend on religious, ethnic, or caste differences in the population.[10] This has been argued in many studies.[11] Religion may have a direct impact on the age at marriage as a system of beliefs, values, or ideas.[12] Alternatively, it may exert an indirect effect via its impact on women's status within the family or community (See Chamie, 1997: 365–82; Obermeyer, 1992: 33–60). The age at marriage may also depend on church sanctions and religious prescriptions.[13] Religion can also affect the search time of finding a suitable mate because of the higher costs to members of some religions of making a wrong marital choice. This argument is applicable in Ramanagaram where the costs of making a wrong choice of marital partner are high. However, whether such costs differ between Hindus, Muslims, and Christians, leading to a higher age at marriage for one religious group *vis-à-vis* the others, is a question that

[10]Carlson, 1979: 341–53; Frisbie, 1986: 99–106; Brien and Lillard, 1994: 1167–204. Brien and Lillard argue that in Malaysia there are differences in marriage age and in fertility between the Malays, the Chinese, and the Indians, even after controlling for socio-economic effects such as a rise in female education and rapid economic growth.

[11]See Sander, 1995: chapter 2; Mcquillon, 1989: 331–46; Ketkar, 1979: 479–88; Jeffery and Jeffery, 1997: chapters 5 and 6.

[12]We have dealt with the normative content of religion on marriage in detail in Chapter 1.

[13]For example, a related issue (which we do not explore in this chapter) is the question of remarriage. The Mysore Population Study of 1961 argued that remarriage in towns such as Ramanagaram was as low as 1 per cent, because religious tradition among higher caste Hindus forbade the remarriage of widows. However, the study noted that remarriage was permitted among Scheduled Castes and that 2 per cent of the Scheduled Caste women in the towns had remarried more than once. Among males, however, remarriage was common. See the UN, 1961: 106–7. Thus, religious attitudes towards remarriage may also affect marriage age.

needs further investigation. In the seventh round of the Indian National Sample Survey undertaken in 1953–4, it was found that Muslim women in Karnataka were marrying one year later than Hindu women, while Muslim men were marrying nearly 1.5 years later than Hindu men (As reported by Caldwell, Reddy and Caldwell, 1983: 344).

In order to assess the influence of religion on the age at marriage for the Ramanagaram data set, three dummy variables were created. The first was for Hindus versus non-Hindus, and the second for Muslims versus non-Muslims, having the Christians as the base category. Third, since this study is particularly concerned with Hindu–Muslim differences, a dummy variable was created for Muslims versus Hindus, excluding the Christians.

The Mysore Population Study and the NFHS argued that in Karnataka, caste has an important influence on the age at first marriage.[14] This is regarded as operating either through custom, or, as in the case of economically disadvantaged castes, through there being a strong economic reason for women to marry at young ages. Although Indian Muslims and Christians also have a sort of 'caste system', in the Ramanagaram sample the widest array of castes was unquestionably found amongst the Hindu respondents.[15] When asked about their caste, it is interesting that Muslim and Christian respondents categorized themselves in religious divisions, providing answers such as 'Mehdavi', 'Sunni', or 'Protestant'. However, since 'caste' for Muslims and Christians was essentially coterminous with 'religion', nothing could be gained by including it as a separate variable in explaining their marriage ages.

Husband's Occupation

The primary occupation of the husband may have an indirect impact on the age at first marriage of the woman. Men who are in skilled jobs may

[14]The Mysore Population Study found that among the Hindus, Brahmin women in the birth cohort 1918–32 had the highest median age at first marriage (16 years) of all castes in the sample. The study also found that among the Christians in Bangalore city, there was a caste-like division. There were Indian Christians, Anglo-Indians, and Europeans. Of these three, the study spoke of 'marked differences between the Indian Christians and the other two. Indian Christians showed greater similarity to Hindus and Muslims, than to Anglo-Indians and Europeans, both in the level and trend of age at marriage'. For more on this, see the *Mysore Population Study*, 1961: 98.

[15]The high castes included *brahmins, gowdas,* and *vokkaligas;* the low castes included *aswajanas, balijas, bestru, kumbhar, kurubas, lingayats, maduvar,* and *viswakarmas;* and the Scheduled Castes included the *ekesu, lambani, ganigas, gangemata, upasadus* and those who did not give a caste name but described themselves as 'SC', i.e. Scheduled Castes.

prefer marrying women who are older, or more educated, or employed outside the home. This may be because such women earn additional income, or raise better 'quality' children. Alternatively, men employed in occupations requiring cheap child labour (such as domestic industry) may marry at a young age, and consequently also marry younger women than others.[16] Farmers may also desire more child labour for farming requirements, although this implicitly assumes that they are unwilling or unable to hire market labour (Thorner, Kerblay and Smith, 1986). On the other hand, if the husband is earning a very high wage, he may be able to afford the costs of keeping a wife and raising a family, thereby reducing female age at marriage.

In order to assess these hypothesized relationships between husband's occupation and age at marriage for the Ramanagaram women, this variable was measured in three ways. First, husband's occupation was measured as taking a value of 1 if the husband was employed in a skilled occupation and 0 if he was employed in an unskilled occupation. Second, it was measured as taking a value of 1 if the man was a farmer, and 0 otherwise. Finally, it was measured as taking a value of 1 if the husband was employed in domestic industry, and 0 if he was employed in any other occupation.

Age at Menarche

The age at menarche is an important demographic variable and it is some-times argued that it exerts an autonomous effect on the age at marriage (Caldwell, Reddy and Caldwell, 1983: 353–5). Trends in the age at menarche have been mainly researched by those working in the field of medicine. The most important finding of this research is that there has been a secular decline in the age at menarche over time in Europe.[17] In a pioneering article in *Nature* in 1973, Tanner argued that there had been a secular declining trend in the age at menarche in five European coun-tries—the UK, Norway, Denmark, the Netherlands, and Hungary. More recent evidence for Denmark, collected by Boldsen, confirms this secu-lar decline in the age at menarche, as well as a significant decline in its variance (Boldsen, 1992: 167–73). Though we will not go more deeply into this research area, various studies have concluded that trends in

[16]This has been argued theoretically in proto-industrial populations in Europe as described in Kriedte, Medick and Schlumbohm, 1981. However, the empirical findings do not provide support for this view: see Ogilvie and Cerman, 1996.

[17]Tanner, 1973: 95–6; Frisch, 1982: 1033–35; Ostersehlt and Dankerhopfe, 1991: 647–54; Boldsen, 1992: 167–73.

the age at menarche are related to changes in stature and nutrition, and that there is seasonal variation in menarche with different mean ages at menarche for girls born in different seasons.[18]

In the demographic research on south India, Caldwell, Reddy and Caldwell found that marriage traditionally took place shortly after menarche (1983: 350–5) due partly to a belief in divine sanctions[19] and partly to a common social custom which forbade a girl attaining menarche from continuing to perform agricultural work or paid work for other households; she was allowed to resume such work only after marriage. This created an economic pressure to marry early. The Mysore Population Study found that 42 per cent of women born in Karnataka between 1893 and 1902 were married before the age of 13 years (UN, 1961: 93). By comparison, Caldwell, Reddy and Caldwell found that in 1980 only 1 per cent of 10-year-olds, and 31 per cent of 15–19-year-olds, were married, indicating a high percentage of girls who were not being married as children, but who were probably being married a few years after menarche, rather than immediately after it (1983). Jeffery and Jeffery (1997) argue that traditionally in north India, as well, marriage shortly after menarche is popular though there is normally a gap of several months between marriage and cohabitation.

In the present study, the Ramanagaram women were asked about the age at which they attained menarche. Some women remembered the exact time of menarche if it took place close to an important event in the family or a major festival, holiday, or birthday. Others remembered the class that they were studying in if they were at school at the time and were able to give precisely the year of the onset of menarche.[20]

In order to test the hypothesis of a secular decline in the age at menarche for the Ramanagaram sample, a five-year moving average of the age at menarche among the women of the sample was calculated and a linear trend line plotted through this graph. This procedure does not show any rise or decline in the age in menarche over time. In fact,

[18]Boldsen, 1992: 167–73. Boldsen tests the theory that the onset of menarche peaks in the seasons of winter and summer, but finds no evidence for this in Denmark. She does however suggest that the seasonality of menarche is probably due to the seasonality of births.

[19]For example, Hindu scriptures such as the *Dharma sastras* advise that marriages of girls should not be delayed long after puberty. They recommend that girls be kept unmarried for a maximum of three years after puberty, and then only if suitable husbands cannot be found for them. For more on this see, Radhakrishnan, 1947: 169.

[20]It has been found that women's recalled ages at menarche are very reliable. For more on this, see Livson and McNeill, 1962: 218–21.

the age at menarche appears to fluctuate more or less around the same level, approximately 14 years, for all birth cohorts in the sample. This does not exclude the possibility that age at menarche influenced the age at marriage, but it excludes the possibility of a systematic influence caused by change over time.

The hypothesis that the gap between menarche and marriage was widening over time was tested by plotting a linear trend line through a graph which looked at the gap between menarche and marriage against the year of marriage. The result showed that for the women of the Ramanagaram sample, the gap between the age at menarche and the age at marriage increased from about two years for women who married in the 1940s to almost five years for women who married in the late 1990s.

Given the theoretical arguments concerning the relationship between the age at menarche and the age at marriage, the age at menarche was included as a variable in the multivariate models estimated later in the chapter.

Marital Consanguinity

Another factor postulated as influencing marriage age is the extent of consanguinity between spouses in a population. In Karnataka in particular and in south India more generally, consanguineous unions are quite common even today;[21] this is not the case in north India (Bittles, 1994: 561–84; Agarwal, 1994: 391–402). The NFHS estimated that 36 per cent of ever-married women in Karnataka had married a relation and that rural women were more likely to marry relatives than urban ones (IIPS, 1995: 54–5. See also Rao, Inbaraj and Jesudian, 1972: 174–8; Rao and Inbaraj, 1977: 281–8). Consanguinity was also more common for Hindus (37 per cent) and Muslims (31 per cent) than for Christians (22 per cent). In Karnataka, the nature of the consanguineous relationship varies between religious communities. For example, Muslims have traditionally married first cousins while Hindu women have traditionally married their maternal uncles. It is possible that this may have led Hindu women to marry at a younger age so as not to further delay marriage for their uncles (Bittles, Cobles and Appaji Rao, 1993: 111–16).

The existence of consanguinity between spouses can be attributed to five causes (Bittles, 1994: 561–84). First, it may be influenced by cultural

---

[21]See Srinivas, 1965: 146–50; Conklin, 1973: 53–63; Epstein, 1973: 197; Hill, 1982: 204; Caldwell, Reddy and Caldwell, 1983: 343–61; Bittles, Cobles and Appaji Rao, 1993: 114–15; Janakarajan, Olsen and Seabright, 1996.

traditions. Second, it may be necessitated by the reduced need for dowry payments in consanguineous unions, where payments are often of lower value or non-obligatory (Govinda Reddy, 1988: 263–8; Centerwall and Centerwall, 1966: 1160–67). Third, with improvements in public health that ensure increased numbers of children surviving to marriageable age, and therefore a larger number of potential partners to be found within the family itself, marriage to a close relative may be made easier. A fourth reason for consanguineous unions is the desire to maintain full control over ancestral landholdings. Finally, consanguineous marriage may be one form of risk-diversifying behaviour in which the household minimizes risk by retaining income strictly in the hands of family members as well as enjoying better opportunities for monitoring the behaviour of other family members.

Given these theoretical considerations, it seemed important to take this variable into account in Ramanagaram. Marriage between relatives was widely prevalent in the Ramanagaram sample; 40 per cent of women had married a relative,—38 per cent of Hindus, 41 per cent of Muslims, and 47 per cent of Christians. At the 95 per cent confidence level, the differences in marrying relatives was not found to be statistically significant between any of the three religious groups. The exact nature of the relationship with the husband before marriage in the 80 consanguineous marriages is reported in Table 6.1. For the sample as a whole, the most popular forms of consanguineous marriage was to first cousins on both the mother's and father's sides. Also, 23 per cent of women had married their maternal uncles; these were mainly Hindu, as this relationship is disallowed by Islam.

TABLE 6.1: MARITAL CONSANGUINITY BY RELIGION, RAMANAGARAM SAMPLE (1996)

Nature of consanguineous relationship	All women		Hindus		Muslims		Christians	
	No.	%	No.	%	No.	%	No.	%
First cousin on father's side	14	17.5	4	9.5	8	25.8	2	28.6
First cousin on mother's side	30	37.5	13	31.0	15	48.4	2	28.6
Maternal uncle	18	22.5	16	38.1	2	6.5	0	0.0
Other blood relation	4	5.0	4	9.5	0	0.0	0	0.0
Other non-blood relation	1	1.3	1	2.4	0	0.0	0	0.0
Second cousin on father's side	7	8.8	2	4.8	3	9.7	2	28.6
Second cousin on mother's side	6	7.5	2	4.8	3	9.7	1	14.2
Total consanguineous marriages	80	100.0	42	100.0	31	100.0	7	100.0

In the present study, marital consanguinity was measured by a dummy variable which took the value 1 if the woman had married a relation and 0 otherwise. An alternative way of measuring consanguinity was also attempted. This was the coefficient of inbreeding which is a statistical measure of the proportion of gene loci at which an individual is homozygous, and is used to describe the mean level of inbreeding in a population.[22] It takes a value between a minimum of 0 (unrelated) and a maximum of 0.125 (double first cousin or uncle–niece marriages, where partners have two sets of grandparents in common). The average coefficients of inbreeding for the three communities were 0.03 for the Hindus, 0.03 for the Muslims, and 0.02 for the Christians, which are all high by the standards of other populations (Bodmer and Cavalli-Sforza, 1976: 361–79).

Other Factors

It has been argued that the age at marriage in urban areas is higher than it is in rural areas, mainly because of the higher average educational and employment status of women in urban areas, and peer-level effects whereby a higher age-at-marriage norm in some urban communities influences members of these communities to adopt similar behaviour patterns (Shapiro, 1996: 89–103). This variable is not used in the multivariate analysis conducted later in this chapter mainly because of the proximity of the five villages surveyed to Ramanagaram town and the close associations between the town and the villages (as discussed in Chapter 4).

Age at marriage may also depend on the welfare system. For example, in some pre-industrial European societies one could get poor relief from the village or town community, and this reduced the incentive to have many children for welfare and insurance purposes (Ogilvie, 1997; Chapter 8). In developing societies such as India, where children are valuable means of insurance in old age and there is no widespread or national system of social security, women who are never married, or do not have children, are often in a precarious position. This creates an economic compulsion that may result in early and near-universal marriage (Dasgupta, 1993a: 323). This variable was not included in the multivariate models because it does not vary sufficiently across the sample.

Another factor thought to influence the age at first marriage includes the family system and the manner in which marriage is arranged. This

---

[22]For more on the calculation of the coefficients of inbreeding, see Bodmer and Cavalli-Sforza, 1976: 361–79. I am grateful to D.N. Rao and N. Appaji Rao of the Department of Biochemistry, Indian Institute of Science, Bangalore for enabling me to understand better how these coefficients are calculated and used in empirical work.

refers particularly to whether a new family is expected to set up an independent household, or if young couples live in extended or multiple family households with parents and other siblings. Traditionally, the latter system will have the effect of lowering the age at marriage because couples do not have to wait until they can afford to buy or rent a separate dwelling, or inherit one, before getting married. This factor is quite important because it has been shown, in studies of pre-industrial Europe, that waiting to own a dwelling had a significant impact on raising the marriage age. This was because couples were required to marshall their own resources and set up independent households after marriage, rather than living with parents (Laslett, 1988: 236). These resources were to be marshalled through life-cycle service, with young men and women working as servants or 'trainees' with other households or production units. In such situations, the individuals were required both to give up a portion of the product of their labour to their employer, and at the same time to accumulate and save funds for marriage. The system of life-cycle servants served the dual purpose of inculcating values of thrift and saving in individuals, and fostering independence in order to be able to own separate dwellings and eventually set up separate households (Laslett, 1983). The obvious consequence of such a system was that marriage was delayed until such time as couples saved enough to marry and set up separate households, and this led to the quite high marriage ages observed for both men and women in pre-industrial Europe. However, because the structure of the family system and the way in which marriage was arranged did not vary significantly across the Ramanagaram sample, this variable was not included in the multivariate analysis conducted below.

The existence of polygyny can also influence the age at marriage (Hern, 1992: 53–64). It is possible that in societies where polygyny is popular, age at marriage for women is lower.[23] In the Ramanagaram sample, this factor is unimportant mainly because there were only four polygynous marriages (less than 2 per cent of the entire sample).

The age at marriage may also depend on attitudes towards sexual activity outside marriage and the fate of illegitimate children. In societies such as Ramanagaram where sexual activity outside marriage is generally considered taboo, at least among Muslims, Christians, and higher-caste Hindus, couples who wish to be sexually active have to marry, and this will tend to lower marriage age. This variable also did not vary significantly

---

[23]This factor is relevant indirectly in the Indian context as right-wing political propaganda has routinely spoken of the 'excesses' of Muslim fertility due to the religious sanction for polygyny.

across women in the Ramanagaram sample and therefore it was not included in the models of marriage age presented later in this chapter.

Female autonomy in decision-making, the status of women in the household, and the extent of female mobility in the community may all affect age at marriage. It is possible that in areas where a purdah system operates, women are less geographically mobile, and that coupled with lower female autonomy, this results in lower ages at first marriage (Vlassoff, 1992: 195–212, Jeffery and Jeffery: 1997). It must also be recognized that a woman's preferences may diverge from her family's preferences and that the extent of female autonomy will influence to what extent women's preferences regarding the right time to marry are realized. This variable was not included explicitly in the multivariate models of marriage age because it is highly correlated with the religion dummies and the education variables, and is in any case difficult to measure accurately.

Finally, the age at marriage may depend on the inheritance system, particularly whether unmarried women are able to inherit land. If unmarried women are not allowed to inherit land, there may be a tendency for early marriage in order to gain access to land.[24] In Karnataka, inheritance is patrilineal. The only exception is the Bant community in the south Canara district of Karnataka, who practise matrilineal/bilateral inheritance.[25] This variable was not used in the multivariate models conducted in the following section, firstly because it was rare for unmarried women to inherit land in Ramanagaram, and secondly, because other measures of income were also being used in the econometric models of marriage age.

As this brief survey shows, a wide range of variables can in theory affect the age at marriage. However, only certain variables have been included in the econometric analysis which follows, as some variables do not vary across women in the same society or it is not possible to obtain empirical measures for them.

TRENDS IN MARRIAGE AGE

There is a small existing literature on marriage age in Karnataka which focuses on explaining the rise in the age at first marriage over the last

[24]Agarwal, 1994. Agarwal argues that while in legal terms women have won extensive rights to inherit and control land, in practice this is not quite so. She writes that of those women who do own land, fewer exercise effective control over it.

[25]Agarwal, 1994: chapter 3:II:2: 116–17. Agarwal argues that in south India the practice of matrilineal/bilateral inheritance is also documented among the Nangudi Vellalars, Nayars, and Tiyyars of Tamil Nadu and the Phadiyas and Chettis of Wynad district on the Kerala–Tamil Nadu border.

century or so.[26] The Mysore Population Study found that the age at first marriage in all the zones covered by the survey increased from 14.0 years for women in the birth cohort 1893–1902 up to 15.5 for women in the birth cohort 1928–32 (UN, 1961: 91). The NFHS found that between 1961 and 1993, the singulate female age at first marriage in Karnataka rose from 16.4 years to 19.6 years.[27] However, in the cross-section of 187 ever-married women studied in Ramanagaram, the mean age at first marriage was 17.3 years, reflecting the fact that women were of varying age-cohorts. Interestingly, the age at first marriage is higher for Muslims and Christians at 17.6 years, compared to 16.9 years for the Hindus. However, the 0.7 year difference between the Hindu and Muslim and the Hindu and Christian mean ages at first marriage is not statistically significant at the 95 per cent confidence level.[28] Also, the mean age at cohabitation for the women of the Ramanagaram sample is not very different from the mean age at first marriage. These findings are wholly consistent with the argument that, on average, there is a very small gap between marriage and cohabitation in south India (Basu, 1993: 85–95).

Table 6.2 presents data on the distribution of women's age at first marriage for Karnataka state and for the Ramanagaram sample. The most interesting feature of Table 6.2 is that over 50 per cent of women in both Karnataka state and the Ramanagaram sample have married before the legal age of 18 years.

Caldwell, Reddy and Caldwell suggested that the age at first marriage increased over the last century for women in Karnataka for a number of reasons. These included the decline of child marriage, the shift from bridewealth to dowry, the decline in marriages to relatives, a rise in life

[26]These include the Mysore Population Study, 1961: 88–108; Goyal, 1975; Caldwell, Reddy and Caldwell, 1983: 343–61; National Family Health Survey 1992–93: Karnataka, 1995: 47–55.

[27]IIPS, 1995: 47. The Mysore Population Study, conducted in 1961, found that there was not much change in the male age at first marriage for men in the birth cohort 1893–1902 and 1923–27. The male age at first marriage for these cohorts was 23.3 and 24.1 years respectively. The study also argued that most men married between 18 and 30 years, and that it was unusual for a man to marry before the age of 18 years. See UN, 1961: 95.

[28]The difference between Hindus and Muslims is not significant at the 5 per cent level. At a higher level of significance, say 12 per cent, it is difficult to gauge if the size of this impact on fertility outcomes would be large, even if Hindus and Muslims married at the same age and retained their age-specific fertility, because it is difficult to hold other factors constant. If we do not hold other factors constant, the resulting figure would merely be equivalent to a cross-tabulation of religion against fertility outcomes. Thus, although the question is an interesting one, it is not possible to assess the size of the impact on Hindus and Muslims (assuming it is statistically significant, which it is not) because it is necessary to hold other factors constant. It must be emphasized again that, at the mean, the t-test shows that the impact could easily be zero.

TABLE 6.2. AGE-SPECIFIC FIRST MARRIAGE, KARNATAKA (1998);
RAMANAGARAM SAMPLE (1996)

Woman's age at first marriage (years)	% of women (Karnataka)	% of women (Ramanagaram)
0–7	4.3	0.5
8–12	17.9	4.9
13–17	42.9	50.0
18–22	26.5	34.8
23–27	7.3	8.7
28–32	1.0	0.6
Over 32	0.1	0.5
Total	100.0	100.0

Source: Batliwala et al., 1998, p. 193.

expectancy, a rise in the belief that pre-menarchic girls are immature, the difficulty in finding suitable grooms, changes in perceptions regarding the age which is commonly regarded as 'the threshold to maturity', the greater 'educational and occupational heterogeneity' in society caused by the diminished influence of caste in deciding occupation, increased education of girls, and increased migration which made it increasingly difficult for parents of daughters to find suitable matches, by causing a 'classic marriage squeeze'.[29]

There is evidence in support of some of these hypotheses. There is evidence that child marriage has declined in recent times. The Infant Marriage Prevention Regulation was passed in 1894, prohibiting marriage of girls below 8 years of age and boys before the age of 14 years. After the Sarda Act was passed in British India in 1929, Mysore state also enacted a legislation fixing the minimum age at marriage for girls at 14 years, and for boys at 18 years. However, the effort failed. In 1955, a revision of the Hindu Marriage Law which had validity throughout India established the minimum age at marriage for girls at 15 years and for boys at 18 years. The Mysore Population Study, 1961 also found that the percentage of those women marrying under the age of 13 years had fallen from 34 per cent for women in the birth cohort 1893–1902, to 18 per cent for women in the birth cohort 1928–32 (UN, 1961: 93). There is evidence that the practice of giving and taking dowry, which has been mainly a

---

[29]This is because each succeeding generation is larger than the one before it due to increased life expectancy and better health facilities with time. See Caldwell, Reddy and Caldwell, 1983: 343–61.

post-Independence phenomenon, has gained predominance from the 1960s onwards (Tambiah, 1973: 100–10; Rao, 1993: 666–77). There is evidence from the National Family Health Survey that marital consanguinity, though it has shown declines elsewhere in south India, is still widespread in Karnataka.[30] With reference to the 'classic marriage squeeze', in the Ramanagaram sample mothers did mention the problem of finding suitable grooms for their daughters, though rarely concern over finding suitable brides for their sons. This is despite the fact that Karnataka, like India as a whole, has had a steadily declining sex ratio over time.

However, very few studies have primarily focused on differences by religion.[31] This analysis of the Ramanagaram sample in this study will attempt to redress some of the gaps in the existing research on the determinants of marriage age in Karnataka, by using OLS estimation procedures to identify the factors which influence the age at first marriage in this sample of Ramanagaram women.[32] Age at marriage is measured as the woman's age at the time of her first marriage for all ever-married women in the sample (N = 187).[33]

A MODEL OF THE DETERMINANTS OF THE AGE AT FIRST MARRIAGE

As discussed in the preceding theoretical section, nine variables were identified as being potential influences on the age at first marriage of the Ramanagaram women. These were the education of the woman, the education of her spouse, total household expenditure (as a proxy for

[30]IIPS, 1995: 54–5. See also Bittles, Cobles and Appaji Rao, 1993: 114–15. For evidence on the decline of consanguineous marriage in one other sample survey see Janakarajan, Olsen and Seabright, 1996.

[31]One exception to this is the Mysore Population Study of 1961, which found that there were differences in the age at first marriage by religion. Marriage age for Hindu women in the birth cohort 1888–97 was 12.9 years. The comparable figure for Muslim women was 15.1 years. On the other hand, the age at first marriage for Hindu women born in the birth cohort 1928–32 was 15.3 years, while the comparable figure for Muslim women was 15.8 years. Thus, it emerged from the study that Muslim women had a higher age at first marriage than the Hindu women covered in the study. Muslim men, too, were marrying later than Hindu men. For men in the birth cohort 1888–97, mean age at marriage was 22.7 for Hindu men and 24.3 years for Muslim men. This increased to 23.4 years for Hindu men and 24.9 years for Muslim men for those in the birth cohort 1918–27. See *Mysore Population Study*, 1961: 96–8.

[32]Sander, 1995. Sander uses OLS regression procedures to investigate the effect of several factors, including religion, on fertility in America.

[33]Ever-married women' refers to those women who were married, widowed, or separated at the time of the survey.

income), the woman's age at menarche, the year in which the woman's marriage took place, the religion in which the woman was brought up, the woman's caste, whether her marriage was a consanguineous union or not, and the primary occupation of the woman's husband.

At the first stage, the nine variables were placed in a multiple regression and some alternative ways of measuring them were explored. Thereafter, a number of zero restrictions were successfully imposed on the model according to the results of successive F-tests. This yielded the 'best' preliminary model of the determinants of female marriage age in Ramanagaram.

However, this preliminary model only allowed for religion to exert a shift effect on the age at first marriage. In order to assess whether it also exerted slope effects, that is, whether the effect of various socio-economic variables on age at first marriage varied across religious groups, a second stage of analysis was undertaken, in which Hindu and Muslim interaction terms were created, to form a total of 36 explanatory variables. Of the variables discussed earlier, only the variable on caste was excluded, because it pertained to the Hindus only. This variable was, however, used in a multiple regression model of marriage age among the Hindu women only.

Of the preliminary model specifications explored (but not reported here), the one which best explains variation in the age at marriage in Ramanagaram showed that the significant determinants of female marriage age were women's secondary education, husband's primary education, age at menarche, whether the husband performed a skilled occupation, year of marriage, and total expenditure. In this model, a one-year increase in female secondary education is associated with a 0.34 year rise in female marriage age; a one-year increase in husband's primary education is associated with a 0.24 year rise in female marriage age; a one-year increase in the age at menarche is associated with a 0.43 year increase in marriage age; an additional later year of marriage is associated with a 0.11 year increase in marriage age; if the husband performs a skilled occupation, the woman married two and one-half years later on average; and a Rs 100 rise in total expenditure is associated, on average, with a 0.05 year increase in female marriage age. The model explained 50 per cent of the variation in the age at marriage in the sample.

The most interesting feature of the preliminary model is that after controlling for the effect of other socio-economic variables, *religion exercises no independent effect on the age at marriage*. However, it is necessary to examine if the effect on marriage age of various socio-economic attributes differs across religious groups. That is, it is necessary to examine if the regression lines for Hindus, Muslims, and Christians have different slopes, different intercepts, or both.

At the first stage, the most general equality to be tested is whether the factors affecting marriage age are the same for Hindus as for Muslims. This hypothesis was tested by comparing the coefficients in the models estimated for the sub-samples of the Hindus and the Muslims separately (that is, the 'unrestricted' model) against the coefficients in the model estimated for the pooled sample of Hindus and Muslims combined (i.e. the 'restricted' model). The sub-sample regressions were estimated by beginning with the general preliminary model, and estimating it for Hindus and Muslims separately.[34] The estimation procedure then used successive F-tests of zero restrictions on the deleted variables. The results of this procedure for Hindus are reported in Table 6.3, and for Muslims in Table 6.4. The sample size for Christians was too small (N=14) to estimate the model successfully for Christians only. The 'pooled' regression on Hindus and Muslims was likewise estimated using the same 11-variable general starting model. The results of this estimation are reported in Table 6.5.

TABLE 6.3: OLS ESTIMATES OF THE DETERMINANTS OF THE AGE AT FIRST MARRIAGE, HINDUS ONLY (RAMANAGARAM, 1996)

Regressor	Coefficient		Standard Error	T Ratio [Prob.]
Constant (CONST)	−350.956	c	62.338	−5.630 [0.000]
Woman's education				
Secondary education of woman (SEDU)	0.421	c	0.143	2.944 [0.004]
Husband's occupation				
Husband's occupation is skilled (SKILL)	2.774	c	0.928	2.991 [0.004]
Age at menarche				
Age at menarche (AGEMEN)	0.584	b	0.226	2.581 [0.011]
Income				
Total expenditure (EXPNRS)	0.005		0.005	0.929 [0.355]
Year of marriage				
Year of marriage (YRMAR)	0.181	c	0.032	5.708 [0.000]
$\bar{R}^2$	0.547			
Residual sum of squares	892.621			

Notes: 1. Dependent variable is AGEMAR: the woman's age at first marriage in years. Sample: 103 ever-married Hindu women.
2. [a]= Significant at the 0.10 level; [b]= Significant at the 0.05 level; [c]= Significant at the 0.01 level.

[34]Note that compared with model 3, there are 11 rather than 13 explanatory variables in the sub-sample regressions because the Muslim and Hindu religion dummies are excluded.

TABLE 6.4: OLS ESTIMATES OF THE DETERMINANTS OF THE AGE AT FIRST MARRIAGE,
MUSLIMS ONLY (RAMANAGARAM, 1996)

Regressor	Coefficient		Standard Error	T Ratio [Prob.]
Constant (CONST)	−85.384	b	44.665	−1.912 [0.060]
Woman's education				
Secondary education of woman (SEDU)	0.611	c	0.155	3.951 [0.000]
Husband's occupation				
Husband's occupation is skilled (SKILLED)	3.532	c	1.051	3.360 [0.001]
Age at menarche				
Age at menarche (AGEMEN)	0.702	b	0.327	2.148 [0.035]
Income				
Total expenditure (EXPNRS)	0.007	a	0.003	1.984 [0.052]
Year of marriage				
Year of marriage (YRMAR)	0.046	a	0.023	1.990 [0.051]
$\bar{R}^2$	0.481			
Residual sum of squares	605.746			

Notes: [1]Dependent variable is AGEMAR: the woman's age at first marriage in years. Sample: 70 ever-married Muslim women.
[2] c = Significant at the 0.01 level; b = Significant at the 0.05 level; a = Significant at the 0.10 level.

TABLE 6.5: OLS ESTIMATES OF THE DETERMINANTS OF THE AGE AT FIRST MARRIAGE,
POOLED MODEL OF HINDUS AND MUSLIMS (RAMANAGARAM, 1996)

Regressor	Coefficient		Standard Error	T Ratio [Prob.]
Intercepts				
Hindu religion dummy (HINDU)	-3.547		2.462	-1.440 [0.152]
Muslim religion dummy (MUSLIM)	-2.858		2.411	-1.185 [0.238]
Woman's education				
Secondary education of woman (SEDU)	0.735	c	0.104	7.096 [0.000]
Income				
Total expenditure (EXPNRS)	0.005		0.003	1.598 [0.112]

(contd...)

(Table 6.5 continued)

Regressor	Coefficient		Standard Error	T Ratio [Prob.]
Husband's occupation				
Husband's occupation is skilled				
(SKILL)	2.482	c	0.690	3.598 [0.000]
Age at menarche				
Age at menarche (AGEMEN)	0.739	c	0.194	3.805 [0.000]
Year of marriage				
Year of marriage (YRMAR)	0.004	b	0.002	2.197 [0.029]
$\bar{R}^2$	0.443			
Residual sum of squares	1823.9			

Notes: [1]Dependent variable is AGEMAR: the woman's age at first marriage in years. Sample: 173 ever-married Hindu and Muslim women.
[2] c= Significant at the 0.01 level; b = Significant at the 0.05 level; a = Significant at the 0.10 level.

An F-test was used in order to test if the restricted and unrestricted models are the same.[35] The test showed that the way in which the explanatory variables affect marriage age for Hindus and Muslims is identical.[36] This implies that it is worthwhile to analyse the differences in the socio-economic determinants of marriage age between Hindus and Muslims.

Such an analysis was then undertaken by means of a multiple regression with interaction terms which included observations from all three religious groups. The general starting model included the initial starting-point variables of the preliminary model, plus Hindu and Muslim interaction terms with each of the starting-point variables.

[35]This statistic took the following form:

$$F(k, n-2k) = \frac{RSS^{Restricted} - RSS^{Unrestricted} / k}{RSS^{Unrestricted} / n - 2k}$$

where k is the number of regressors in the pooled model, $2k$ is the number of regressors in the unrestricted model, and n is the number of observations in the pooled model. The unrestricted residual sum of squares ($RSS^{Unrestricted}$) equals the residual sum of squares for the Hindus-only model (RSS^{Hindu}) plus the residual sum of squares for the Muslims-only model (RSS^{Muslim}). Therefore, the value of the F-statistic is:

$$F(12,163) = \frac{1823.9 - 1498.3675/7}{1498.3675/163} = 5.059$$

The critical value of $F(7,163)$ at the 0.05 significance level is 2.01. Since, $F(7, 163) = 5.059 > 2.01$, this implies that we can reject the null hypothesis.
[36]Note that the F-statistic is rejected even at the 0.01 level (F = 5.059 > 2.64).

Successive variable deletion tests, using a joint F-test of zero restrictions on the coefficients of groups of variables, were imposed on this general model. This yielded the specification shown in Table 6.6.

In order to compare the behaviour of the Hindus with that of the

TABLE 6.6: OLS INTERACTION MODEL OF THE DETERMINANTS OF THE AGE AT FIRST MARRIAGE, ALL RELIGIONS, RAMANAGARAM SAMPLE (1996)

Regressor	Coefficient		Standard Error	T Ratio [Prob.]
Intercepts				
Constant (CONST)	-381.5090	c	102.0155	-3.7397 [0.000]
Muslim religion dummy (MUSLIM)	295.9298	c	112.2234	2.6370 [0.009]
Hindu religion dummy (HINDU)	198.2441	a	110.9455	1.7869 [0.076]
Woman's education				
Woman's secondary education (SEDU)	-0.275		0.217	-1.266 [0.207]
Secondary education for Muslims (MSEDU)	0.888	c	0.269	3.300 [0.001]
Secondary education for Hindus (HSEDU)	0.750	c	0.256	2.932 [0.004]
Age at menarche				
Age at menarche (AGEMEN)	0.978	a	0.591	1.654 [0.100]
Age at menarche for Muslims (MAGEMEN)	-0.273		0.663	-0.413 [0.680]
Age at menarche for Hindus (HAGEMEN)	-0.267		0.618	-0.433 [0.666]
Income				
Total expenditure (EXPNRS)	0.009	c	0.003	3.080 [0.002]
Total expenditure for Muslims (MEXPN)	-0.002		0.005	-0.543 [0.588]
Total expenditure for Hindus (HEXPN)	-0.005		0.004	-1.116 [0.266]
Husband's occupation is skilled				
Husband's occupation is skilled (SKILL)	1.282		1.780	0.720 [0.473]
Muslim husband's occupation is skilled (MSKILL)	2.246		2.078	1.081 [0.281]
skilled (HSKILL)	0.814		2.023	0.403 [0.688]

(contd...)

Regressor	Coefficient	Standard Error	T Ratio [Prob.]
Year of marriage			
Year of marriage (YRMAR)	0.195 ᶜ	0.053	3.680 [0.000]
Year of marriage for Muslims			
(MYRMAR)	–0.149 ᵇ	0.058	–2.560 [0.011]
Year of marriage for Hindus			
(HYRMAR)	–0.099 ª	0.057	–1.732 [0.085]
R̄²	0.530		

Notes: ¹Dependent variable is AGEMAR: the woman's age at first marriage in years. Sample:
187 ever-married Hindu, Muslim, and Christian women. Base category: Christians
²ᶜ = Significant at 0.01 level; ᵇ = Significant at 0.05 level; ª = Significant at 0.10 level.

Muslims and Christians, restrictions were imposed on the parameters of the final interaction model and Wald tests were performed to test the validity of these restrictions.

The first set of hypotheses tested concerned the effect of women's secondary education on marriage age. Secondary education has a significant effect on marriage age for Hindus and Muslims. A one-year increase in secondary education increased Hindu women's age at marriage by 0.48 years[37] and increased Muslim women's marriage age by 0.61 years. However, there was no difference in the effect of secondary education on marriage age between the two religious groups. These results are all wholly consistent with the results in Tables 6.3 and 6.4.

The next set of hypothesis tested concerned the effect of the age at menarche. Only one of the three age-at-menarche variables (AGEMEN) was significant separately, and only at the 0.10 level. One possible reason for this finding is that the age at menarche is comparatively invariant relative to the age at marriage. The mean age at menarche in the sample is more or less the same for all religious groups, approximately 13.5 years. While the age at menarche varied between ages 11 years and 16 years, the age at marriage varied much more widely, from age 7 years to age 35 years. In the marriage models for Hindus and Muslims estimated separately, the age at menarche is a very important variable in explaining age at marriage, with coefficients significant at the 0.05 level. According to Table 6.3, a one-year increase in the age at menarche results in a 0.58 increase in the age at marriage for Hindu women; according to Table

[37]Note that since the model is estimated with interaction terms, the effect of secondary education on marriage age for Hindus is calculated by adding the coefficient on SEDU to the coefficient on HSEDU. This procedure is adopted for calculating the effects of all other interaction explanatory variables throughout this chapter.

6.4, a one-year increase in the age at menarche raises the age at marriage by 0.70 for Muslim women. Moreover, the size of these coefficients is similar to that found on the menarche variables in the interaction model in Table 6.6. These results considered together suggest that the age at menarche is important in explaining age at marriage.

The importance of the age-at-menarche variable was further borne out by the results of the Wald tests, which showed that while the age at menarche *is* a significant influence on the age at marriage for Hindus and Muslims, there was *no* difference statistically in the effect of menarche on marriage between Hindus and Muslims. The findings from these tests indicate that the effect of age at menarche on age at marriage is similar between Hindus and Muslims.

The next set of hypotheses tested pertained to the total expenditure variables. In the sub-sample regressions, expenditure did not significantly affect marriage age for Hindus; for Muslims the estimated coefficient is significant only at the 0.10 level. In the interaction model, a Wald test showed that that there is no statistically significant difference in the effect of expenditure on marriage age between Hindus and Muslims. As we can see from Table 6.4, for Muslims, even though expenditure is significant at the 0.10 level, the coefficient is extremely small, about 0.007, which is not very much different from that for the Hindus (which is 0.005). Thus, total expenditure does not appear to exercise an effect on Muslim marriage age that is significantly different from its effect on Hindu marriage age.

The next set of hypotheses concerned the 'husband's occupation is skilled' variable. The sub-sample regressions in Tables 6.3 and 6.4 show that for both Hindus and Muslims considered separately, the skill variable is highly significant with a large positive coefficient (2.8 for Hindus and 3.5 for Muslims). The sizes of these coefficients is similar to those estimated in the interaction model, at 2.1 for Hindus and 3.5 for Muslims. The fact that these variables have significant coefficients in the sub-sample regressions, and the fact that an F-test rejects the hypothesis that all three should be excluded from the model, supports the view that husband's skilled occupation does have an important effect on marriage age, despite the insignificant t-ratios on each variable separately in the interaction model. A Wald test showed that husband's occupation being skilled did not have a significantly different effect on age at marriage for Hindus than for Muslims. Thus, the skill variable does appear to be a significant determinant of marriage age for both Hindus and Muslims, but there is no difference between the two religious groups.

Finally, the effect of the year-of-marriage variables was tested. For Hindus and for Muslims, the year of marriage is a significant determinant of marriage age. This finding is borne out in the sub-sample regression on Hindus only in Table 6.3, and on Muslims only in Table 6.4. Finally, a Wald test showed that the effect of the year of marriage on age at marriage for Hindus is not significantly different from its effect for Muslims.

One possible reason for the importance of the year-of-marriage variable might be legislation concerning the age at marriage in Karnataka. According to the Child Marriage Restraint Act of 1978, the minimum legal age for marriage in India is 18 years for women and 21 years for men.[38] However, the NFHS documented that for Karnataka as a whole in 1995, 51 per cent of women in the 20–4 year age group had married at the age of 18 years or younger. This proportion was as high as 59 per cent in the rural areas and 36 per cent in the urban areas. What the report stated of Karnataka as a whole was: 'Evidently many marriages in Karnataka do not abide by the legal regulations regarding age at marriage' (IIPS, 1995: 51). If we consider mean age at marriage alone, many women in the Ramanagaram sample appear also not to have followed the legal prescription of 1978. The mean age at marriage for those marrying after 1978 was 18.2 years, while the mean age at marriage for those marrying before 1978 was 15.5 years. However, in order to see this issue more clearly, a five-year moving average for age at first marriage by year of marriage was calculated. This indicated a sustained rise in marriage age. In order to see if the observed rise in marriage age may have been partly in response to the change in the law, the percentage of women who married after the age of 18 years according to marriage year in five-year intervals was also calculated. As evident from Figures. 6.1 and 6.2, after 1978 there does seem to be a gradual increase in marriage age, with a greater percentage of marriages taking place after the age of 18 years, which may be related to the passing of the law restraining child marriage.

Finally, let us examine whether the intercepts are different across the three religious groups. A Wald test implied that the intercept for Muslims was different from that for the Christians, and that the intercept

---

[38]Historically in India, early marriage and child marriage have been recognized as 'social problems' and early social reformers were involved in campaigns to increase male and female marriage age. In 1872, the Civil Marriage Act was passed largely due to the efforts of a social reformer in Bengal, Ram Mohan Roy. Later, in British India, the Sarda Act of 1929 fixed the legal marriage age for men at 18 years and for women at 14 years. The latter was raised to 15 years in 1949. However, where the 1978 Child Marriage Restraint Act differs from past legislation is that child marriage was made an offence punishable by law.

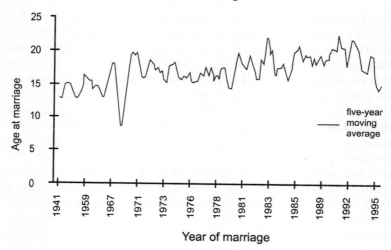

FIG. 6.1: FIVE-YEAR MOVING AVERAGE FOR FEMALE AGE AT FIRST MARRIAGE,
RAMANAGARAM SAMPLE, 1996

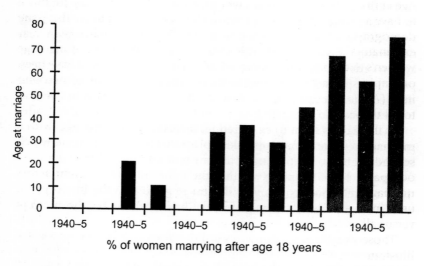

FIG. 6.2: PERCENTAGE OF WOMEN MARRYING AFTER 18 YEARS OF AGE,
RAMANAGARAM SAMPLE, 1996

also differed significantly between Christians and Hindus. However, a Wald test showed that the intercept for Hindus is not significantly different from the intercept for Muslims. These results taken together suggest that Hindus and Muslims do not have significantly different intercepts, but that the intercept for Christians is significantly different from those for both Hindus and Muslims. Membership of the Hindu instead of the Muslim religion does *not* have a significant effect on female age at marriage independently of socio-economic differences between the two religious groups. However, in the context of a model of the age at marriage, in which the dependent variable, and indeed all of the explanatory variables take values strictly greater than zero, it is not possible to draw interpretative conclusions from the *size* of the intercept coefficients. This quantitative evidence is consistent with the qualitative evidence presented earlier (in the shape of remarks made by the Ramanagaram women) which suggest that there was little difference between Hindus and Muslims in terms of women's ideas about the correct age at which to marry.

CONCLUSIONS AND IMPLICATIONS FOR POLICY

Age at first marriage is a vital demographic variable that is widely held to have a profound impact on women's fertility. However, while much demographic research has focused on the age at marriage as an explanatory factor in models that seek to identify the determinants of women's fertility in India, there is relatively little work, whether theoretical or empirical, that looks into the determinants of the age at marriage itself (As also remarked in Singh, 1992: 123–30). This chapter attempts to fill this gap.

In the Ramanagaram sample, the only factors that influenced female marriage age were the educational level of the woman, especially secondary education; whether the woman's husband had a skilled occupation; the woman's age at menarche; the year in which the marriage took place; total monthly household expenditure (which was used in this study as a proxy for income); and religion (Christianity versus all others, but not Hinduism versus Islam).

Those variables that were *not* significant are interesting in that they illustrate where the Ramanagaram dataset is at variance with the other theoretical and empirical literature on marriage age. Of the variables considered in our regression models, the marital consanguinity variables, no matter how they were measured, were insignificant. As discussed, consanguineous marriage, especially the uncle–niece union, is thought to reduce female marriage age, mainly because of the large age gap between spouses. The widespread acceptance of consanguineous marriage in Karnataka, particularly in rural areas, has been noted in many empirical studies and consanguineous unions made up almost 40 per cent of the marriages in the Ramanagaram sample.

However, neither measure of consanguinity was found to be a statistically significant predictor of marriage age in the Ramanagaram sample. Although marital consanguinity may be a cultural tradition typical to south India that has reinforced greater female autonomy there because it keeps the woman close to her natal family, and although it may function as an important means of reducing dowry and as a way of diversifying risk for rural households, the Ramanagaram sample provides no statistical evidence that it reduces marriage age.

Husband's education is also theoretically supposed to affect marriage age, and did have a significant effect in the preliminary model, but not in the interaction model. Different theories have hypothesized diametrically opposite effects for this variable. Groom's education is hypothesized to *increase* female marriage age because better-educated men prefer to marry women who are older, whether because they desire a better-educated spouse, because they believe that it is better to marry someone who is more mature, because they believe that a better-educated wife would earn more, or because they believe she will cause their children to be better educated. But, men's education may *decrease* female marriage age if better educated men are able to afford to marry earlier in life. Also, if a wife is supposed to be near her husband's age or younger than her husband, then the wife's age at marriage may be lower if the husband's is.

Husband's primary education was not a statistically significant determinant of marriage age for any of the three religions in the interaction model. One reason for this finding may be that the effect of men's education is being picked up by other variables such as husband's skilled occupation.

One way in which husband's occupation was measured was by whether the husband performed a farming-related occupation. Historically, in the case of pre-industrial Europe, it has been suggested that if the husband was a farmer, he was likely to marry later because he needed to wait until he or his bride inherited (or accumulated enough savings to purchase) a farm, thereby increasing both male and female marriage age. Alternatively, it has been suggested that in order to obtain more child labour for the family farm, men who were farmers married earlier and married younger women. In the econometric models this variable was not significant, perhaps because farming was not the only occupation in Ramanagaram which used some amount of child labour. Many occupations (particularly those connected with the silk industry, such as boiling cocoons in the silk-reeling units and silkworm rearing) also required large quantities of child labour. Moreover, in Indian society a man does not need to wait to achieve economic independence through inheritance before he marries, but can cohabit as a married man with his own parents.

Another measure of husband's occupation was if a man was employed in domestic industry. This variable is hypothesized to decrease female marriage age because additional child labour may be required for such occupations, again a hypothesis widely advanced for pre-industrial Europe. In the econometric models this variable was not significant, again perhaps because child labour was important in so many income-earning occupations and in household activities in Ramanagaram.

Moving onto the variables which did emerge as significant determinants of female marriage age in Ramanagaram, let us first consider husband's skilled occupation. Theoretically, this variable is expected to exert an impact on female marriage age in different ways. First, there is a hypothesis that if a husband holds a skilled occupation rather than an unskilled one, he will tend to marry an older bride because he prefers to wait for a better educated bride due to 'positive assortative mating'. Second, in a skilled occupation a man can earn additional income and raise better 'quality' children, which may lead him to delay marriage so as to reduce child 'quantity'. Third, a 'skilled occupation' is a measure of 'effective education' or human capital investment. The implication of this finding is that there is a 'pure work influence' on female marriage age even after controlling for education. Fourth, men in skilled occupations may want to devote some years building up their careers before getting married, increasing their own ages at marriage, and hence leading them to marry older women. Finally, men in skilled occupations may be more influenced by their colleagues or peers in the workplace who are marrying later as well. Husband's skilled occupation did emerge as a significant influence in the models of marriage age estimated for sub-samples of Hindus and Muslims. If we examine differences in the effects of husband's skilled occupation on female marriage age by religion, there is no statistically significant difference in the effects of husband's skilled occupation on marriage age between any of the three religious groups.

The next variable which was significant was the education of the woman. Theoretically, female education is hypothesized to exert a powerful positive effect on female marriage age for a variety of reasons (Birdsall, 1989: 23–50; Appleton, 1996: 139–66). Women's secondary education was also highly significant in the interaction model. It exerted a significant and positive impact for Hindus separately and Muslims separately, although there was no statistically significant difference in its effect between the two religions. Interestingly, this variable is insignificant among the Christians, possibly because there was not much variation in education among Christians. From the qualitative information gathered during my fieldwork, it seemed likely that it was university education which exerts a significant effect on the Christians' marriage age, although this could not be tested econometrically because the sample size of the Christians was too small.

There are several reasons why secondary education may exert a larger effect than total education. First, higher education may have delayed marriage because of the tendency of women with such an education to have a longer search process, and their greater capacity to bear the search costs of doing so. Higher education also increases the opportunity cost of women's time (both in employment and the opportunity costs of leisure) and increases both productivity at home and in the market. It is also possible that when girls in Ramanagaram are in secondary school, which they enter at age 11 or 12 years, they are old enough to be amenable to educational teaching about marriage age. When girls are in high school, they are able to read about the benefits of small families themselves or are influenced by the media (such as radio and television) on these matters. This was particularly evident to me during my fieldwork because the Anganwadi teachers were required to have passed the SSLC examination in order to teach, and many of the single girls who had not as yet completed their SSLC were keen to do so in order to become courtyard teachers. Most planned to marry only after completing their secondary education.

The income variable, measured as total expenditure, emerged as very significant in the models of marriage age presented here. Theoretically, income is thought to exert either a negative or a positive impact on marriage age. It may increase marriage age for those women who earn higher incomes because these women expect to obtain fewer gains from marriage. On the other hand, higher incomes earned by men may enable them to support a wife with no income or to afford to have additional children, consequently leading to lower marriage ages for women. The income variable (measured as total expenditure) had a highly significant positive effect on marriage age. These findings have several implications. First, 'income of destination' may indeed have been a good proxy for income of origin, since it exerts a measurable effect on marriage age. Secondly, the fact that the positive effects of income outweigh the negative effects imply that it makes sense, at least in Ramanagaram, for the rich to marry later and the poor to marry earlier. This may be due to two causes. First, as suggested by the literature on income and marriage age, women who have higher incomes have lower expected gains from marriage, and hence may be marrying later. Secondly, the poor may require children for old-age support and insurance to a greater degree than richer parents with other means of saving and insurance, leading to lower ages at marriage for women who are from poor families in order to ensure that enough children are born to guarantee effective insurance cover. However, there is no statistically significant difference in the effect of this variable on marriage age between Hindus and Muslims.

Age at menarche also had a significant positive effect on marriage age, one which did not vary across religious groups. There are several possible reasons for this. First, menarche may be a sign of a woman being 'grown up' enough to marry 'soon'. Second, it may be a sign that a girl is now reproductively fertile and needs to be married off to prevent illegitimate pregnancies. The qualitative evidence collected during my fieldwork suggests that both of these factors may have been at work. Most important, however, was that two key desired characteristics in a potential bride in Ramanagaram were physical strength and long hair. This was because, for the rigorous life which many of the Ramanagaram women had to lead after marriage, stamina and strength were required to keep up with household activities. The women explained that this was also compounded by the fact that because both boys and girls were being sent to school, married women were bearing the burden of additional work formerly performed by children. Given the lack of alternative labour to help with household tasks, women were required to take on huge burdens in terms of time and stamina on themselves. Hence, because physical strength increased household productivity, it was a highly desired characteristic for young women, contributing greatly to their eligibility in the marriage market. Another desired characteristic which was also reflected in Chapter 5 in which we saw that one of the key items of personal expenditure for the Ramanagaram women was coconut oil, was long hair, which was prized as an asset. Interestingly, both desired characteristics—physical strength and long hair—are directly related to better nutrition and health, which in turn are medically known to be reflected in early menarche. The positive relationship between age at marriage and age at menarche therefore may have been because menarche is a good proxy for a woman's health and nutritional status and hence her desirability in the marriage market.

Year of marriage was included in the model as a possible proxy for changes in social norms and/or legislation over time, both of which would be postulated theoretically to increase marriage age. The econometric findings showed that a one-year later year of marriage was associated with a significant increase in marriage age for all three religious groups.

The implications of the significant effect exerted by the year of marriage variable must be considered more carefully. With the imposition of the Child Marriage Restraint Act in 1978, there was a change in the practice of child marriage, with an average of 54 per cent of the women who married after 1978 in the Ramanagaram sample doing so after the age of 18 years, compared to an average of 27 per cent for those women who married before 1978. Although the law is still not wholly complied with, it does appear to have exerted some influence on people's behaviour. This is borne out by the opinions expressed by some of the Ramanagaram women. For example, Sardamma of village C said 'My daughter can study as much as she wants to for now, and she must get married only at 18.' On the other hand, the law is certainly still being violated, as illustrated by Chandramma of village B who said that for her daughter 'it is best that she should get married at 15–16. As she is currently that age, I am looking out for an alliance for her'. The fact that we see the 'time' effect operating on age at marriage even after controlling for variations in other factors such as education, income, and occupation may mean that the 1978 law is being better enforced.

An alternative interpretation of the positive effect of year of marriage on age at marriage is that the changes over time may be being brought about by changes in the set of expectations, social norms, and customs governing age at marriage and female status in the home, especially with regard to the 'proper time to marry' for women in younger birth cohorts. This is because for 'social behaviour' (such as fertility may be), an individual's utility-maximizing level of that behaviour is an increasing function of the average level of that activity undertaken by all others in a social reference group.

We find some support for the influence of norms in the responses to two questions on daughters' age at marriage in the Ramanagaram questionnaire. The women who had married daughters were asked at what age their daughters had been married, and for those who had unmarried daughters, at what age they desired their unmarried daughters to be married. For all women who had married daughters, the mean age at which the daughters had married was 17.5 years. For those who had unmarried daughters, the proposed mean age at marriage was 18.9 years. It is interesting that both these figures are higher than the mean age at marriage for ever-married women in the sample as a whole (17.3 years), again indicating that the 'normal' female marriage age may be rising. The positive effect of year of marriage on age at marriage was observed among all three religious groups, with no significant difference in the effect between Hindus and Muslims, but a significantly larger effect among Christians.

The main purpose of this study is to identify differences between religions in the determination of demographic indices. Theoretically, religion has been hypothesized to have a direct impact on the age at first marriage via its function as a system of beliefs or values, and an indirect impact via its impact on women's status (See Sander, 1995 for differences between Catholics, Protestants, and Baptists in America; Thornton, 1979: 131–42; Jeffery and Jeffery, 1997: 212–54).

The religion variable was eliminated in the preliminary model of marriage age in Ramanagaram. Controlling for other socio-economic variables, religion by itself had no significant effect on female marriage age in Ramanagaram. The interaction model then showed that there were also no differences between Hindus and Muslims in the effects of other socio-economic variables on marriage age. That is, the factors which determine marriage age in Ramanagaram do not differ between Hindus and Muslims. However, there were some differences in the socio-economic influences on marriage age between Christians and the two other religious groups.

These findings provide no empirical support for the concerns which have been put forward by the more extreme right-wing political parties in India since the 1990s about the so-called 'Islamic' effects on marriage, according to which Muslim women have much lower autonomy (and hence lower marriage age) than other religious groups. The analysis conducted for Ramanagaram shows that any observed difference in female marriage age across religious groups can be explained by other socio-economic differences between these communities such as access to secondary education, income, age at menarche, year of marriage, and husband's occupation.

These findings have important implications for government policy, insofar as they include targeting religious leaders and the socio-economic characteristics of religious groups that affect the timing of marriage. For example, government policy should be more proactive about encouraging parents to adhere to the Child Marriage Restraint Act. The 1995 NFHS data show that 58 per cent of women in all of India were marrying before the minimum legal age at marriage. The findings of the present study support targeting socio-economic characteristics such as women's education and employment in order to delay the timing of marriage. Media campaigns can be used to influence customs or ideas about the 'proper' time to marry, and to discourage husbands from undertaking marriage with very young brides.

These findings also suggest that religious leaders need to be integrated better into population policy and into development policy more widely in order to significantly influence the age at first marriage in India. The most significant ways in which religious leaders may influence the age at marriage are through advocating that individuals adhere to the Child Marriage Restraint Act, and to stress a later marriage age, particularly for women. Religious leaders could also help influence thinking about later marriage by encouraging marriage only after menarche.

This chapter has investigated the determinants of the female age at marriage on the grounds that it is an important proximate determinant of women's fertility and a vital variable in explorations of economic demography in a society in which most reproduction occurs within marriage. Despite these facts, beyond the early theoretical economic models of marriage put forward in the 1970s and early 1980s, there has been little attempt, at least in the realm of economics, to integrate the theoretical literature on the determinants of marriage age with the discipline encouraged by concrete empirical findings.

This chapter has attempted to contribute to an understanding of the determinants of the timing of marriage in an economic and demographic context. First, it has attempted to highlight the most important theoretical and empirical issues that emerge in assessing the determinants of marriage age through a survey of the economic, socio-anthropological, and medical literature that does exist. Secondly, it has carried out a detailed econometric investigation of the empirical evidence obtained from one taluk in Karnataka to investigate whether, in addition to the factors which have conventionally been used to account for differences in marriage age among populations, religion also plays a role.

It was found in this chapter that after controlling for other socio-economic factors such as income, education, age at menarche, and year of marriage, the religion in which the woman was raised *did not* exert an effect on the age at marriage in Ramanagaram. Nor did the effects of other socio-economic factors on marriage age differ between Hindus and Muslims. Discussions of fertility in poor countries have stressed that it is important to increase female age at marriage in order to lower fertility. This chapter supports the conclusion that in order to achieve this end, increasing the educational level of women, particularly secondary education, is essential. Skilled occupations and rising incomes also seem to play a role in delaying marriage. The age at marriage is also influenced by biological factors such as the timing of menarche. However, this study also recognizes that social factors such as the role of custom (which may be what is reflected in the significant 'year of marriage' variable) may come to bear on marriage decisions as well. This chapter has integrated economic argument and econometric analysis with a consideration of wider sociological factors to identify the most important determinants of female marriage age in India.

chapter seven

~

The Determinants of Contraceptive
Use in India

I have never adverted to the check suggested by Condorcet without the most marked disapprobation. Indeed I should always particularly reprobate any artificial and unnatural modes of checking population, both on account of their immorality and their tendency to remove a necessary stimulus to industry.[1]

There are two opposing views of the interaction between fertility regulation and the fertility transition. The first view is that fertility will decline in response to the supply of family planning services. The other is that fertility will decline in response to the decline in the demand for children (Pritchett, 1994: 1–2). This debate is particularly relevant for southern and western India where in the past two decades there have been rapid declines in fertility, often approaching replacement levels, as in the case of Tamil Nadu. It is still unclear as to what extent these declines are due to the provision of family planning services, to socio-economic changes in education and women's employment, to changes in the institutional structure, to changes in ideas and norms, or to some combination of all of these factors.

The decision whether or not to practise contraception is based on the individual's evaluation of the costs and benefits of adopting a contraceptive method. The costs of practising contraception include factors such as the actual monetary costs of using a method, the time spent in travel-

---

[1]Malthus, 1817: 393, as quoted in Folbre, 1992: 114. Although clearly Condorcet was in favour of contraception, as Folbre argues, 'Whether or not he was prudish, Malthus endorsed traditional religious views of contraception that other political economists of his day were willing to criticise.' See Folbre, 1992: 114.

ling, payments to providers such as family planning clinics or hospitals, and psycho-social factors such as disapproval of other family members (Bongaarts, 1997a: 13; see also Bongaarts and Bruce, 1995: 57–75). The benefits of practising contraception are the reduced cost of additional children, as well as the reduced maternal health risks associated with repeated pregnancies.

In India, according to the 1991 Census, 44 per cent of couples are using a method of family planning. Of the Hindus, 42 per cent are currently using a contraceptive method, compared with 28 per cent of Muslims and 34 per cent of Christians. In the Ramanagaram survey, women were asked if they had ever used any method of birth control. The question was answered in the affirmative by 53 per cent of ever-married women in the whole sample, 86 per cent of Christians, 57 per cent of Hindus, and 40 per cent of Muslims. These percentages suggest that it is possible that religion does affect contraceptive use in Ramanagaram. However, it is also possible that the underlying characteristics of the three religious groups are what accounts for these differences.

This chapter will not deal with whether the supply of contraception and contraceptive usage acts as an independent determinant of fertility because the dataset available for Ramanagaram is drawn from a sample over which contraceptive access is uniform and, indeed, very good. This is because the government family planning movement in Karnataka is well-organized and covers all parts of the state. A detailed micro-level dataset such as the one collected in Ramanagaram is more suited to the study of what characteristics of women influence their decision whether to use contraception, and that is the question this chapter will explore.

This chapter is organized as follows. The first section reviews the literature on the importance of family planning programmes, whether the decision to use contraception ought to be studied separately from the decision whether to have a child, and the theoretical determinants of contraceptive use. The next section examines the empirical findings on contraceptive use in Ramanagaram. The third section considers the empirical evidence from the survey on fertility preferences in Ramanagaram. The fourth section estimates a LOGIT model of the determinants of contraceptive use. The fifth section presents the conclusions and implications for policy.

THEORIES OF THE DETERMINANTS OF CONTRACEPTIVE USE

Existing views of the importance of contraceptive use within the theory of fertility comprise two broad streams: that which dwells on the supply-side determinants of contraceptive use such as family planning programmes,[2] and that which deals with demand-side determinants such as the role of desired fertility (See *The Economist*, 1994: 21–3). The first body of theory stems from the work of Easterlin and others;[3] the Easterlin synthesis framework acknowledges a role for both demand and supply-side factors: contraceptive use is determined both by the desire to achieve certain fertility outcomes and the costs of using contraception.

The fundamental issue which demographers and economists debate about is whether contraceptive use ought to be studied independently of fertility choice. This discussion has taken the form of debates about the impact and relative success of family planning programmes in effecting fertility transitions (Bongaarts, 1997b: 422–43). In 1960 only 10 per cent of women in developing countries were using any form of fertility control, whereas by 1994 the figure had risen to 51 per cent (*The Economist*, 1994: 22). Figures such as these have led demographers to argue that there is a 'KAP-gap' (a gap in women's knowledge of, attitudes towards, and practice of birth control) and an 'unmet need' for contraception (Bongaarts, 1991: 293–313; Thapa, 1993: 4). This has been one of the most important arguments in favour of continuing investment in large-scale family planning programmes (Bongaarts, 1991: 293–313; Guilkey and Jayne, 1997: 173–89).

However, the role of family planning programmes in the fertility transition has also been criticised by economists such as Pritchett and others who contend that desired fertility and the demand for children are the key factors in explaining changes in fertility, and that the supply of contraception is relatively unimportant (Pritchett, 1994: 1–55, Westoff, 1988: 225–32).

In essence, it is correct to argue that access to family planning alone does not have an impact on contraceptive adoption. However, as Bongaarts has suggested, family planning programmes not only provide access, but also aid in '[t]he diffusion of knowledge about fertility regulation and the social acceptability of private control over reproductive behaviour (which) have probably been more important in raising contraceptive use than has the mere physical accessibility of methods (Bongaarts, 1997a; Bongaarts, 1997b: 427. See also Cleland and Wilson, 1987: 5–30).

[2]For example, Parker Mauldin argues that 'There is considerable empirical evidence that large-scale family planning programs, when well-managed, have a substantial effect on fertility.' See Parker Mauldin, 1983: 289.

[3]Easterlin, 1975: 54–63; Bourgeois-Pichat, 1967: 160–3; Chen, Hicks, Johnson and Rodriguez, 1990: 408–24.

Moreover, as Egerö argues, 'The very act of providing services changes the context within which people operate, and could in certain situations be an important 'ideational' preparation for the couple-based decision-making about birth control simply by making birth control an open public issue' (1994: 25). This suggests that the role of family planning programmes is not only about access but also about information.

Moreover, a combination of theories is needed to explain the rapid decline in fertility in Bangladesh and Indonesia in the past two decades, and the declines in fertility which we observe in Tamil Nadu, Karnataka, and Andhra Pradesh in India in the 1980s and 1990s, which have occurred at times independently of other demand-side socio-economic factors such as female education (as in the case of Andhra Pradesh).[4]

For these reasons, it seems more appropriate to argue that *both* the demand for children and the supply of contraception play an important role in the fertility transition:

Making contraception more widely available will make it easier for women to have only the number of children they want, and to do so in safe and efficient ways. But changing the number they want to have will need a subtle mix of education, economic development, land reform and improvements in the lot of women (*The Economist*, 1994: 23).

Investigating if contraceptive use exercises a completely autonomous role on fertility is difficult, mainly because the investigation must be conducted in areas which have differential access to contraception. However, another option is to investigate empirically a testable model which introduces variables which may affect the decision to use contraception independently of the determinants of fertility. This chapter carries out such an analysis for the Ramanagaram sample. We therefore go on to discuss which factors may affect the decision to use contraception.

One of the most important factors postulated as influencing this decision is women's and men's education. Studies on a number of countries have argued that couples with more schooling have a wider knowledge of contraceptive methods, use the methods better, and are better able to assimilate information about availability, correct use, side effects, and costs of using contraception.[5] In addition, women with some

---

[4]Retherford and Ramesh, 1996; Koenig et al., 1992; Egerö, 1994; Cleland and Wilson, 1987: 5–30.

[5]Rosenzweig and Schultz, 1989: 457–77; Ainsworth, Beegle and Nyamate, 1996: 85–122; Chen, Hicks, Johnson and Rodriguez, 1990: 408–24; Schuler, Hashemi and Riley, 1997: 563–75; Guilkey and Jayne, 1997: 173–89; Shapiro and Tambashe, 1994; Jejeebhoy, 1992; Castro Martin, 1995: 187–202; Cochrane, 1979.

education have a stronger bargaining position within the family when it comes to decisions about contraception. These conclusions are supported by studies on south India conducted in the 1960s and in the 1990s.[6] In the LOGIT models presented later in this chapter, this variable is measured in terms of the total number of years of education of the woman.

Several studies also argue that husband's education is an important determinant of contraceptive use and that it exerts an impact most particularly at low levels of husband's and wife's schooling, a conclusion substantiated by other studies.[7] Husband's education, measured in terms of the total number of years of education, is used in the LOGIT models presented later in this study.

Contraceptive choice may be affected by the occupations of women (Kraft and Coverdill, 1994: 593–602). For example, women who are employed may be more likely to use contraception either for birth spacing or for birth limitation, if their occupations are incompatible with child rearing (Dharmalingam and Morgan, 1996: 187–201). Women who are employed in a skilled occupation may also use contraception more. In the econometric models presented later in this chapter, this variable is measured in three ways: first, so as to take the value 1 if the woman was employed in a home-related occupation and 0 otherwise; second, so as to take the value 1 if the woman was employed in a silk-related occupation and 0 otherwise; and third, so as to take the value 1 if the women was employed in a skilled occupation and 0 otherwise.

Contraceptive choice may also be affected by the occupations of men. Men who are employed in skilled occupations may encourage their wives to use contraception more if they want fewer or better-'quality' children. Men who are employed in domestic industry may encourage their wives to use contraception less, if more children are required for their labour. Finally, if a man is employed as a farmer, he may encourage his wife to use contraception less, if children are required for the family farm. In the econometric models presented, this variable is measured in three ways: so as to take the value 1 if the man was employed in a skilled occupation and 0 otherwise; so as to take the value 1 if the man was employed in domestic industry and 0 otherwise; and so as to take the value 1 if the man was a farmer and 0 otherwise.

Contraceptive use may also be affected by income. Families with higher incomes may be more likely to use contraception because they may be able to afford better access to contraceptive services. Alternatively,

[6]UN, 1961: 163; Dharmalingam and Morgan, 1996: 187–201; IIPS, 1995: 88

[7]Ainsworth, Beegle and Nyamate, 1996: 85–122; Cochrane and Guilkey, 1995: 779–804; Omondi-Odhiambo, 1997: 29–40.

they may have a higher opportunity cost of the value of their time spent in leisure which may reduce their demand for children and increase contraceptive use to achieve lower desired fertility outcomes. This variable is included in the econometric models presented later in this chapter and is measured in terms of total monthly expenditure, total monthly food expenditure, and in terms of an index of ownership of items of consumer equipment.

The decision to use contraception may also depend on the age of the woman. Studies of contraceptive use argue that women in their mid-thirties to mid-forties, who have completed their childbearing, may have the highest demand for contraception compared with women who have not as yet completed their families (Visaria and Chari, 1998). Certainly, women who are older will have grown up in a cohort in which norms and values were more unfavourable to contraception than they were for younger women. This variable is measured in the econometric models in terms of the woman's age in years at the time of survey.

Contraceptive choice is affected by the institutional structure and by ideas and norms about contraceptive use. For example, the extent to which women have access to information and their natal kin after marriage, and cultural constructs such as patriarchy (Schuler, Hashemi and Riley, 1997: 563–75) may have an important impact on their ability to enjoy greater autonomy and use contraception (Omondi-Odhiambo, 1997–29). The influence of ideas and norms on the decision to use contraception is supported by statements made by the Ramanagaram women. For example, when questioned about the ideal number of children, Kamalamma, aged 45 years, said, 'Two is about right. The government tells us through the family planning programme. I got myself operated after two children. I do not know if the population is growing too fast, but we are all told that we should only have two.'[8] The woman's age variable, which is included in the econometric models, may also capture the effect of changes in social norms over time.

Related to the role of norms and social mores, another factor which may influence contraceptive use is religion. For example, in their study of Bangladesh, Schuler, Hashemi and Riley find that Hindu women are re more likely to use a contraceptive method than Muslim women

---

[8]The importance of the media is also observed in studies of fertility in other countries. For example, Ibrahim and Ibrahim argue that in Egypt, over 70 per cent of Egyptian women acquire their knowledge about family planning from the television and that this is one of the most important factors accounting for fertility declines in Egypt in the 1980s and 1990s. See Ibrahim and Ibrahim, 1998: 19–52.

(1997: 563–75). The Mysore Population Study found that in Karnataka post-partum abstinence was on average longer for Hindu than for Muslim women, with obvious contraceptive implications.[9] Amin, Diamond and Steele's study of Bangladesh found that religion is an important predictor of contraceptive use, but primarily via the religious practices of the community, rather than through individual religious observance (1996). Religion is included in the econometric models presented later in this chapter.

There are two ways in which family composition may affect the decision to use contraception. One way is the effect on contraceptive use of undertaking a consanguineous marriage. It is possible that a woman who marries a relative may be more likely to consult with her extended family on matters relating to contraception. Alternatively, since consanguineous marriages in India have traditionally involved a large age gap between spouses, this may contribute to reducing inter-spousal communication on contraception, which may decrease contraceptive use. This variable is included in the econometric models presented later and is measured in terms of a dummy variable which takes the value 1 if the woman married a relative but 0 otherwise; and in terms of the coefficient of inbreeding (discussed in the preceding chapter).

The second measure of family composition that might influence the decision to use contraception is the presence of extended family (Muhuri and Menken, 1997: 279–94). For example, it is conventionally argued that female extended family members such as mothers and mothers-in-law have an important role to play in influencing a couple's decisions about using contraception (Srinivas, 1989; 123–44). Most often, the hypothesized direction of influence is thought to be negative. In this chapter, the influence of the extended family is measured in terms of the total number of female extended family resident in the household. The influence of female extended family on women's decisions to use contraception is also discussed in detail in the qualitative evidence presented in the next section. Hence two measures of family composition are included in the econometric models presented—a dummy variable that examines whether the woman has undertaken a consanguineous marriage, and a measure of the total number of female extended family resident in the household.

Another factor which may influence a woman's decision to use contraception is her autonomy and her mobility, as measured by her free-

---

[9]UN, 1961: 137. Desired fertility between Hindus and Muslims was, however, similar at 3.7 births for Hindus and 3.8 births for Muslims. See UN, 1961: 141.

dom of movement and of interaction with others.[10] For example, greater autonomy for women may encourage them to join credit programmes more readily than others, or it may lower the levels of the 'unmet need' for contraception (Schuler, Hashemi and Riley, 1997: 573; Morgan and Niraula, 1995: 541–61). This variable was included in the econometric models in the form of a question which asked women if they perceived that access to a contraceptive method (provided by government services) was easy. However, a more in-depth qualitative examination of how women's autonomy in Ramanagaram influenced the decision to practise family planning is also carried out in the next section.

Another factor postulated as affecting contraceptive use is the preference for sons because son-preference may be expected to result in higher contraceptive use for families with more sons than daughters.[11] These findings are also supported by studies on a number of other countries, including India.[12] The Ramanagaram women themselves made statements indicating that the decision to use contraception was affected by the desire for sons. For example, one Hindu woman, Vasantakumari, aged 24 years, remarked, 'I will have an operation (sterilization) after I have a son. I will still try for a boy ... because I have three girls, who will look after me otherwise?' This variable was not included in the econometric models because it is endogenous in a model of contraceptive choice where the dependent variable is whether or not the woman had ever used contraception.

The incidence and period of breastfeeding may also affect contraceptive use. A longer period of breastfeeding may reduce the necessity for using temporary or permanent methods of contraception. Informal discussions with the women of Ramanagaram suggested that there were no significant differences between Hindus and Muslims in the number of months of breastfeeding after birth. The percentage of women who breastfed their children was 98 per cent among the Hindus, 96 per cent among the Muslims, and 100 per cent among the Christians. In any case, breastfeeding must be regarded as endogenous with contraceptive adoption and cannot therefore be included in the model as an exogenous determinant of the latter.

Another factor thought to influence contraceptive practices is infant

[10]Although autonomy is defined more widely in Chapter 8. See also Dyson and Moore, 1983: 35–60; Basu, 1992; Balk, 1994: 21–45.

[11]Using a sample of 8979 households from Egypt and non-linear maximum likelihood estimation procedures, Aly and Shields argue that contraceptive use increases dramatically at each parity as the number of sons increases. See Aly and Shields, 1991.

[12]Schuler, Hashemi and Riley, 1997: 563–75; Morgan and Niraula, 1995: 541–61; IIPS, 1995: 89–90.

mortality. A decline in infant and child mortality generates a larger demand for contraceptive methods to regulate fertility, because of the increased survival of children into adulthood (Gulati, 1992: 157–72; Retherford and Ramesh, 1996. For evidence from elsewhere see Guilkey and Jayne, 1997: 173–89). This variable is not included in the econometric models presented later because the infant mortality rate is unlikely to have varied greatly (or perceptibly) within Ramanagaram, and it would in any case have been impossible to assign an infant mortality rate to each woman in the sample. However, it is possible to estimate the mean level of infant and child deaths by religious group for the Ramanagaram sample, and the number of children ever born net of child deaths. These estimates are shown in Tables 7.1 and 7.2.

Table 7.1 shows infant mortality by religion in the Ramanagaram sample. A statistical test shows that this difference is not significantly different between Hindus and Muslims. Total children ever born net of infant mortality is also not significantly different to the differences between Hindus, Muslims, and Christians in total children ever born. This is shown in Table 7.2. Tables 7.1 and 7.2 show that taking into account figures for infant mortality in the sample does not significantly alter the inherent differences between Hindus, Muslims, and Christians in the mean level of their fertility.

Another factor which may affect contraceptive use is the degree of participation of men in decision-making about fertility (Omondi-Odhiambo, 1997: 29). Since some traditional and modern methods of contraception do require the husband's consent, approval, and financial support (or all three), it is important to take men's ideas about contraception into account when devising a family planning strategy. This is also important because in many less developed societies there is very

TABLE 7.1: INFANT MORTALITY BY RELIGION, RAMANAGARAM SAMPLE (1996)

Infant mortality	All women	Hindus	Muslims	Christians
Mean	0.15	0.15	0.21	0.00
Standard deviation	0.03	0.04	0.05	0.00

TABLE 7.2: CHILDREN EVER BORN NET OF INFANT MORTALITY, RAMANAGARAM SAMPLE (1996)

Children ever born net of infant mortality	All women	Hindus	Muslims	Christians
Mean	2.87	2.51	3.51	2.46
Standard deviation	0.13	0.15	0.22	0.33

limited inter-spousal communication on fertility and couples may not always concur in their perceptions about contraceptive adoption (Omondi-Odhiambo, 1997; Caldwell and Caldwell, 1990; Biddlecom, Casterline and Perez, 1996). In the econometric models presented here, this variable is not used because it is highly correlated with husband's education and occupation, and indeed, the level of participation by men may even be a result of the level of education. However, the role of husbands in decision-making about contraception in the Ramanagaram sample is discussed in detail in the qualitative evidence presented in the next section.

Of the factors postulated in the literature as being important determinants of contraceptive choice, therefore, ten have been regarded as appropriate for inclusion in the econometric models estimated here for Ramanagaram. These are woman's education, husband's education, income, woman's occupation, husband's occupation, marital consanguinity, woman's current age, woman's reported perception of access to contraceptive methods, resident female extended family, and religion.

THE PATTERN OF CONTRACEPTIVE USE

Before analysing the determinants of contraceptive use in Ramanagaram, it is important to examine the pattern of such use, as well as the Ramanagaram women's attitudes towards contraception. In the survey, the Ramanagaram women were asked if they had ever used any method of birth control. The question was answered in the affirmative by 53 per cent of ever-married women in the whole sample, 86 per cent of Christians, 57 per cent of Hindus, and 40 per cent of Muslims. According to the 1991 Census, 44 per cent of Indian couples are effectively protected by family planning methods (Madras Communications Institute, 1994). There are significant regional differences, however, with rates as high as 50 per cent in Tamil Nadu, Andhra Pradesh, and Karnataka, but only 20 per cent in Uttar Pradesh (Rutherford and Ramesh, 1996; IIPS, 1995: 79–80). The Ramanagaram sample is therefore a typical example of the experience of the south Indian states.

The survey asked Ramanagaram women which method of birth control they adopted, and their responses are shown in Table 7.3. The most popular means of birth control was the sterilization (tubal ligation) operation.[13] For example, one woman, Padma, aged 23 years, from

[13]This finding was also corroborated in interviews with doctors in Ramanagaram *taluk*, March 1996.

TABLE 7.3: BIRTH CONTROL METHOD USED, IN RAMANAGARAM SAMPLE (1996)

Method used	All women		Hindus		Muslims		Christians	
	No.	%	No.	%	No.	%	No.	%
Copper T	5	5.1	5	8.5	0	0.0	0	0.0
Mala D (pills)	18	18.2	8	13.6	7	25.0	3	25.0
Nirodh (condoms)	6	6.1	3	5.1	2	7.1	1	8.3
Operation	66	66.7	41	69.5	18	64.3	7	58.3
Mala D + operation	4	4.1	2	3.4	1	3.6	1	8.3

Ramanagaram town, remarked, 'I will have an operation after three children. Currently, I do not use any birth control techniques.' However, some women did have their reservations. For example, Gangamma, a Hindu mother of five, aged 33 years, from Ramanagaram town, remarked, 'I am scared of undergoing the operation. That is why I have five children.' Another woman, Puttibai, aged 35 years, from village A, remarked, 'The population is less today because operations are in vogue, but I will not have it because they are said to be painful.'

This predominance of the tubal ligation method is similar to findings from the NFHS which reported that female and male sterilization is the most widely-known contraceptive method in Karnataka, and that knowledge of spacing methods is comparatively low.[14] Female sterilization accounts for 87 per cent of total current contraceptive practice in Karnataka, 79 per cent of all contraceptive use in Tamil Nadu, and 95 per cent in Andhra Pradesh, but only 66 per cent in Uttar Pradesh.[15]

In the Ramanagaram sample, spacing methods were more popular among the Christians and Muslims than among Hindus. The second most popular method of family planning in the sample was birth control pills, which was used by one-quarter of Muslim and Christian women, but only by 14 per cent of Hindu women. By contrast, only Hindu women used the intra-uterine device (IUD).

Why is a permanent method of contraception so favoured by the women of Ramanagaram, as indeed by women in other Indian states?

[14]IIPS, 1995: 79–80. A 'modern' method refers to intra-uterine devices (IUDs), pills and condoms.

[15]IIPS, 1995: 88; Retherford and Ramesh, 1996. The median age at sterilization is 25.2 years in Karnataka and sterilization operations after the age of 35 years are quite rare (approximately 4 per cent). This finding is similar to the case of Tamil Nadu where the median age at sterilization is 26.2 years. The comparable figure for Andhra Pradesh is 24.5 years and for Uttar Pradesh is 29.6 years.

One contributory factor is that most family planning services are performed by the public sector which emphasizes permanent methods of birth control, and hence sterilization is less costly and more easily available than other methods. Another contributory factor is the very small degree of communication among couples about contraception, discussed further on. The tubal ligation method is a contraceptive method which a woman can adopt without the need to discuss it with her husband or seek his consent. The tubal ligation method also involves fewer costs in terms of post-operative care, making this option attractive to women who live further away from medical infrastructure, as well as to service providers (Visaria and Chari, 1998: 53–112).

Couple communication in Karnataka is very low, with an estimated 58 per cent of women in Karnataka ever discussing contraception with their husbands (IIPS, 1995: 104). In the Ramanagaram sample, couple communication was even less frequent, with only 36 per cent answering that they ever discussed contraception with their husbands, 37 per cent of Hindus, 23 per cent of Muslims, and 93 per cent of Christians.

Earlier the importance of female autonomy in influencing women's decision to use contraception was discussed. Moreover, recent studies of family planning in India suggest that before adopting a contraceptive method, 'women generally seek the opinion of parents, husband and in-laws, in that order, and accept contraception only if these three parties approve' (Visaria and Chari, 1998: 97). The Ramanagaram questionnaire therefore asked women which persons they consulted about family planning. Their responses are reported in Table 7.4.

The most popular responses were that the woman took the decision

TABLE 7.4: PERSON(S) INFLUENCING DECISIONS ABOUT BIRTH CONTROL, RAMANAGARAM SAMPLE (1996)

Persons	All women		Hindus		Muslims		Christians	
	No.	%	No.	%	No.	%	No.	%
Couple	95	50.8	44	42.7	38	54.3	13	92.9
Couple+parents-in-law	2	10.7	2	1.9	0	0.0	0	0.0
Couple+nurse	1	0.5	0	0.0	1	1.4	0	0.0
Woman	36	19.3	26	25.2	10	14.3	0	0.0
Woman+mother-in-law	1	0.5	1	1.0	0	0.0	0	0.0
Woman+doctor/nurse	3	16.0	2	1.9	1	1.4	0	0.0
No response	49	26.2	28	27.2	20	28.6	1	7.1
Total	187	100.0	103	100.0	70	100.0	14	100.0

either together with her husband or alone. Although half the sample reported taking the decision to use contraception with their husbands, it must be remembered that over 60 per cent of women said that they did not discuss contraception with their husbands at all. It seems likely that this contradiction arises from many women's desire to display loyalty towards their husbands by reporting that they took the decision to use contraception together, whether or not they were actually doing so. It may also indicate that though communication was taking place, it was partial and limited. Finally, it may reflect the influence of the media, since family planning campaigns on radio and television continually urged couples to discuss birth control with each other.

In order to specifically assess the influence of female extended family members and friends, the women were asked with whom they would discuss family planning, apart from their husbands, among five options: mother-in-law, sister-in-law, sister, mother, and friends. The responses to this question are shown in Table 7.5.

TABLE 7.5: INFLUENCE OF EXTENDED FAMILY MEMBERS (FEMALE) OR FRIENDS ON
FAMILY PLANNING, RAMANAGARAM SAMPLE (1996)

Female extended family member	All women		Hindus		Muslims		Christians	
	No.	%	No.	%	No.	%	No.	%
None	53	28.3	37	35.9	12	17.1	4	28.5
Mother	37	19.7	21	20.4	10	14.2	6	42.8
Friends	25	13.3	15	14.5	8	11.4	2	14.2
Mother-in-law	25	13.3	11	10.7	13	18.6	0	0.0
Sister	24	12.8	10	9.7	11	15.7	3	21.4
Sister-in-law	6	3.2	3	2.9	3	4.3	0	0.0
Nurse	1	0.5	1	0.9	0	0.0	0	0.0
Others	6	3.2	4	3.8	0	0.0	2	14.2
Breakdown of 'others'								
Aunt	1	0.5	1	0.9	0	0.0	1	7.2
Daughter/daughter-in-law	1	0.5	1	0.9	0	0.0	0	0.0
Niece	1	0.5	1	0.9	0	0.0	0	0.0
Co-sister*	2	1.1	1	0.9	0	0.0	1	7.2
Total	201	100	111	100	75	100	15	100

Note: *husband's brother's wife

Mothers, friends, mothers-in-law, and sisters were the chief confidants on family planning matters, and this was true for all three religious groups. Qualitative evidence suggests that one reason sterilization operations are such a popular method of contraception in Ramanagaram is partly because female extended family or women-friends urge women to undergo these operations after they have achieved what is perceived to be an ideal family size of two or three children. For example, Devamma, a mother of three sons and two daughters, aged 51 years, a housewife from village C, said, 'I encouraged my daughter and daughters-in-law to have two children quickly and go in for the operation. Then they are not troubled any more. The girls have to go in one morning and come back later by *auto* (a three-wheeled motorized vehicle). They take some rest and then they do not have to bother any more. There is no problem as with the pills, which they may not remember to take. After all, why should they be burdened with so many children as I?'

This study is concerned primarily with the impact of religion on demographic outcomes. The NFHS found that approval for family planning in Karnataka was highest among the Christians (92 per cent) compared with Hindus (84 per cent) and Muslims (81 per cent) (IIPS, 1995: 107). All 201 women in the Ramanagaram Sample were asked about what they thought was the position of their religion on contraception. The first question was, 'Does your religion permit contraception?', and the responses to it are shown in Table 7.6.

Over half the sample said that they thought that their religion permitted contraception: 100 per cent of the Christians, 81 per cent of the Hindus, but only 1 per cent of the Muslims. However, there was considerable variation in Muslim women's presentation of what they regarded as the Islamic ban on contraception. Shamsheda, aged 33 years, and a Muslim mother of four children, said, 'Whatever God gives is his will.' But another Muslim woman from Ramanagaram, Hussain Bi, aged 63 years, mother of seven children, said, 'God's will is fine, but how do we

TABLE 7.6: RELIGION AND CONTRACEPTION RAMANAGARAM SAMPLE (1996)

Response	All women		Hindus		Muslims		Christians	
	No.	%	No.	%	No.	%	No.	%
Yes	106	52.7	90	81.0	1	1.3	15	100.0
No	78	38.8	4	3.6	74	98.6	0	0.0
Don't know	17	8.5	17	15.3	0	0.0	0	0.0
Total	201	100.0	111	100.0	75	100.0	15	100.0

Note: Persons were asked if their religion permitted contraception.

support the (larger) family?' A leading Muslim social worker explained the position of Islam on contraception to me as follows: 'Everyone is having an operation. The Koran says that we can take pills when the stomach [womb] is empty, but when there is a birth [conception], we can't take the tablets. We need to reconsider this.'

The women were then asked what their personal views were concerning the position of their religion on birth control. This second question was a very sensitive one and many women were reluctant to answer this openly. The women were for the most part happy to answer questions on this issue in general terms, but more hesitant when questioned on specific, individual preferences. This must be understood in the context of Ramanagaram society. In a small community such as Ramanagaram taluk, where the priests and mullahs wielded considerable power both in terms of their religious position and their high social standing, it was not very easy for the women to divulge openly (to what must be perceived as an urban stranger alien to their context) their true feelings on an issue as sensitive as religion and family limitation. Thus, there is perhaps a case to be made here that revealed preferences and stated preferences were different. Nevertheless, keeping this caveat in mind, it is possible to analyse the women's responses, which are shown in Table 7.7.

Perhaps the sensitive nature of this question is reflected in the large proportion (37 per cent) who said that they had 'no view'. Among the Hindus in the sample, although 36 per cent agreed with the position of their religion, there were 45 per cent who said that they held no view. For example, Gauramma, a Hindu woman aged 26 years from village C, remarked, 'Our religion does not say anything, hence I have not hesitated to have an operation.' The number of Hindus who said that they had 'no view' is much higher (45 per cent) than among the Christians (7 per

TABLE 7.7: VIEW REGARDING POSITION OF RELIGION ON BIRTH CONTROL, RAMANAGARAM SAMPLE (1996)

Response	All women		Hindus		Muslims		Christians	
	No.	%	No.	%	No.	%	No.	%
Agree	74	36.8	40	36.0	22	29.3	12	80.0
Disagree	29	14.4	4	3.6	24	32.0	1	6.6
Don't know	20	9.9	14	12.6	5	6.6	1	6.6
Did not answer	4	1.9	3	2.7	1	1.3	0	0.0
No view	74	36.8	50	45.0	23	30.7	1	6.6
Total	201	100.0	111	100.0	75	100.0	15	100.0

cent) and Muslims (31 per cent) probably because, as we saw in Chapter 3, Hinduism does not say very much scripturally about birth control.

The other interesting difference across religious groups is in the percentage disagreeing with the position of their religion on contraception. This was only 14 per cent for the whole sample, but a shocking 32 per cent for Muslims, compared to 7 per cent for Christians and 4 per cent for Hindus. This finding is interesting, because, as we have seen earlier, although there is debate about whether or not theologically Islam permits contraception, the perception among Muslim women in Ramanagaram is unambiguously that it does *not* permit birth control. Muslim women who did limit their fertility implicitly contrasted the position of priest and theological writings, as in the case of Shahzamma, aged 35 years, from Ramanagaram town, who remarked, 'I am educated, therefore I have a small family. We do not need to consult the priest because everything is written in the Shariat.' A Hindu woman, Saraswati, aged 38 years, from Ramanagaram town remarked, 'The Muslim religion does not allow contraception, unlike us Hindus.' These findings suggest that insofar as religion does influence contraceptive choice, it is through local community influences, and the manner in which theological beliefs are interpreted to women, rather than through the actual theological content of the religion worldwide.

In Karnataka, as indeed in many other Indian states, all forms of family planning services are provided through government hospitals and urban family welfare centres in urban areas and through PHC and subcentres in rural areas. Family planning services are also available from private hospitals, private clinics, and non-governmental organizations. Sterilization operations and IUD insertions are conducted mostly in government hospitals, PHCs, and in sterilization camps which are organized periodically by the government hospitals. Modern methods of contraception are available through both government and private sources; government health outlets supply 83 per cent of users. Sterilization operations are performed almost exclusively at government facilities which conducts 95 per cent of male sterilizations and 87 per cent of female sterilizations (IIPS, 1995: 111–26).

The Ramanagaram questionnaire asked several questions in order to find out whether women felt there was an 'unmet need' for family planning. First, women were asked how frequently they visited their local family planning health centre or hospital. Their responses are reported in Table 7.8. Of the entire sample, 37 per cent said that they never went to the local hospital. This is in contrast to the doctors' views that women with IUD ought to visit their doctors fortnightly, while those using other contraceptive methods ought to visit them weekly. Mothers were also

TABLE 7.8: FREQUENCY OF VISITS TO FAMILY PLANNING CENTRE/LOCAL HOSPITAL BY
EVER-MARRIED WOMEN, RAMANAGARAM SAMPLE (1996)

Frequency of visits	All women		Hindus		Muslims		Christians	
	No.	%	No.	%	No.	%	No.	%
Do not go at all	69	36.8	37	35.9	29	41.4	3	21.4
Nurse comes to house	50	26.7	32	31.1	13	18.6	5	35.7
Go when ill	24	12.8	12	11.6	10	14.3	2	14.2
Often	20	10.7	4	3.8	12	17.1	4	28.6
Not often	15	8.0	12	11.7	3	4.3	0	0.0
Rare	4	2.1	4	3.8	0	0.0	0	0.0
Sometimes	4	2.1	4	3.8	0	0.0	0	0.0
Only in old age	2	1.1	0	0.0	2	2.9	0	0.0
Daily	1	0.5	0	0.0	1	1.4	0	0.0
Total	187	100.0	103	100.0	70	100.0	14	100.0

asked to bring in their children on thursdays for check-ups and vacci-
nations (Oral communication provided by doctors from Ramanagaram
town). It has been suggested in other studies that doorstep delivery is
an important way to reduce fertility because it reduces the costs of contraception (Arends Kuenning, 1997: 1). The 27 per cent of women who
responded that they depended on the nurse who came round once a
fortnight to provide family planning services suggests that the system
of doorstep delivery of contraceptives is effective in Ramanagaram. This
was more prevalent among the Hindus (31 per cent) and Christians
(36 per cent) than among the Muslims (19 per cent). One Hindu
woman, Sowbhagyamma, aged 20 years, from Ramanagaram town remarked, 'It is easy for us to get contraception as the nurse comes once
in two weeks to give us pills.' Compared with Hindus and Christians, a
higher percentage of Muslim women (41 per cent) said that they did not
go to the health centre at all. The most important result of these findings
is that irrespective of religion, health care and contraceptive services are
available in Ramanagaram, either through the hospital or through the
nurses who regularly visited both town and villages.

Women were also asked how easy it was for them to obtain at least
one method of contraception. Their responses are shown in Table 7.9.
These responses indicate that contraceptive services were easily available
in Ramanagaram *taluk* and that the nurses who visited their localities
once a fortnight were an important aspect of this access.[16] The 'not

[16]Doctors interviewed in Ramanagaram taluk said that Copper-Ts were in 'short supply'.

TABLE 7.9: EASE OF OBTAINING CONTRACEPTION, RAMANAGARAM SAMPLE (1996)

Response	All women		Hindus		Muslims		Christians	
	No.	%	No.	%	No.	%	No.	%
Easy	71	37.9	42	40.7	20	28.6	9	64.3
Nurse provides	18	9.6	13	12.6	5	7.1	0	0.0
Not easy	5	2.7	4	3.8	0	0.0	1	7.1
Cannot get	2	1.1	0	0.0	2	2.9	0	0.0
Not applicable*	91	48.7	44	42.7	43	61.4	4	28.5
Total	187	100.0	103	100.0	70	100.0	14	100.0

Note: *This stands for those who said that they did not currently use contraceptive services
    and thus had no need to obtain them from any particular source.

applicable' category, is twice the size, in terms of percentages, for Muslim women as it is for Christian women. This suggests that contraception was used much less by the Muslim women than by women of other religions, at least before controlling for the influence of other factors, but that this was *not* because it was difficult to obtain.

In conclusion, these findings show that just over half the sample had used a method of contraception, the most popular of which for all religions was the sterilization (tubal ligation) operation. The decision to use contraception was influenced by husbands and by other female family members and friends, but many women took the decision alone. Religion appeared to play a part in influencing family planning but women were hesitant to reveal their views about this openly. A greater proportion of Muslim women than of Hindus or Christians disagreed with what they perceived to be the position of their religion on contraception. Finally, contraceptive services are perceived as being widely available, though Muslim women used the doorstep delivery of contraceptives less than others. Together, these findings suggest strongly that the main motivation associated with contraceptive use was its *acceptability* rather than its availability.

FERTILITY PREFERENCES, IDEAL FAMILY SIZE, AND UNWANTED FERTILITY

Interpretation of data on fertility preferences is a matter of debate because at the time of interview women's attitudes towards fertility may not be fully formed. These views may change over time and others may have influenced women's preferences, or at least their expression of them. Women's stated preferences and their revealed preferences may, therefore,

TABLE 7.10: PREFERENCES FOR CHILDREN, RAMANAGARAM SAMPLE (1996)

Boy or girl	All women		Hindus		Muslims		Christians	
	No.	%	No.	%	No.	%	No.	%
Boy	34	54.8	23	63.9	10	43.5	1	33.3
Girl	14	22.6	8	22.2	6	26.1	0	0.0
One of each	2	3.2	1	2.8	0	0.0	1	33.3
Both	4	6.5	1	2.8	3	13.0	0	0.0
Either	8	12.9	3	8.3	4	17.4	1	33.3
Total	62	100.0	36	100.0	23	100.0	3	100.0

diverge. It can nevertheless be useful to explore what women state their fertility preferences to be.

The currently married women in the Ramanagaram sample were asked, first, if they wanted another child. In the entire sample, 33 per cent of married women answered yes. The responses were almost identical between Hindus (at 35 per cent) and Muslims (at 33 per cent), although lower among Christians (at 21 per cent).[17]

The women who did want another child were then asked if they preferred a boy or a girl. Their responses are reported in Table 7.10. By far, most women wanted a boy, at more than half of the whole sample. Preference for boys was highest among the Hindus, and lowest among the Christians. This strong preference for sons is similar to other studies of fertility preferences for Karnataka which show 44 per cent of mothers wanting boys and only 16 per cent wanting girls (See IIPS, 1995: 111–26).

The women gave a variety of reasons for their preferences, which are shown in Table 7.11. For the sample as a whole, the most popular reasons for desiring an additional child were for insurance purposes (32 per cent), in order to have a child of the opposite sex to existing children (24 per cent), and to provide help to the mother (10 per cent). There was little difference in response by religion. Jayalakshmi, a 27 year-old Hindu woman from village A, who was a mother of one son and who wanted her next child to be a daughter, said rather poetically that she wanted two children, 'One for love and one for property—a girl for *aasé* (love) and a boy for *aasti* (to bequeath property) is perfect for us.' Lakshmi, a Hindu woman, aged 20 years, who was single, said that she wanted two

[17]These responses are similar to the 30 per cent of women in Karnataka who said that they wanted another child, reported in the *National Family Health Survey 1992–93: Karnataka*, 1995: 111.

TABLE 7.11: REASONS FOR DESIRING ANOTHER BOY OR GIRL, RAMANAGARAM
SAMPLE (1996)

Reason	All women		Hindus		Muslims		Christians	
	No.	%	No.	%	No.	%	No.	%
1 enough	1	1.6	1	2.7	0	0.0	0	0.0
1 more nice	1	1.6	1	2.7	0	0.0	0	0.0
3 nice	1	1.6	1	2.7	0	0.0	0	0.0
1 boring	1	1.6	1	2.7	0	0.0	0	0.0
Both nice	4	6.5	1	2.7	2	8.7	1	33.3
For husband	1	1.6	0	0.0	1	4.3	0	0.0
Girls expensive	2	3.2	1	0.0	1	4.3	0	0.0
God's will	5	8.1	0	0.0	5	21.7	0	0.0
In-law pressure	2	3.2	1	2.7	1	4.3	0	0.0
Insurance	20	32.3	13	36.1	6	26.1	1	33.3
Like girls	1	1.6	0	0.0	1	4.3	0	0.0
Help mother	6	9.7	5	13.8	1	4.3	0	0.0
Nice	1	1.6	1	2.7	0	0.0	0	0.0
No kids	1	1.6	1	2.7	0	0.0	0	0.0
Opposite sex	15	24.2	9	25.0	5	21.7	1	33.3
Total	62	100.0	36	100.0	23	100.0	3	100.0

children, 'a girl for the *aarti* (lighting the oil lamp for prayer in the home) and a boy for *keerti* (family prestige)'.

Pursuing the theme of gender preference, the entire sample of Ramanagaram women were asked if the birth of a boy was better news, worse news, or similar news to the birth of a girl (see Table 7.12). Although 43 per cent of the sample believed that the birth of a boy was better news, 48 per cent said that they were indifferent. The highest son-preference was expressed by the Muslims (at 51 per cent), but it was nearly as high among the Hindus (at 42 per cent); only the Christians expressed low son-preference (at 13 per cent). One woman, Jayantibai, aged 24 years, from Ramanagaram town, who was the wife of a silk unit owner, remarked, 'My first-born was a son, so I did not feel bad. So, I am indifferent between the birth of a girl or a boy from now onwards.' But even among the son-preferring Muslims there were divergent views, such as that of Najmunissa, aged 60 years, from Ramanagaram town, who said, 'I always wanted a girl. I had six sons instead. I always wanted

TABLE 7.12: PREFERENCES BETWEEN BOYS AND GIRLS,
RAMANAGARAM SAMPLE (1996)

Category	All women		Hindus		Muslims		Christians	
	No.	%	No.	%	No.	%	No.	%
Boy better	87	43.2	47	42.3	38	50.6	2	13.3
Indifferent	96	47.8	53	47.7	30	40.0	13	86.6
Boy worse	7	3.5	3	2.7	4	5.3	0	0.0
Did not answer	11	5.5	8	7.2	3	4.0	0	0.0

fewer boys and at least one girl, because for the mother, girls are so much closer.'

These answers seem to contradict those given to the questions on preferences for a boy versus a girl as the next child, discussed in Table 7.10. It appears that when women are asked in abstract terms if the birth of a boy is better than that of a girl, as in Table 7.12, they are reluctant to express son-preference and opt to say that they are indifferent, whereas when women who were currently married and desired another child were questioned specifically if they desired their next child to be a boy or a girl, a majority preferred sons to daughters. One reason for these contradictory findings may be that media campaigns which encouraged families not to discriminate against the girl-child made women reluctant to divulge their true feelings, preferring instead to claim 'indifference'. This is again an example of stated preferences diverging from revealed preferences. Perhaps what is most significant, however, is the very small proportion of the sample—of whatever religion—who said that the birth of a girl was better news.

On comparing Table 7.10 with Table 7.12, son-preference for the next child seems far stronger for Hindus than for Muslims (as shown in Table 7.10), but son-preference in general seems stronger for the Muslims (as shown in Table 7.12). However, it is important to be aware that while Table 7.12 depicts responses for all 201 women, Table 7.10 shows only the responses of the 62 women who wanted another child. The empirical impact of son-preference cannot be explored in an econometric model of contraceptive choice because it is endogenous to the decision to use a contraceptive method. However, it can be, and indeed is, explored in the models of fertility presented in Chapter 8. The greater degree of son-preference among Hindus may also account for the higher levels of infant mortality and under-5 mortality found among Hindus than among Muslims in all of India. Although we do not go into the relationship between religion, infant mortality, and son-preference more deeply here, this is an important area for future research.

The women were also asked if their husbands wanted another child. This may seem odd at first sight, given the reported infrequency of couple communication on fertility planning. However, this question is important as an indication of the influence of husbands over wives' fertility decisions. The responses are shown in Table 7.13.

In the sample as a whole, some two-thirds of women said that their husbands did not want another child, with fairly similar percentages among the Hindus and Muslims but substantially higher percentages among the Christians. The other striking finding was the 12 per cent of Muslim wives who reported that their husbands specifically wanted another boy, as compared to very small percentages giving this answer in the other two religious groups.

In order to assess the extent of use of birth control strategies in the sample population, all ever-married women were asked if the birth of their children had been planned or not. For the sample as a whole, a majority (71 per cent) reported that the birth of their children had been unplanned. There was considerable variation by religion, with this answer being given by 80 per cent of Muslims, and 70 per cent of Hindus, but only 21 per cent of Christians.[18]

'Unwanted' births are those births which occur after a woman has attained her desired family size and one study has estimated them as 22

TABLE 7.13: ISSUE OF ANOTHER CHILD,
RAMANAGARAM SAMPLE (1996)

Response[1]	All women		Hindus		Muslims		Christians	
	No.	%	No.	%	No.	%	No.	%
No	105	66.9	59	68.6	36	62.1	10	76.9
Yes	37	23.6	20	23.3	14	24.1	3	23.1
Yes, boy	11	7.0	4	4.7	7	12.1	0	0.0
Yes, girl	4	2.5	3	3.5	1	1.7	0	0.0
Total	157[2]	100.0	86	100.0	58	100.0	13	100.0

Notes: [1]Women were asked if their husbands wanted another child.
   [2]Thirty married women did not answer this question because they said that they did not know their husband's views. The non-answers varied by religion, given by 17 Hindus, 12 Muslims, and 1 Christian woman.

[18]However, it must be borne in mind that the sample size of ever-married Christians is small relative to those of ever-married Hindus and Muslims.

TABLE 7.14: IDEAL NUMBER OF CHILDREN DESIRED
RAMANAGARAM SAMPLE (1996)

Category	All women		Hindus		Muslims		Christians	
	No.	%	No.	%	No.	%	No.	%
Yes	145	77.5	80	75.5	52	74.3	13	92.8
No	40	21.3	22	20.7	17	24.2	1	7.1
Don't know	2	1.1	1	1.0	1	1.4	0	0.0

Note: Evern-married women were a asked if they have an ideal number of children they desire.

per cent of observed fertility in a sample of twenty developing countries in 1990 (Bongaarts, 1997a). 'Unwanted' fertility is calculated using ideal family size. The Ramanagaram women were asked two sets of questions to ascertain their ideal family size. The first was, 'Do you have a desired or ideal number of children? If so, what is it?' Their answers are reported in Table 7.14. Almost identical proportions of Hindu and Muslim women (at about 75 per cent) said that they did have an ideal number of children but the percentage was much higher among Christian women (at 93 per cent). Women were often amused by this question, as in the case of one Muslim woman from Ramanagaram, Sofia, aged 40 years, a mother of five children, who remarked, 'What is the point of asking me about what I would have desired? If I had that much sense, I would have cut off my childbearing at two!'

The precise numbers of children that the women said they desired are shown in Table 7.15. The difference in the means between Hindus and Muslims, Muslims and Christians, and Hindus and Christians was not statistically significant at the 95 per cent confidence level. This is

TABLE 7.15: IDEAL NUMBER OF CHILDREN, RAMANAGARAM SAMPLE (1996)

Ideal number of children	All women		Hindus		Muslims		Christians	
	No.	%	No.	%	No.	%	No.	%
Mean	2.51		2.48		2.65		2.21	
1	10	4.9	7	6.3	1	1.3	2	13.3
2	72	35.8	38	34.2	24	32.0	10	66.6
3	44	21.8	26	23.4	16	21.3	2	13.3
4	16	7.9	8	7.2	8	10.6	0	0.0
5	3	1.5	1	0.9	1	1.3	1	6.6
Don't know	55	27.4	31	27.9	24	32.0	0	0.0
God gives	1	0.5	0	0.0	1	1.3	0	0.0

TABLE 7.16: Unwanted fertility, Ramanagaram sample (1996)

Unwanted births	All women	Hindus	Muslims	Christians
Mean	0.85	0.55	1.44	0.07
Median	0	0	1	0
Mode	0	0	0	0
Maximum	7	7	7	4
Minimum	−4	−4	−3	−2

interesting because if the Hindu and Muslim women, who show higher fertility than the Christians (as we will see in Chapter 8), also desire similar numbers of children to the Christians, then it is essential to investigate those factors which are preventing Hindu and Muslim women from achieving their desired family size.

'Unwanted fertility' is measured either as the 'unwanted' component of the total fertility rate expressed in births per woman (Bongaarts, 1997a) or as the number of living children less the ideal number of children stated by the respondent. The latter measure of unwanted fertility can be calculated for the Ramanagaram sample, as shown in Table 7.16. The mean for the entire Ramanagaram sample closely resembles the 0.8 found for rural women in Karnataka by the NFHS (IIPS, 1995: 125–6). The mean for Muslim women is strikingly high compared to that for Hindus and Christians. This difference in the mean level of unwanted fertility between Hindus and Muslims and between Muslims and Christians is statistically significant at the 95 per cent level, which suggests that Muslims in Ramanagaram are perhaps still more uneasy about contraceptive practice than Hindu and Christian women, despite the disagreement of some Muslim women with the perceived religious requirements of Islam on contraception. By this measure, there is substantial 'unwanted' fertility in the Ramanagaram sample. However, since this measure does depend crucially on women's stated 'ideal' number of children, and there may be a discrepancy between stated and revealed preferences, this finding should be interpreted with caution, especially in the light of the evidence of easy access to contraception provided by women's answers to the other survey questions.

In order to approach the same question in a different way, the Ramanagaram women were asked if they would have wanted fewer children than they currently had. Their responses are reported in Table 7.17. In the entire sample, just over three-quarters of women said that they did not want fewer children, but answers varied significantly by religion,

TABLE 7.17: DESIRE FOR FEWER CHILDREN
RAMANAGARAM SAMPLE (1996)

Responses	All women		Hindus		Muslims		Christians	
	No.	%	No.	%	No.	%	No.	%
Yes	34	18.2	8	7.8	24	34.3	2	14.3
Yes, wanted daughters	1	0.5	1	1.0	0	0.0	0	0.0
Yes, wanted two children	1	0.5	1	1.0	0	0.0	0	0.0
Yes, wanted fewer boys	1	0.5	0	0.0	1	1.4	0	0.0
Yes, wanted fewer girls	1	0.5	1	1.0	0	0.0	0	0.0
Yes (total)	38	20.3	11	10.7	25	35.7	2	14.3
No	142	75.9	88	85.4	42	60.0	12	85.7
No, want more girls	1	0.5	0	0.0	1	1.4	0	0.0
No (total)	143	76.5	88	85.4	43	61.4	12	85.7
Don't know	6	3.2	4	3.9	2	2.9	0	0.0
Total	187	100.0	103	100.0	70	100.0	14	100.0

Note: Even-married women were asked if they wanted fewer children.

with about 85 per cent of Hindus and Christians giving this answer, but only 61 per cent of Muslim women. Most women of all religions apparently did not want fewer children than they had already. This finding is in striking contradiction to the estimates of unwanted births just discussed. When directly questioned, women were very loyal to existing children and did not want to suggest that any of them were actually 'unwanted'. However, when asked in abstract terms about their ideal family size, women gave answers implying unwanted births averaging almost one child per woman. These findings highlight that women's stated preferences and their revealed preferences can diverge considerably, and point to the fact that estimates of unwanted fertility depend crucially on the manner in which questions about these issues are asked.

The fertility preferences of Ramanagaram women were further explored by asking women why they did or did not want fewer children. Some women wanted fewer children but felt constrained by the demands of their families, as in the case of Nagamma, aged 36 years, the mother of four young daughters, from village D, who remarked, ' I have four daughters. I am trying for a son because my parents-in-law are pressuring me. Our religion says we need a son to look after us. But, I would definitely have liked fewer daughters. I do not send the girls to school now because my parents-in-law disapprove. Even though I know differently, I must listen to them. But I will definitely send my girls to school after they (in-laws) die.' The diverse range of reasons which women gave in response to this query is presented in Table 7.18.

For the sample as a whole, the most popular reason for desiring fewer children was that children were expensive to raise. The next most popular reason was the desire for fewer girls. The main reasons for not desiring fewer children were that two children was just right and that the current

TABLE 7.18: REASONS FOR WANTING/NOT WANTING FEWER CHILDREN,
RAMANAGARAM SAMPLE (1996)

Reasons	All women (No.)	Hindus (No.)	Muslims (No.)	Christians (No.)
Reasons for not wanting fewer children				
1 each nice	3	0	0	3
1 enough	1	1	0	2
1 lives here	1	1	0	0
1 nice	3	3	0	0
2 enough	7	2	5	0
2 nice	18	12	3	3
2 right	1	0	1	0
3 enough	5	3	2	0
3 nice	9	4	4	1
4 nice	1	1	0	0
God's will	5	0	5	0
God's will and insurance	1	0	1	0
Happened	2	2	0	0
Income	1	1	0	0
Insurance and help mother	1	1	0	0
Insurance	17	12	5	0
Like all	2	0	2	0
Many will help with work	1	0	1	0
Love all	1	1	0	0
Large family is nice	1	1	0	0
Help mother	2	1	1	0

(contd...)

Reasons	All women (No.)	Hindus (No.)	Muslims (No.)	Christians (No.)
Nice	1	1	0	0
Currently have only 1 child	2	2	0	0
Currently have only 2 children	1	0	1	0
Planned	16	9	6	1
Wanted 3	1	0	1	0
Will do work	1	1	0	0
Reasons for wanting fewer children				
8 excessive	1	0	1	0
All are boys	1	0	1	0
Expensive	21	6	15	0
Girls expensive	2	0	2	0
Wanted less girls	5	1	4	0
Opposite sex	4	2	2	0
Pressure from parents-in-law	1	1	0	0
Don't know	2	1	0	1
Total	187	103	70	14

number of children would serve as a means of insurance in old age. God's will was another reason, cited by 7 per cent of Muslim women.

To summarize, it appears that the Ramanagaram women did have opinions on desired fertility, which were similar across religions, and that this figure was lower than actual family size. However, when specifically questioned if they would have wanted fewer children themselves, most women answered 'no'. In my view, this apparent contradiction was related to the *ex ante* general and *ex post* specific nature of the questions asked. When asked in general terms if they had an ideal or desired family size, the women were willing to express their opinions freely. Yet they also recognized that they could not have had less children because of certain constraints. The women, therefore, attempted to justify the existence of already born children with very similar reasons to those put forward in response to an earlier question about whether boys were to be preferred to girls (for example: insurance *vis-à-vis* expense). It appears that the Ramanagaram women recognized the need for children, specifically in order to contribute to the household's activities or insurance in old age but also realized that additional children (particularly daughters) would be expensive to rear. Shivalingamma, a Hindu woman, aged 32 years, from village C, gave explicit statement to the different cost-benefit calculations involved: 'If the family is large, everyone can pitch in to collect water, firewood etc., but it also costs more to support a large family. So, I do not know which is better. Perhaps we need to balance the two.' Thus, though the Ramanagaram women reported an ideal family size which was smaller than the actuality, they were also able to justify their actual large families on various counts. However, the contradictory nature of the same women's replies to different questions casts worrying light on the nature of the evidence on which most estimates of 'ideal' or 'unwanted' fertility appear to be based in the contraceptive choice literature. Depending on how the question is posed, the same woman will give different answers, depending on whether she is focusing primarily on costs or on benefits, whether she is asked for a general normative statement or a concrete positive one, whether she feels she is likely to be approved of by the questioner for certain answers, and many other unmeasurable factors.

A LOGIT MODEL OF CONTRACEPTIVE USE

To identify determinants of contraceptive use in Ramanagaram, a LOGIT model of contraceptive choice was estimated. A LOGIT model was used because the dependent variable, namely, *ever-use of contraception by the woman*, was dichotomous. If a woman had ever used any method of contraception, she was assigned a value of 1; if she had never used a contraceptive method, she was assigned the value 0.

For the reasons discussed in the first section of this chapter, the explanatory variables used were the education of the woman, her husband's education, various measures of the household's income, various measures of the woman's occupation, various measures of her husband's occupation, various measures of marital consanguinity, the woman's current age, the woman's perception of access to government contraceptive services the number of female extended family members, and various measures of religion.

The preliminary LOGIT models estimated (but not reported here) used backward elimination based on the value of the likelihood ratio. The procedure involved two stages. First, 11 models which did not include interaction terms between the religion dummies and the other regressors were estimated, with the purpose of arriving at the best specification of certain regressors for which alternative measures were available. The 'best' specification of the model was selected on the basis of goodness of fit and specification tests for heteroscedasticity, model specification, and collinearity. Then, at the second stage, the best of these models was selected, and each independent regressor was interacted with the two religion dummies.

Of all the preliminary regression models estimated, the model which emerged as the best specification showed that the woman's education, husband's education, the perception of access to government services, the number of female extended family members resident, the woman's age, whether the woman was Muslim, and whether the woman was Hindu were the most significant determinants of the probability of contraceptive use.

According to this model, a greater degree of education for the woman and for her husband both increase the probability of contraceptive use. The model also predicts that if a woman is older, she is less likely to use contraception. If there is one more female family member resident, the woman is less likely to use contraception. If the woman perceived that contraceptive access provided by government services was easy, she was more likely to use contraception. Finally, the model predicts that if a woman is either Muslim or Hindu, she is less likely to use contraception than if she is Christian, although a Wald test established that this effect is not significantly different between the two groups.

Having established that Hindus and Muslims do not have significantly different intercepts, it is also important to examine whether religion affects the *slope* of the regression, that is, whether the socio-economic factors which affect contraceptive use act differently for the three religious groups. In order to investigate this, interactive terms between the other explanatory variables and the Hindu and Muslim dummies were introduced into the model. At every stage of the regression procedure, a restriction was imposed which hypothesized that the coefficients on a particular regressor and all its interaction terms were equal to zero. This hypothesis was tested by using a likelihood ratio test and the model was re-estimated on the basis of the outcome of this test.[19] The final model estimated using this procedure is reported in Table 7.19.

The first variable which emerged as significant is the number of years of education for the woman, which had a significant and positive impact on contraceptive use for all three religions in Ramanagaram.

---

[19]The likelihood ratio (LR) test was of the form: LR = $2[L(H_1) - L(H_0)] \sim \bar{\Lambda}^2$ (r) where $L(H_1)$ is the maximized value of the log likelihood function under the unrestricted model; $L(H_0)$ is the maximized value of the log likelihood function under the restricted model; and r is the number of restrictions.

TABLE 7.19: LOGIT MAXIMUM LIKELIHOOD ESTIMATION OF THE DETERMINANTS OF CONTRACEPTIVE USE, ALL RELIGIONS, RAMANAGARAM SAMPLE, (1996)

Regressor	Coefficient	T Ratio [Prob.]	Marginal effect
Constant (CONST)	−2.8762	−2.2666 [0.025][a]	–
Woman's education			
Number of years of education (EDCN)	0.5697	2.6584 [0.009][c]	0.1367
Number of years of education for Muslims (MEDCN)	−0.5281	−2.3006[0.023][b]	0.0099
Number of years of education for Hindus (HEDCN)	−0.4500	−2.0259[0.044][b]	0.0287
Husband's education			
Husband's years of education (EDCNSP)	0.3460	1.2408[0.216]	0.0829
Muslim husband's years of education (MEDCNSP)	−0.0986	−0.3572[0.721]	0.0594
Hindu husband's years of education (HEDCNSP)	−0.2358	−0.8465[0.398]	0.0264
Ease of access to government services			
Ease of access (EASYCON)	0.0102	0.0038[0.997]	NR[3]
Ease of access for Muslims (MEASY)	4.0397	1.3233[0.187]	NR[3]
Ease of access for Hindus (HEASY)	2.8578	1.0536[0.294]	NR[3]
Female extended family			
Female extended family resident (FEXFAM)	−0.4435	−2.2640[0.025][b]	−0.1064
Muslim female extended family resident (MFEXFAM)	0.2428	0.7461[0.457]	−0.0481
Hindu female extended family resident (HFEXFAM)	–	–	–
Woman's age			
Woman's age (AGE)	−0.0085	−0.3751[0.708]	−0.0021
Muslim woman's age (MAGE)	−0.0679	−1.8768[0.062][a]	−0.0183
Hindu woman's age (HAGE)	–	–	–

Notes: [1]Dependent variable is CTPRUSE : 1=woman had ever-used a contraceptive method; 0=woman had never used a contraceptive method. Sample consists of: 187 ever-married Hindu, Muslim, and Christian women. Base category is Christians.
[2]Marginal effect = coefficient*scale factor. This is evaluated at the sample mean of the regressor.
[3]NR is not reported because the explanatory variable is a dummy variable.
Two Hindu interaction terms (HWOMAN and HFEXFAM) were excluded from the model because of their perfect correlation with other regressors. As the model could not be estimated by retaining them, it was necessary to exclude them.
[a]indicates significant ignificant at the 0.10 level, [b]indicates significant at 0.05 level and [c]indicates significant at the 0.01 level.

MODEL STATISTICS

Scale factor for the calculation of marginal effects	0.23990
Maximised value of the log likelihood function	−90.8589
Mean of CTPRUSE	0.54011
Mean of fitted CTPRUSE	0.49733
Goodness of fit	0.75401
Pesaran-Timmermann test statistic	−2.8630 [0.004]
Pseudo R-Squared	0.29576

Calculated at the sample means, a one-year increase in total education increases the probability of contraceptive use by 0.01 for Muslims, by 0.14 for Christians, and by 0.03 for Hindus.[20] However, a Wald test showed that the effect of total education on the probability of contraceptive use did not differ significantly between Hindus and Muslims. Analogous tests, however, established that the effect of women's education on contraceptive use did differ significantly between Christians and Hindus, and between Christians and Muslims, with a much larger marginal impact of education on contraceptive choice for the Christians than for women of the other two religions. One possible explanation for why education is much more important for Christians than for Hindus or Muslims may be that education has increasing returns in contraceptive use and Christian

[20]It may be recollected that when reporting the value of the LOGIT coefficient for Muslim and Hindu interaction terms, this is equal to the stated coefficient for a particular attribute plus the value of the coefficient on the base category of that attribute. Thus, the coefficient for total education for Muslims is equal to the coefficient on MEDCN plus that on EDCN; the coefficient for Hindus is equal to that on HEDCN plus EDCN and so forth. It is this value of the coefficient which is multiplied by the scale factor to get the value of the marginal effect for interaction terms.

women have more education, on average, than Hindu or Muslim women.

The set of variables that measured the total education of the husband had to be retained in the model as a group, on the basis of the likelihood ratio test. A Wald test showed that husband's education did affect contraceptive use for Hindus and for Muslims, although not for Christians. Calculated at the sample means, a one-year increase in husband's total education increases the probability of contraceptive use by 0.06 for Muslims and by 0.03 for Hindus. A Wald test also showed, however, that husband's education does not have a different effect on contraceptive use for Muslims than for Hindus, nor between Christians and Hindus, or between Christians and Muslims.

The presence of female extended family members resident in the household significantly decreased the probability of using contraception among Hindu and Christian women, but had no effect for Muslims. For Hindu and Christian women, calculated at the sample mean, one additional female family member reduced the probability of contraceptive use by 0.11. However, this difference between Hindus, Christians, and Muslims was not statistically significant.

The dummy variable that measured women's qualitative perceptions about access to government services did not emerge as significant for any of the three religious groups. This is consistent with the qualitative finding that family planning services are widely available in Ramanagaram, as in the state of Karnataka in general.

Finally, a woman's age was found to affect contraceptive use. Calculated at the sample means of all other variables, if a woman was Muslim, her being one year older decreased the probability of her using contraception by 0.02. The fact that younger Muslim women are more likely to use contraception may be testimony to the influence of the family planning programme in changing norms in Ramanagaram. A Wald test showed that the effect of a woman's age on contraceptive choice did not differ significantly among religious groups.

Finally, it must be noted that the religion dummies for Hindus and for Muslims were deleted from the model on the basis of a likelihood ratio test. This finding is very interesting from the point of view of the present study because it is in contrast with the preliminary model in which the Muslim and Hindu religion dummies were significant. In the preliminary model, the Muslim and Hindu dummies had a negative effect on contraceptive use, although the effect did not differ significantly between Hindus and Muslims. The findings from the interaction model suggest that although the Hindu and Muslim religion have an effect on contraceptive use in Ramanagaram, it is expressed primarily through differences in how socio-economic 'characteristics' of the individual members of different religions affect their contraceptive use. Moreover, as we saw in Chapter 3, there is debate about the influence of Islamic prescriptions on the acceptibility of using contraception by Muslim women and some ambiguity about the influence of Hinduism on contraception. However, in this model, Hinduism is not having an effect on contraceptive use which is significantly different from the effect of Islam. The findings from the econometric models suggest that rather than theological doctrines, it may be the manner in which religion is being *interpreted* to women by the community which is influencing their contraceptive use, via the decisions they make about other aspects of their lives, such as their education. This finding is also consistent with the qualitative evidence presented earlier in this chapter which suggested that community interpretations of religion may be more important than religious observance in explaining contraceptive use.

The LOGIT coefficients and analysis of the marginal effects suggest that similar combinations of factors account for patterns of contraceptive use among the three religious groups. Among Hindus, the factors positively affecting the probability of using contraception are the education of the woman, her husband's education, and perception of access to government services, while the factors affecting it negatively are the number of female family members resident. The woman's age is unimportant. For Muslims, the factors positively affecting the probability of using contraception are women's education, husband's education, and perception of access to government services, while the factor negatively affecting the decision to use contraception is the woman's age. The presence of female resident family members has no significant influence. Finally, for Christians, the factor affecting the probability of contraceptive use positively is the woman's education, while the factor affecting contraceptive use negatively is the number of female extended family members resident in the household. Those factors which had no impact were husband's education, the woman's age, and the perception of access to government services.

If we consider comparisons across pairs of religions, the estimated regression lines for Hindus compared with Christians, and for Muslims compared with Christians, differ in terms of intercept and in terms of slope mainly because of differences in the effect of women's education. Hindus and Muslims did not differ in terms either of intercept or of slope, indicating that the factors which affect decisions about contraception in Ramanagaram do not vary significantly between Hindus and Muslims.

CONCLUSIONS AND IMPLICATIONS FOR POLICY

The extent of contraceptive adoption has concerned demographers and family planning policy in developing countries since the mid-1950s. This chapter has sought to examine the determinants of contraceptive use based on data from India. The analysis began by examining the theoretical determinants of contraceptive use more widely. The next step involved examining the findings concerning contraceptive use and practice in the Ramanagaram sample, women's fertility preferences, and 'unwanted' fertility. The main conclusions derived from this part of the analysis was that just over half of the sample had ever used a method of contraception, and that of the women who had used contraception, almost two-thirds had opted for the tubal ligation method. Inter-spousal communication about family planning was low, but women did discuss these issues with other female extended family members and friends. As nurses regularly visited the localities studied, access to at least one method of contraception was reported to be comparatively easy. Finally, when questioned about the impact of religion on contraception, though some women were hesitant to reveal their views, Muslim women thought that their religion did disapprove of contraception, and as many as one-quarter of them disagreed with this position. This proportion was much larger than that found among Hindus and Christians. This suggests that the absence of theological prohibitions in Islam on contraception is irrelevant, since these Muslim women *think* that there are such prohibitions.

The information collected about the Ramanagaram women's fertility preferences showed the importance of distinguishing revealed preferences from the stated ones. On average, ideal family size in Ramanagaram was 2.5 for all three religious groups, and 'unwanted' fertility averaged 1 child for all women. The larger actual family size was, however, rationalized and justified on several counts, particularly insurance reasons, which was also manifest in a pronounced preference for sons. The final part of this chapter estimated a LOGIT model of the religious and socio-economic determinants of contraceptive choice.

Let us begin by considering the factors which were found not to affect the probability of contraceptive use. The income of the household was not found to be a significant determinant of contraceptive choice, perhaps because its effect is cancelled out by various substitution effects. Another possible reason is that because access to contraception is very good in Ramanagaram, women's purchasing power, as measured by income, has no impact on contraceptive use.

Second, husband's occupation, distinguished as farming-related and domestic-industry-related, was not a significant predictor of the probability of contraceptive use. Marriage to a relation also appears not to affect a woman's decisions about contraception, a finding which is consistent across all three religious groups. Interestingly, the finding that consanguinity exercises no effect on contraception seems in contrast with the other econometric findings such as the significant effect of the female-extended-family variable reported earlier. In combination, the findings from these variables suggests that while extended family (as measured through members resident) can exert an impact on demographic outcomes, the same may not be true of the influence of extended family, as measured through the influence of inbreeding, in south India.

Different measures of women's occupation (distinguished as home-related, skilled, and silk-related), exerted no effect in the interaction model. It may be that because access to contraception is so widespread and its benefits are so well-known in the region, whether or not a woman used contraception was not determined by her employment status. Or it may be that so many of the Ramanagaram women were employed, as discussed in Chapter 5, that there is not enough variation in these variables to account for differences in contraceptive use.

It has been hypothesized that if the husband is better educated, he will encourage his wife to adopt a contraceptive method in order to limit and space births, because he is concerned about his wife's health, or because he wishes to attain a low fertility goal. In the interaction model, Wald tests established that this variable was important for Hindus and for Muslims. This indicates that even after controlling for women's education, husband's education influences the decision to use contraception. This finding is vital from the perspective of family planning policy because it indicates that men should be targeted, whether through the education system, through the health system, or through the media, if it is desired to influence contraceptive adoption by their wives. This finding is also consistent with the qualitative information from Ramanagaram which suggested that couples should be encouraged to communicate more about family planning, and that for couples who say that they communicate already, care must be taken to ensure that communication is not partial and limited, but substantial.[21]

The women's qualitative perceptions about access to government services did not emerge as significant in the interaction model, probably because most women in the Ramanagaram sample had easy access to contraception. However, more general evidence collected from qualitative

---

[21]One way of doing this is to ascertain men's and women's views about contraception, as argued by Biddlecom, Casterline and Perez, 1996.

questioning and group discussions with the women seems to suggest that access may still have been a major issue for the remainder.

Let us now turn our attention to those factors which exercised a consistently significant effect on the decision to use contraception. The first such factor was women's education. It is hypothesized that as women become better educated, they are likely to be better informed of contraceptive techniques, use information about contraception better, and discuss contraception with others. Moreover, the higher opportunity cost of their time makes them demand fewer children and use contraceptives to achieve their lower fertility goals. Education may also change women's values in a direction consistent with less rejection of family planning. The effect of education on contraceptive use was not significantly different between Hindus and Muslims, but was significantly higher for Christians, compared to the other two religions. One possible reason for this finding may be that education exercises a greater impact on the decision to use contraception for a population with a high average level of education, and then only after a certain level of education has been reached. Because Christians had a much higher average level of education (9.2 years) than Hindus or Muslims (5.5 years), it is possible that they were more susceptible to this sort of educational impact on contraception.

The next factor which was significant for Hindus and Christians in the final interaction model was the presence of female family members in the household. Conventionally, demographers have argued that the role of the female extended family, and especially the mother-in-law, has been to encourage high fertility and discourage contraceptive use among young brides. Another reason is that the mother's extended family may look after her children at low real and opportunity-cost, thereby cutting the cost of having more children, which in turn discourages the use of contraception. This appears to be borne out by the econometric finding that for Hindus and Christians only, if a woman had one additional female family member resident this reduced her probability of contraceptive use. However, it emerges from the *qualitative* evidence collected during my fieldwork that female extended family and other female associates may be performing a role with respect to contraception which is quite different to that postulated in much of the earlier literature on the subject (and which contradicts directly the econometric findings of the present study). For example, Naseema, aged 45 years, a Muslim mother of 7 children, from Ramanagaram town, remarked, 'We need to improve ourselves, have fewer children. I wish people had spoken to us when we were young, now there is so much difficulty ... the family planning people keep telling us the population is growing. We should have more responsibility.' It was similar among Hindu women, for example, one Hindu woman, aged 51 years, from Ramanagaram town, stated quite clearly that she encouraged all her daughters and daughters-in-law to 'have their children and stop with an operation'. Such remarks suggest that attitudes favouring low fertility (and the associated contraceptive practices) have gained widespread acceptance within parts of south Indian society in the 1990s. This factor may be an important contributing factor to the fall in fertility in south India in recent years, although one which is hard to measure except by micro-level fieldwork of the sort carried out in the present study.

However, it must be acknowledged that the role of female extended family on the decision to use contraception is an issue on which the qualitative and quantitative findings from Ramanagaram are at odds with one another. There are two possible explanations for this. The first is that quantitatively, female extended family may be exercising a negative effect on the decision to use contraception not because there is a direct causal link between these two factors, but because there is an indirect connection, that is, some other underlying factor may be affecting both variables. For example, it may be that those who live with extended family are also those who come from more traditional and conservative homes in which the use of contraception is discouraged. The other possibility is that female extended family members are actually discouraging the use of family planning, but that women are not willing to admit it openly in a questionnaire survey. In any case, the contradiction between the econometric and qualitative findings do suggest that this whole relationship requires further research.

At this stage one can only speculate about the possible impact of these qualitative findings on demographic behaviour in the future. One possibility is that female extended family may be an important channel for lower fertility via 'diffusion effects' on the childbearing of younger female relatives. Research on the manner in which these diffusion effects operate in rural Indian societies, via learning effects, language or the effects of social capital, is still in its infancy, but the findings from the present study do suggest that these diffusion effects are important. Moreover, as far as religious differentials in the adoption of contraception are concerned, as the impact of a 'pure religion effect' on the decision to use contraception diminishes, the demographic behaviour of religious communities may be expected to converge, provided this is combined with improvements in educational infrastructure and socio-economic development more widely.

The last variable which was a significant determinant of contraceptive use was the woman's age. Muslim women were found to have a higher probability of ever having used contraception if they were younger. This is probably because younger women are more exposed to family planning messages than older ones. The woman's age may also be proxying for changing norms over time.

Finally, we consider religion. In the preliminary models, the Hindu religion and the Muslim religion did emerge as a negative influence on contraceptive use; however, in the interaction model this effect disappeared. This suggests that Hindus and Muslims do not have significantly different intercepts. It was discovered that the estimated regression lines for Hindus and Muslims also did not differ in terms of slope. However, in the interaction model, the estimated regression lines differed in terms of intercept and in terms of slope between Hindus and Christians and between Muslims and Christians. Thus, it is probably the differences between Christians and the other two religious groups which accounts for the initial significance of the Hindu and Muslim religion dummies in the preliminary regression model.

The differences between the quantitative and qualitative findings from Ramanagaram are also important in that they provide a unique insight into the changing ways of thinking which may have a significant impact on demographic behaviour in the future. The qualitative evidence presented in this chapter suggests that the decision to use contraception may be influenced by the manner in which Islam and Hinduism is being interpreted for women by the local community in Ramanagaram. This was clearly evident to me when I interviewed the local mullah of Ramanagaram,[22] who stated that he strongly objected to women working outside the home, which he said was against the Shariat. He said that he disapproved of a leading woman parliamentarian at the time as a role model for Muslim women. More particularly, he stated that he did not encourage birth control, but rather believed that children were 'gifts of God'.

We have already observed that Muslim women in Ramanagaram believed that contraception was not encouraged by their religion, and that in fact over one-quarter of Muslim women disagreed with this position. For example, a Muslim woman, Fatima, aged 52 years, from Ramanagaram, who was educated to the Masters level, remarked, 'I had two births and then got myself operated. My husband encouraged me. We have a responsibility to restrict our fertility. ... In twelve years the

---

[22]By a happy coincidence, the wife of the mullah was admitted to have a baby in a private clinic the day I went to interview the lady doctor at the clinic. Seizing the opportunity, I informally interviewed the mullah.

population has increased a lot. I feel sick looking at the numbers. I follow the Koran, what is correct, but ... I am trying to propagate small family norms. But you see, men are selfish. They do not allow girls to study. Husbands do not like wives in control of their lives or their fertility.'

Quantitative and qualitative evidence from the present study also suggests that individual beliefs held by men and women about whether their religion prescribes or proscribes contraceptive use (whether or not their religion actually does so) may be fundamental to demographic decisions. The effect of religion may also be exercised through the local religious community, particularly through religious leaders. However, this is expressed not in terms of a 'pure theological effect' on the decision to use contraception, but in terms of decisions taken about socio-economic matters, such as whether to continue an education, by individual members of different religions. In addition, socio-economic factors appear to affect the contraceptive decision-making of Christians in Ramanagaram differently to other religious groups.

These findings have important implications for future demographic patterns in India, and suggest that there are likely to be three main trends. First, with better education in particular and with economic development more widely, the effect of religion is likely to play a less important role in influencing contraceptive choice and thereby demographic behaviour. Moreover, with a greater role for diffusion effects in influencing fertility, for example via the role of the media, popular misconceptions about the precise effects of the theological content of Islam or Hinduism on birth control and other demographic issues are likely to be clarified and information made more widely available. This may have an impact both on fertility preferences by altering preferences for greater numbers of children, or children of a particular sex, and on reducing unwanted fertility by making information about contraceptive methods more readily accessible. Finally, with the diminished influence of religion and a narrowing of the socio-economic differentials between religious groups, the demographic behaviour of different religious communities in India is likely to converge; this is likely to be similar to the narrowing of religious differentials in contraceptive use in other societies.

These findings also have important implications for policy. First, it may be necessary for population policy to target religious and community leaders. Religious leaders may have a particularly important role to play in urging couples to use contraception, and to influence fertility preferences by promoting a small family norm. Religious leaders could also work in tandem with village panchayats to address issues that concern access to methods of contraception and to provide information about them, particularly to vulnerable populations. Religious leaders may also have a role to play in promoting 'information, education, and communication' about family planning. These leaders would also be very effective if asked specifically to target men or adolescent populations, who are not as widely involved in more conventional population policy. The second more general policy implication of the findings from Ramanagaram is that without systematically controlling for socio-economic status and other factors, it is impossible to make generalizations about contraceptive adoption by religion, as is often heard from religious leaders speaking about members of their own community who are said to have committed a 'travesty of faith' by practising family planning; or from more right-wing Indian politicians who make blanket statements about contraceptive acceptance and adoption by members of other religions. Third, policy initiatives directed at altering patterns of contraceptive adoption may need to target some of India's different religious groups in different ways, since in Ramanagaram the socio-economic factors determining people's existing contraceptive use vary between Christians and other religions, although not between Hindus and Muslims. So for example, it would be desirable to target education and employment particularly for women, to use the media to counteract son-preference, to target older women who often exert an influence on younger female members of the family, and to target men in order to integrate them better into the family planning programme. The present study emphasizes the importance of holding socio-economic factors constant when attempting to evaluate the impact of religious faith on demographic outcomes, and the importance of recognizing the influence of the community in enforcing popular and preconceived notions about religious injunctions on birth control. In fact, it is the neglect of such a procedure that causes serious misrepresentations of demographic phenomena in developing countries such as India, and which is the more fundamental travesty, one that this chapter has attempted to overcome.

chapter eight

~~~

The Determinants of Fertility in India

This chapter analyses the socio-economic and demographic determinants of fertility in India. It begins with a review of the relevant literature on the determinants of fertility. It then undertakes an econometric analysis of the factors influencing variations in fertility among the 201 women interviewed in the Ramanagaram survey, concluding with a consideration of the implications of these findings for theoretical models of fertility in religiously differentiated societies.

The discussion that follows categorizes the factors influencing fertility into what are conventionally termed the 'proximate determinants' and the 'nonproximate determinants' or 'nonproximate developmental factors' in fertility change.[1] In the two preceding chapters, we analysed the factors influencing two important proximate determinants of fertility: nuptiality and contraceptive use. This chapter focuses on the influence of the nonproximate determinants.

PROXIMATE DETERMINANTS AND NONPROXIMATE DEVELOPMENTAL INFLUENCES

The proximate determinants of fertility are those intermediate variables through which changes in fertility are effected (Bongaarts, 1978: 105–32; Srinivasan, 1995: 577–86). Nonproximate determinants affect fertility through their impact on the proximate variables.[2] The relationships

---

[1]The term 'nonproximate determinant' is used by Bongaarts, while, in the context of India, both terms are used interchangeably by Srinivasan. See Bongaarts, 1978: 105–32; Srinivasan, 1995: 577–86.

[2]An illustration of the way in which the nonproximate determinants affect fertility via the proximate determinants can be found in studies of historical demography. Wrigley and

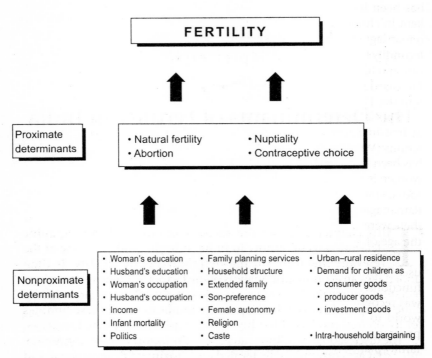

FIGURE 8.1: PROXIMATE AND NONPROXIMATE DETERMINANTS OF FERTILITY CHANGE

between actual fertility, the chief proximate determinants of fertility, and some of the main nonproximate determinants are schematically represented in Fig. 8.1.

Natural fertility is defined as the total fertility of a couple who have which has not practised any method of deliberate control either to increase birth-spacing or to curtail total family size. Natural fertility has a number of components: sterility, menarche, intra-uterine mortality, breastfeeding, postpartum abstinence, and so on. Historically in India, natural fertility

---

Schofield argue that fertility trends in England from 1541–1816 followed real wage trends with a lag of forty years, so that the increase in fertility in England after 1750 occurred when nuptiality responded with a lag to the rise in real wages in the early eighteenth century. Goldstone argues that in England before 1700 changes in real wages determined fertility by affecting the proportions marrying, though in later cohorts fertility was determined by a sustained fall in the age at marriage. For more on this debate, see Wrigley and Schofield, 1981; Goldstone, 1986: 5–33.

has been low, averaging 6 births per woman, mainly because it was kept in check by cultural practices (such as the prohibition of widow remarriage) and a high incidence of diseases which diminished biological fecundity (Srinivasan, 1995: 58). However, with improvements in health care and life expectancy in the 1960s and 1970s, natural fertility in India increased from 6 births per woman in the 1930s to 7 in the 1970s and 9 in the 1980s (Srinivasan and Jejeebhoy, 1981: 103).

Nuptiality, reflected in the proportions married and the female age at first marriage, is the second important proximate determinant of fertility (Wrigley and Schofield, 1981; Goldstone, 1986: 5–33). This factor has been hypothesized to affect fertility because a later marriage age for women is associated with lower fertility. This factor is highly relevant for India, since marriage is near-universal. As we saw in Chapter 5, for the Ramanagaram sample, the mean age at first marriage was 17.3 years, and there were no women in the sample who had remained unmarried past the age of 49 years.

The third important proximate determinant of fertility is contraceptive use. Contraception performs both birth-spacing and birth-limitation functions. In India, the importance of this factor in the control of fertility was recognized at an early date and India was the first country in the world to launch an official government-sponsored family planning programme (in 1951). Moreover, as a part of this programme, the first family planning centre in Karnataka was set up in Ramanagaram in 1952.

Induced abortion, the willingness and ability of women to terminate unwanted births, is the final proximate determinant of fertility. It may be influenced by socio-economic factors such as income, by technological factors such as the availability of safe abortion methods, by religious and cultural factors such as attitudes toward the moral acceptability of abortion, and by legal factors such as the laws regarding termination of pregnancies. In previous chapters we have already looked at nuptiality and contraceptive use in detail. We have not considered natural fertility or induced abortion primarily because of paucity of data on these two factors.

Infant and Child Mortality

A first important nonproximate developmental factor is infant and child mortality. There are two hypotheses concerning the effects on fertility of higher infant mortality. First is the 'child survival hypothesis' which argues that if parents live in an area of high child mortality, they will have more children because they expect to lose a high percentage of offspring to death.[3] Second is the 'child replacement hypothesis', which assumes that if a child dies, parents are anxious to replace it as soon as possible (Scrimshaw, 1978: 383–403). Lower mortality both reduces the number of births necessary to achieve desired reproductive outcomes, and reduces the costs to parents of investing in children, by reducing the risk that such investments will be lost through child deaths. This is an especially important consideration in the context of the 'quantity–quality' model of fertility (Becker and Lewis, 1973: 279–88; Schultz, 1990: 599–634). This variable is not included in the econometric models presented later in this chapter because it did not vary significantly among the women covered in the Ramanagaram sample, and because in any case it would be impossible to assign an infant mortality rate to each woman in the sample.

Education

Education is another important nonproximate influence on fertility. A wide array of empirical studies have shown that greater education, especially secondary education for women, contributes significantly to declines in fertility, even after controlling for other variables.[4] There are a number of avenues through which female education is hypothesized to influence fertility. First, attending school or university may itself delay marriage. Secondly, it may mean women have better knowledge of contraception and greater efficiency in using it. Thirdly, educated women have healthier babies and lower child mortality, which in turn lowers their fertility.[5] Fourthly, educated women are more likely to work in jobs in the modern sector, thereby increasing the time costs of having children.[6] Fifthly, education is likely to have a favourable effect on a woman's influ-

[3]Birdsall and Griffin, 1988: 29–55. For evidence from other countries, see Olsen, 1987; Ketkar, 1979: 479–88; Duraisamy 1988: 293–316.

[4]See Cochrane, 1979; Cochrane, 1983: 992–1026; Dasgupta, 1995a: 1879–1902; see also Caldwell, 1980: 225–255; Caldwell, Reddy and Caldwell, 1985: 29–51; Nag and Kak, 1984: 661–678; Appleton, 1996: 139–166; Duraisamy, 1988: 293–316; Shapiro, 1996: 89–103; Ajayi and Kekovole, 1998: 113–56. Birdsall and Griffin postulate that women with very few years of primary schooling have slightly higher fertility than those with no education, but that as the number of years of education increases beyond primary levels, the number of children declines. See Birdsall and Griffin, 1988: 29–55.

[5]According to Singh, Casterline and Cleland, educated women achieve desired family size better as they are more successful in preventing excess births by using contraception. The World Fertility Survey also found that while desired family size may not vary by educational level, actual family size does. See Singh, Casterline and Cleland, 1985: 113–35.

[6]Female employment itself does not necessarily reduce fertility. Only those women who perform jobs which are incompatible with child rearing are likely to show reduced fertility. See Standing, 1983: 517–46.

ence on all household decisions, including additional childbearing. Sixthly, education influences the ability of mothers to produce higher 'quality' children, who are more expensive to raise, which increases the unit costs of higher child 'quantity' (or higher fertility).[7] The interaction between quantity and quality is such that an increase in quality and a decrease in quantity encourages greater substitution away from child quantity and towards child quality (Becker, 1981: 93–113).

Female education was included in the econometric models of fertility in this study, in two alternative measures: first, in terms of the total number of years of education; and second, the number of years of primary, secondary, and university education separately.

The education of the woman's husband has also been postulated as an important determinant of fertility. An increased level of husband's education increases the opportunity cost of women's time. It may also contribute to the desire for fewer, but better 'quality' children because higher education for the man raises the relative price of child quantity (and lowers the price of a unit of child quality), which increases the demand for child quality relative to the demand for other goods. A higher level of education for the husband may also lead him to prefer a wife who is more highly educated or has a skilled job, factors which themselves may contribute to lower fertility. In this study, husband's education was measured in two ways: in terms of the husband's total number of years of education, and in terms of the number of years of husband's primary education, secondary education, and university education.

Employment

Female labour force participation is another important nonproximate influence on fertility and is closely related to education. Women who work have fewer children because the opportunity cost of children for them is higher (Birdsall and Griffin, 1988: 29–55). Higher women's wages have the same effect on the time cost of children whether or not women work, because higher wages increase the opportunity cost of leisure. However, female employment is neither a necessary nor a sufficient condition for fertility reduction. This is because women's employment depresses fertility only if women work in jobs which are incompatible with child rearing (for example, in cities, or in the modern sector) (Standing,

---

[7]For example, the 1961 UN study noted that ever-married women in Bangalore city, aged more than 45 years with high school or university education, gave birth, on average, to 4.0 children, compared with 5.3 children for women with no education, and 5.5 children for women with primary education (p. 122).

1983: 517–46). In rural areas, female employment does not necessarily depress fertility because it is often compatible with child rearing.[8] This issue is particularly relevant to Ramanagaram, where so many women were employed in the silk industry (Standing, 1983: 517–46). It is also argued that in order to depress fertility, it is necessary to raise both the productivity of women inside the home and their earnings in the market outside (See also Duraisamy, 1988: 293–316). This is important because it improves women's bargaining position within the household by widening their exit options, whether or not women actually take up work outside the home (Dasgupta, 1995a: 1879–902).

In this study, employment for women was measured in three different ways. The first was through a dummy variable which took the value 1 if the woman said she had a primary occupation and 0 otherwise. The second was through a dummy variable which took the value 1 if the woman was employed in a silk-related occupation, and 0 otherwise. The latter was tested for two reasons: first, because in Ramanagaram taluk the silk industry is the main source of livelihood for a large part of the population; and second, because some stages in the silk manufacturing process are dominated by women workers and child labour. There is a large literature on proto-industry (market-oriented rural domestic industry) which postulates that it creates incentives for higher fertility (Kriedte, Medick and Schlumbohm, 1981: 58–9). Therefore, it seemed important to analyse if employment in this industry was related to fertility behaviour in the taluk. Finally, a third dummy variable was defined which took the value 1 if the woman was employed in a skilled occupation (such as a teacher) and 0 otherwise.

The occupation of the woman's husband is also an important predictor of women's fertility, though the manner in which it is supposed to affect fertility is complex. It is theorized that if the husband is employed in a skilled occupation, his wife is likely to have fewer children. This is because a man will tend to prefer a wife who is also employed in a skilled occupation, who is better educated, or who is older at the time of marriage. Alternatively, it has been postulated that at higher wage rates men can afford to marry earlier and raise more children, hence increasing

[8]In a very early article on female employment in cottage industry and fertility, Jaffe and Azumi argued that female employment in cottage industries may have actually increased fertility in Puerto Rico and Japan in the 1950s. They argued that women employed in agriculture had the highest fertility, while those employed in non-agricultural industry which was carried on very near the woman's home, enabling women to combine work and child rearing, resulted in considerably higher fertility than if the woman worked away from the home. See Jaffe and Azumi, 1960: 52–63.

their fertility. It has also been postulated that if the husband's primary occupation is farming, there may be greater need for children to work on the family farm, increasing the demand for children. There may also be a higher demand for children if men are employed in domestic industry, for the same reasons as adduced for the employment of women in domestic industry.

In order to test these competing theories, three variables relating to husband's primary occupation were created. First, a dummy variable was created which took the value 1 if the husband had a farming occupation and 0 otherwise; the expected sign of the coefficient on this variable is positive. Second, a dummy variable was created which took the value 1 if the husband had a skilled occupation and 0 otherwise; the expected sign of the coefficient on this variable is negative. Thirdly, a variable was created which took the value 1 if the husband was employed in domestic industry and 0 otherwise; the expected sign of the coefficient on this variable is positive.

Income

The pure 'income effect' raises the demand for all normal goods, including children. This is thought to be the reason why at very low levels of income, as incomes rise, fertility rises. As income keeps rising, fertility is subsequently observed to fall because at higher incomes various 'substitution effects' come into play, reducing the demand for children by increasing the price of children relative to other goods, and thus parents substitute away from them. These 'substitution effects' operate in a number of ways: by increases in the opportunity cost of parent's time, by the 'quantity–quality' trade-off, and by increased access to substitutes for various 'child services' such as insurance and welfare. Thus, the effect of income on fertility is first to increase fertility due to the operation of a pure 'income effect', and then to depress fertility due to 'substitution effects'.

Consequently, in empirical analyses of income and fertility, one seldom observes the pure 'income effect', mainly because the 'substitution effects' soon cancel it out (Schultz, 1982: 137–50; Duraisamy, 1988: 293–316). Five different measures of income were calculated for the Ramanagaram sample: total monthly expenditure, per capita monthly expenditure, total monthly foodgrains expenditure, per capita monthly foodgrains expenditure, and an index which measured the ownership of items of consumer equipment. The regression models estimated in this chapter use total monthly expenditure, total monthly food expenditure, and the index of consumer equipment ownership as measures of income. Per capita expenditure and per capita foodgrains expenditure are not used because they are calculated by taking total family size into account and are therefore endogenous in a model of fertility. However, in order to control for the fact that some households' total expenditure (or total food expenditure) may be higher than that of other households not because they are richer, but because there are more members living in the household, we also use (as discussed further on) the total number of female extended family members (or total number of extended family), both of which are highly correlated with total household size, as an additional explanatory variable in the models, in order to control for family size (The correlation coefficient is 0.87).

Women's status and female autonomy

Another important nonproximate influence on fertility is women's status and female autonomy. Various studies have postulated that an increase in female autonomy or control of resources leads to a fall in fertility.[9] Women's status is also believed to influence fertility in two ways. First, it can increase child survival due to a mother's increased ability to provide better nutrition and medical care, and it will tend to increase the value of daughters in a society, which may consequently increase nutritional and health investments in them. Many studies have argued that mortality and women's status are linked (Standing, 1983: 517–46; Dyson and Moore, 1983: 35–60).

The second set of ways in which women's status is thought to affect fertility is that it tends to increase the age at first marriage, to reduce the importance of son-preference and the patriarchal family structure, to encourage women's access to contraception, and to diminish the extent to which women have to resort to high fertility in order to gain power and prestige within the family or the wider community.[10] Finally, across India with some exceptions, it is possible to observe a broad north–south dichotomy with areas of low female autonomy (and high birth and death rates) prevalent in north India, and comparatively high female autonomy (and low birth and death rates) prevalent in south India.[11] This variable

[9]Mason, 1993: 19–42; Dharmalingam and Philip Morgan, 1996: 187–201; Drèze and Sen, 1995; Malhotra, Vanneman and Kishor, 1995: 281–305; Steele, Amin and Naved, 1998.

[10]Standing, 1983: 517–46; Cochrane, 1983; Cain, 1984; Dyson and Moore, 1983: 35–60; Mason and Taj, 1987: 611–38; Mason, 1993: 19–42; Cain, Khanam and Nahar, 1979: 432; Srinivas, 1989: 129; Oppong, 1983: 556–7; Dasgupta, 1995a: 1888; Rosenzweig and Schultz, 1982: 803–15; Kennedy and Haddad, 1994; Kennedy and Peters, 1992.

[11]This is Sopher's hypothesis of differences in culture between north and south India. See Sopher, 1980: 289–327. Dyson and Moore's contrasting demographic regimes mirror

was not included separately in the econometric models for two reasons: first, because it is highly correlated with women's education, occupation, and other explanatory variables, and could also well be the *result* of education; and second, because it did not vary sufficiently across Hindus and Muslims in the Ramanagaram sample.

Water and fuel infrastructure

It is hypothesized that poor households have high fertility because children are desired for their contributions of labour income and time spent performing household tasks, especially fuel and water collection. There is considerable evidence in support of the producer goods motive for high fertility.[12]

It has also been postulated that the lack of water and fuel infrastructure in poor countries may create a cycle of overpopulation, poverty, and environmental degradation.[13] This can eventually give rise to a 'tragedy of the commons', when the social costs of the externalities to child rearing outweigh the private benefits of children, resulting in a situation where poverty and depletion of environmental resources is a natural consequence. The present study has sought to explore this hypothesis empirically at the micro level, by investigating in detail how water and fuel were obtained by Ramanagaram households and (in the econometric analysis of the determinants of fertility) whether these infrastructure variables influenced fertility significantly.

There were five main sources of water supply in Ramanagaram: daily filling-up of pots of water from the river or from hand-pumps provided by the municipality; borewells; motor pumps; taps/pipes in the home supplied by the municipality; and ordinary wells. In the sample as a whole, 82 per cent said that they collected pots of water by hand as their primary source of water supply, and this percentage was quite similar across religious groups.

The average number of pots of water required in Ramanagaram per

---

the alleged cultural differences between the northern, mainly 'Aryan', culture and the southern, predominantly 'Dravidian', culture. For more on some of these factors and the contrasts between north India and south India, see Dyson and Moore, 1983; Agarwal, 1994; Malhotra, Vanneman and Kishor, 1995: 281–305; Murthi, Guio and Drèze, 1995: 745–82; Jeffery and Jeffery, 1997.

[12]Dasgupta, 1993a: 358–61; Dasgupta, 1995a: 1879–902; Cain, 1977: 201–27; Duraisamy, 1988: 293–316; Mamdani, 1972; Das Gupta, 1994: 101–33; Vlassoff, 1979: 415–28.

[13]Dasgupta, 1993a: 358–61. Lee and Miller, 1991: 275–97. Dasgupta argues that the breakdown of agreements on common property resources may set off this spiral in poor countries. See Dasgupta, 1995b; Dasgupta, 1993b: 207–43.

day to meet the family's water requirements was 26.3: the Muslims required 27.7, the Christians 26.9, and the Hindus 25.2. It may be recollected that the mean household size in the sample was 5.7 for Hindus,
6.6 for Muslims, and 4.3 for Christians. Thus, the Muslims, who had the
largest households, also had the highest water requirements. The mean
per capita water requirements by religion were almost identical between
Hindus and Muslims (4.5–4.6 pots per person), but 6.2 among the
Christians. One reason why the Christians had the highest per capita
water requirements may be that they were the most likely of all three
religious communities to have water taps in their homes or employ
others to collect water for them (as discussed in the following paragraph).

Table 8.1 shows the responses to the question 'Who collects water?'.
Women and children (especially daughters) are the main water-carriers
in Ramanagaram taluk: 67 per cent of all women collected water on a
daily basis for their own homes, and 47 per cent of all households used
one or more children to collect water. In only 10 per cent of households
were men alone performing water-carrying duties, though a few men
did come under the 'others' category.

TABLE 8.1: WATER COLLECTION IN THE HOUSEHOLD, RAMANAGARAM SAMPLE (1996)

Water collection performed by	All women		Hindus		Muslims		Christians	
	No.	%	No.	%	No.	%	No.	%
Woman	134	66.7	84	75.7	43	57.3	7	46.7
Husband	22	11.0	9	8.1	11	14.7	2	13.3
Daughter(s)[1]	40	19.9	20	18.0	18	24.0	2	13.3
Son(s)[1]	11	5.5	7	6.3	3	4.0	0	0.0
Children[2]	35	17.4	22	11.0	11	14.7	2	13.3
Daughter(s)-in-law[1]	9	4.5	6	5.4	3	4.0	0	0.0
Others[3]	25	12.4	13	11.7	9	12.0	3	20.0
Total number of women[4]	201		111		75		15	

Notes: [1]Very often, more than one daughter, son, or daughter-in-law assisted with water
collection, though the detailed breakdown is not reported here.

[2]In their responses, some women did not distinguish between sons and daughters
and preferred to indicate that 'children' in the household helped with water-collection.

[3]This includes siblings, brothers-in-law, hired coolies and servants, parents-in-law,
joint family members (where the woman did not provide a detailed breakdown),
sisters-in-law, co-sisters, girl neighbour, mother, sons-in-law, and in three cases an
unnamed person.

[4]The women mentioned more than one person who collected water, and hence
the column totals do not add up to 100 per cent.

As regards the religious breakdown, 76 per cent of Hindu women, 57 per cent of Muslim women and 47 per cent of Christian women collected water for their own homes. Moreover, 50 per cent of Hindu households and 47 per cent of Muslim households used children for water-collection, compared with only 26 per cent of Christian households. This is relevant to a discussion of fertility because it appears that those religious communities (mainly Hindus and Muslims) having greater fertility were also those in which children were more widely used for water-collection, although we cannot know whether these are causally related. Even so, women explained that as the daughters of the household were increasingly being sent to school, the water-collection tasks often fell on their mothers. One woman, Devamma, from village C, remarked that while she realized the importance of educating her daughters, yet she was suffering greater tiredness and ill-health, mainly because she did not have enough help with the water and fuel-collection tasks. Although more girls were being sent to school, this process would perhaps have proceeded further and faster by this time if it was not for the water burden that it implied.

Women were also asked, 'How many hours per person per day are required for water collection?' In the sample as a whole, the mean number of hours per person per day required for water collection was 2.2 hours for all women, 2.3 for the Hindus, 2.2 for the Muslims, and 1.5 for the Christians. The differences between the three religious groups was found not to be statistically significant at the 95 per cent confidence level. The closeness of the figures for all three religious groups suggests that the women were acutely aware of the time spent per day collecting water to meet the household's needs. Hence it is certainly possible that labour needed for water collection entered into their fertility calculations.

The Ramanagaram women were also asked about their sources of fuel. Of the women in the sample, the majority (74 per cent) used fire-wood. Even schoolteachers and government office clerks (considered to be more 'prestigious' and monetarily more rewarding occupations for women) used firewood, although these groups often bought it rather than collected it. The large difference in the proportions dependent on firewood between the Hindus (81 per cent) on the one hand and the Muslims (65 per cent) and Christians (66 per cent) on the other is prob-ably explained by the relative prosperity of some Muslim and Christian households who replaced firewood with alternative fuel sources such as kerosene oil or gas.

The firewood requirements of the family were expressed by the women interviewed in terms of *manas*. One mana cost approximately

Rs 8 to Rs 9. Sometimes, when firewood was bought, it was also expressed in terms of *gadis* or carts. For those who owned silk trees, or a saw-mill, there was no question of payment for firewood collection. For others, the firewood was collected by hand from common land in surrounding areas or on the outskirts of the town and no monetary payment was made for it. For still others, it was purchased from the saw-mills. I observed in my fieldwork that most families purchased a fixed amount of firewood per week, and supplemented it with additional wood, if required, which was either purchased again, or cut by hand. The average Ramanagaram family which used wood for fuel needed 6.7 manas every week—6.3 among the Hindus, 7.0 among the Muslims, and 7.8 among the Christians.

Women were asked about who performed firewood collection for the household. In Table 8.2 their answers are alphabetically grouped by family members and group totals for some of the family members who were mainly responsible for fuel collection, in order to facilitate comparisons. This table is presented in detail, both to highlight the range of responses, and to illustrate how firewood collection in Ramanagaram taluk, as perhaps in most parts of India, is a fundamental aspect of daily living and may involve various combinations of all members of the family and household.

TABLE 8.2: COMBINATIONS OF HOUSEHOLD MEMBERS WHO PERFORM FIREWOOD COLLECTION TASKS IN THE RAMANAGARAM SAMPLE (1996)

Household member(s)	All women	Hindus	Muslims	Christians
Brothers-in-law (2)	1	0	1	0
Brothers (1 or 2)	3	0	2	1
Daughter	4	3	0	0
Daughter/daughter-in-law	1	1	0	0
Total daughters	5	4	0	1
Daughter-in-law (2)	2	0	2	0
Father [tractor]	5	4	0	0
Father-in-law/brother-in-law	1	1	0	0
Girl neighbour	1	1	0	0
Husband	42	21	19	5
Husband/daughters (3)	1	0	1	0
Husband/sons (2)	1	0	1	0
Total husbands	44	21	21	5

Household member(s)	All women	Hindus	Muslims	Christians
Children (2)	3	2	1	0
Children (3)	1	1	0	0
Children (4)	2	1	0	0
Children (5)	3	0	3	0
Children (6)/daughters-in-law (2)	1	0	1	0
Children (7)	1	0	1	0
Total children	11	4	5	0
Male joint family members	1	0	1	0
Parents in-law	1	0	1	0
Mother	1	1	0	0
Nephews (2)	1	0	1	0
Son	1	1	0	0
Son {auto}	10	2	8	0
Son [cycle]	1	0	0	1
Son (2)	8	2	5	1
Son (3)	2	0	2	0
Total sons	22	5	15	2
Servant	1	1	0	0
Suppliers	6	6	0	0
Woman	43	33	8	2
Woman/daughters (unspecified)	2	2	0	0
Woman/daughters (3)	1	1	0	0
Woman/daughter-in-law	1	1	0	0
Woman/husband	11	10	0	1
Woman/husband/son	1	1	0	0
Woman/children	1	1	0	0
Woman/co-sister	1	1	0	0
Woman/son (3)	1	1	0	0
Woman [auto]	1	1	0	0
Total women	63	52	8	3

Notes: The number within parentheses indicates the presence of two or more particular household members. Else, this implies a single person only. Sometimes, the women would also describe how the firewood, once collected, was eventually transported back home. This is represented in brackets.

The women themselves, their husbands and their sons were those mainly responsible for firewood collection. But this differed across religions. For Hindus, the women themselves and their husbands were primarily responsible, while in Muslim families, it was mainly the husbands and sons. This is probably due to the strict code of the purdah practised by the Muslim women and girls of Ramanagaram. In the Christian families, husbands, sons, and women themselves collected firewood.

An interesting feature of the Ramanagaram sample is that among the children, there is a broad split down gender lines in the allocation of water-collection and fuel-collection tasks, with daughters routinely collecting water and sons mainly collecting fuel. As one Muslim woman explained, daughters were not normally sent out very far on their own to collect firewood, both for security reasons and because it was a very heavy load to carry. The reluctance to send daughters out for firewood collection was evident across all three religious groups. In Ramanagaram taluk, it was intrinsically less laborious to obtain water, as compared with firewood, due to easy access to the river Arkavati and due to water taps provided by the municipality. If we accept the hypothesis that increased fertility arises because children may be desired as producer goods to help with fuel and water collection, this argument could perhaps explain the observed son-preference among all religious groups, since sons would help with the more labour-intensive fuel collection. This desire for sons may be reinforced if communities observe a strict code of purdah which restricts the mobility of girls and women.

The women were also asked about how many hours the family spent collecting fuel each day. Their responses were remarkably similar across religious groups, at 1.6 hours for Hindus, 1.8 for Muslims, and 1.8 for Christians. The closeness of these figures, as with those for water collection, suggest quite accurate responses and knowledge by the respondents about the time involved for firewood collection.

The econometric analysis of fertility will examine whether the family's fuel and water requirements influenced the total number of children ever born. This is done by creating two dummy variables, the first measuring whether the household collected water in pots by hand, the second whether it collected firewood by hand.

Son-preference

Demographers postulate that the strength of parents preferences for sons may increase fertility in order to obtain the desired quantity of sons.[14]

---

[14]Irudaya Rajan, Mishra and Vimala, 1996: 1980–86. In this article, using Census data for India between 1980 and 1991, they argue that the acceptance of a permanent method

Many studies have shown that evidence exists that some women may not be as interested in the survival of some of their children as in that of the others, as is evident in gender discrimination against daughters relative to sons in the access to food and medical care in some parts of north India, and elsewhere.[15] Given the enormous literature devoted to son-preference in poor countries, from the Ramanagaram data a variable was calculated in order to examine whether the delay in succeeding in giving birth to a son had any impact on fertility. This was done by calculating an index which measured the location of sons in the birth order.

This variable was calculated as follows. A number was assigned to each family, which took the value of the birth order of the *first-born son*. For example, if a woman gave birth to a son, followed by a daughter, followed by another son, the variable took the value '1'. If she gave birth to a daughter, followed by another daughter, then a son, and then another daughter, it took the value '3'. This variable in a sense captures a pure demographic accident. In the multivariate models presented later, it was attempted to examine whether this demographic accident affected total fertility.

To cast some qualitative light on the old-age security motive for fertility, women were also asked with whom they would live after the age of 60 years. Over half of all women preferred to live with their sons in old age, a percentage which was very similar across all religious groups: 57 per cent of Hindus, 55 per cent of Muslims, and 53 per cent of Christians. Only 5 per cent of the women in the sample said they would choose to live alone. However, women did indicate that living with a son was contingent on obtaining a daughter-in-law they could tolerate. One uneducated woman, Gangamma, aged 36 years, of Ramanagaram town, replied, 'If Indira Gandhi herself did not stay with her son because she could not get on with her daughter-in-law, how do I know, when my son marries, if I will obtain a daughter-in-law that I will get on with; and therefore, how can I possibly say who I will stay with in my old age? It is a very stupid question.'

Extended Family

It is also postulated that the presence of extended family or the existence of a kinship network to share the costs of child rearing is an important nonproximate determinant of fertility (Oppong, 1983: 547–89). Hajnal

---

of contraception among Indian couples is strongly associated with the sex composition of the family, in particular the number of sons.

[15]Chen, Huq and D'Souza, 1981: 55–70; Cain, 1984; Mason, 1993: 19–42; Dyson and Moore, 1983: 35–60; Dasgupta, 1993a: 343–70; Cain, 1981: 467.

(1982) argued that in north-west Europe in the past, the costs of raising children were solely borne by parents; by contrast, the 'Asiatic' pattern involved joint households, where the costs of child rearing were borne by many, and hence parents had high fertility. On the other hand, the presence of extended family members may also reduce fertility, both because there is a lack of privacy and because traditional taboos on sexual intercourse at particular times are more likely to be observed by women in extended households, under the scrutiny of in-laws, than among those living in nuclear family households.

Most households in Ramanagaram had extra persons beyond the nuclear family living in the household. These included family members, such as elderly parents or parents-in-law, distant relatives, and servants living permanently in the household. Table 8.3 shows the average household composition for different religious groups in Ramanagaram.

The mean household size for this sample is very similar to the mean household size calculated for Ramanagaram by other studies.[16] The lower household size among the Christians compared to Hindus and Muslims seems to be caused primarily by the lower number of other relatives in their households. This may be because members from the better-educated Christian community are able to migrate easily to other places elsewhere in India; and therefore the possible universe of 'extra kin' resident locally who could be recruited as members of Christian households is lower than for the other two religious groups. There may also be a tendency towards more nuclear families within the Christian community because of its tendency to be the most educated of all the religious groups in Ramanagaram.

TABLE 8.3: HOUSEHOLD COMPOSITION RAMANAGARAM SAMPLE (1996)

Mean number of:	All women	Hindus	Muslims	Christians
Women (wife/female head)	1.0	1.0	1.0	1.0
Husbands (male head)	0.8	0.8	0.8	0.9
Offspring	2.9	2.5	3.5	2.3
Other relatives	1.5	1.6	1.6	0.3
Servants	0.01	0.01	0.01	0.0
Mean household size	5.9	5.7	6.6	4.3

[16]For example, a study of urban infrastructure undertaken in 1995 has calculated that mean household size in Ramanagaram was 5.6. See Government of Karnataka, 1995.

Women were also asked 'Who looks after the children when you are not at home?' Their answers are shown in Tables 8.4 and 8.5.

Nearly 77 per cent of the women interviewed had extended family helping with the child care, though not all these relations were actually

TABLE 8.4: ROLE OF THE EXTENDED FAMILY IN CHILD CARE,
RAMANAGARAM SAMPLE (1996)

Extended family member assisting with child care	All women		Hindus		Muslims		Christians	
	No.	%	No.	%	No.	%	No.	%
Mother	34	16.9	15	13.5	14	18.7	5	33.3
Mother-in-law	45	22.4	25	22.5	17	22.7	3	20.0
Father	3	1.5	2	1.8	1	1.3	0	0.0
Father-in-law	8	4.0	6	5.4	2	2.6	0	0.0
Friend	6	3.0	5	4.5	1	1.3	0	0.0
Husband's brother's wife	6	3.0	4	3.6	2	2.6	0	0.0
Sister	5	2.5	2	1.8	2	2.6	1	6.7
Sister-in-law	6	3.0	3	2.7	3	4.0	0	0.0
Elder offspring	11	5.5	6	5.4	4	5.3	1	6.7
Others	28	13.9	12	10.8	13	17.3	3	20.0
Extended family not used	35	18.7	23	22.3	11	15.7	1	7.1
Total	187	100.0	103	100.0	70	100.0	14	100.0

TABLE 8.5: 'OTHERS' ASSISTING WITH CHILD CARE,
RAMANAGARAM SAMPLE (1996)

'Others'	All women	Hindus	Muslims	Christians
Aunt	1	0	1	0
Brother	1	0	1	0
Daughter	1	0	1	0
Daughter-in-law	4	3	1	0
Husband	6	2	2	2
Joint family	4	0	4	0
Children	1	1	0	0
Maid	1	1	0	0
Midwife	1	0	1	0
School	4	3	1	0
Servant	2	1	0	1
Work at home	2	1	1	0

co-resident in the women's families. The most popular responses for the whole sample taken together were the woman's mother, her mother-in-law, elder offspring, and 'others' (broken down in Table 8.5). The percentage relying on their own mothers varied a great deal among religious groups: lowest for Hindus (13.5 per cent), higher for Muslims (18.7 per cent), and very much higher for Christians (33.3 per cent). By contrast, 22 per cent of women interviewed listed their mothers-in-law as helpers with child care, and this percentage was approximately the same for all religions. Clearly, members of the extended family, widely defined, helped substantially with child care. This variable is therefore included in the econometric models of fertility estimated later on. It is measured as the number of female extended family members resident in the household.

Religion

As discussed in Chapter 3, the impact of religion on fertility can be direct, in the form of religious injunctions to refrain from contraception or to have certain numbers of children in order to continue the lineage, or indirect, in the form of religious norms about such matters as women's status (which may in turn affect fertility).

The Ramanagaram questionnaire contained five questions which focused on the religious characteristics of the women and their families. First, the women were asked how faithfully they practised their religion. They were asked to respond on a scale of 1 to 5, where 1 was 'not at all', 2 was 'not very much', 3 was 'medium', 4 was 'quite a bit', and 5 was 'very much'. Their responses are shown in Table 8.6.

Christians and Muslims rated themselves as being more 'faithful' to their religion than the Hindus. The difference between the Muslims and Christians was not found to be significant, at the 95 per cent level, but the difference between the Hindus and Muslims and that between

TABLE 8.6: FAITHFULNESS IN PRACTISING RELIGION, RAMANAGARAM SAMPLE (1996)

Rank	All women		Hindus		Muslims		Christians	
	No.	%	No.	%	No.	%	No.	%
Mean	3.8		3.2		4.6		4.1	
1	7	3.5	6	5.4	1	1.3	0	0.0
2	23	11.4	21	18.9	1	1.3	1	6.7
3	40	19.9	32	28.8	5	6.7	3	20.0
4	70	34.8	49	44.1	16	21.3	5	33.3
5	61	30.3	3	2.7	52	69.3	6	40.0
Total	201	100.0	111	100.0	75	100.0	15	100.0

TABLE 8.7: IMPORTANCE OF THE PRIEST'S OPINION, RAMANAGARAM SAMPLE (1996)

Rank	All women		Hindus		Muslims		Christians	
	No.	%	No.	%	No.	%	No.	%
Mean	3.0		2.1		4.2		3.6	
1	40	19.9	33	29.7	4	5.3	3	20.0
2	52	25.9	44	39.6	7	9.3	1	6.7
3	26	12.9	20	18.0	5	6.7	1	6.7
4	28	13.9	14	12.6	10	13.3	4	26.7
5	55	27.4	0	0.0	49	65.3	6	40.0
Total	201	100.0	111	100.0	75	100.0	15	100.0

the Hindus and Christians was found to be highly significant. One might speculate that this is a spin-off of 'minority group status' whereby members of a small religion are more assiduous in their faith to it.

The women were then asked about the role of their local priest in their lives. First, they were asked, 'How much does it matter to you what the local priests think of you?' Again they were asked to use a scale of 1 to 5, where 1 stood for 'not at all' and 5 stood for 'very much'. The responses are shown in Table 8.7.

It appears that the Muslims and Christians were also more concerned with the opinions of their priests than the Hindus. The difference between Muslims and Christians was not found to be statistically significant, but the differences between Hindus and Muslims and between Hindus and Christians were found to be highly significant.

The women were then asked if they would ask advice from the local priests about aspects of their lives. The responses to this question are shown in Table 8.8.

TABLE 8.8: ADVICE FROM PRIEST ABOUT ASPECTS OF ONE S LIFE, RAMANAGARAM SAMPLE (1996)

Rank	All women		Hindus		Muslims		Christians	
	No.	%	No.	%	No.	%	No.	%
Mean	3.1		2.2		4.2		3.6	
1	40	19.9	32	28.8	5	6.6	3	20.0
2	50	24.8	43	38.7	6	8.0	1	6.7
3	27	13.4	21	18.9	5	6.6	1	6.7
4	28	13.9	15	13.5	9	12.0	4	26.6
5	56	27.8	0	0.0	50	66.6	6	40.0
Total	201	100.0	111	100.0	75	100.0	15	100.0

The difference in means was statistically insignificant at the 95 per cent confidence level for the difference between Muslims and Christians, but it was significant for the differences between Hindus and Christians and between Hindus and Muslims. Thus, it appears that the Muslim and Christian priests exercised more influence over their communities than the Hindu priests, both in terms of the importance the women placed on their priests' opinions of them and in terms of whether they would ask advice from the priest about aspects of their daily lives.

The Ramanagaram women were then asked how frequently they visited places of worship. Their responses are shown in Table 8.9.

Christian women visited places of worship most frequently, followed by Hindu women and then, a long way behind, by Muslim women. The difference in means between all three groups was significant at the 95 per cent confidence level. There were 37 per cent of women in the sample who said that they visited places of worship quite a bit, but also 27 per cent who said that they did not visit places of worship at all. This was mainly because a large proportion of Muslim women (64 per cent) were not allowed to go to the mosque in Ramanagaram because of purdah restrictions.[17] Thus, all communities seemed to believe in visiting places of worship, though a large percentage of the Muslim women were prevented from doing so by other norms. Even then, Muslim women who

TABLE 8.9: FREQUENCY OF VISITS TO PLACES OF WORSHIP,
RAMANAGARAM SAMPLE (1996)

Rank	All women		Hindus		Muslims		Christians	
	No.	%	No.	%	No.	%	No.	%
Mean	2.8		3.2		2.1		3.9	
1	54	26.8	6	5.4	48	64.0	0	0.0
2	28	13.9	25	22.5	1	1.3	2	13.3
3	32	15.9	26	23.4	3	4.0	3	20.0
4	75	37.3	51	45.9	19	25.3	5	33.3
5	12	5.9	3	2.7	4	5.3	5	33.3
Total	201	100.0	111	100.0	75	100.0	15	100.0

[17]There were 27 Muslim women who rated their frequency of visits to places of worship as 'medium' to 'very much', even though none of them were actually allowed to go to the mosque (and, in fact, did not go there) for prayers. This question was often misinterpreted by Muslim women as referring to how frequently they prayed. Moreover, some Muslim women did visit the burial sites of saints or seers (dargha) nearby which they considered as places of worship.

TABLE 8.10: FREQUENCY OF INTERACTION WITH OTHER RELIGIONS,
RAMANAGARAM SAMPLE (1996)

Rank	All women		Hindus		Muslims		Christians	
	No.	%	No.	%	No.	%	No.	%
Mean	2.1		2.0		2.2		2.3	
1	78	38.8	51	45.9	32	42.6	5	33.3
2	48	23.3	30	27.0	14	18.6	4	26.6
3	29	14.4	14	12.6	13	17.3	2	13.3
4	29	14.4	11	9.9	14	18.6	4	26.6
5	16	7.9	5	4.5	1	1.3	0	0.0
Don't know	1	0.5	0	0.0	1	1.3	0	0.0
Total	201	100.0	111	100.0	75	100.0	15	100.0

were not allowed to visit the mosque prayed simultaneously at home during prayer-time. Thus, the Muslim women's lower level of attendance at places of worship cannot be interpreted as indicating a lesser importance of religion in their lives.

Finally, the women were asked if they interacted with neighbours who did not belong to their religion. The responses are shown in Table 8.10. Although there were some exceptions, the religious groups did not mix very much socially in Ramanagaram. The lower proportions for the Muslims (62 per cent) and Christians (60 per cent) than for the Hindus (73 per cent) is understandable, since the former were minorities in a predominantly Hindu region. But the differences between all three groups, Hindus and Muslims, Muslims and Christians, and Hindus and Christians, were not found to be significant at the 95 per cent level. What is striking is how little even the two 'minority' religions interacted outside their own religious community.

In summary, women in Ramanagaram appear to be religious, the Muslims and Christians more so than the Hindus. The opinions of the priests are important, but more so to Muslims and Christians, who would ask for advice pertaining to their lives, than for Hindus, who would not. All communities worshipped either at home or at places designated for worship, and interactions between those of different religions appears to be limited, though there were pockets where there were exceptions.[18]

[18]The women were also asked two questions about the religiosity of their offspring, although their responses are not reported here. These questions were 'Are your children religious too and do they go to the temple/mosque/church/worship at home?' and 'Do they practise religion to your satisfaction?'

In order to test empirically the effect of religion on fertility in the econometric analysis, the following measures of religion were used. First, a dummy variable was defined that took a value of 1 if the respondent was Muslim and 0 if otherwise. Second, a dummy variable was defined which took the value 1 if the respondent was Hindu and 0 otherwise. The Christians were the base category. Third, a dummy variable was defined which looked only at Hindu and Muslim respondents, leaving out the Christians, and took a value of 1 if the respondent was Muslim and 0 if the respondent was Hindu; because the Christians were excluded, the sample size was reduced to 173 ever-married women. Fourth, a qualitative 'index of piety' was created, which was calculated as each woman's mean response to the five questions in the questionnaire relating to her personal evaluation of her religiosity (discussed earlier).

Marital Consanguinity

Marital consanguinity is also postulated as affecting fertility (as also discussed in Chapter 6). However, we need to recognize two effects of consanguinity on fertility which work in opposite directions. First, there is the possibility of greater autonomy for the woman by marrying into the natal family, and thereby residing matrilocally; this would tend to reduce fertility. Second, there is the larger number of years of childbearing potential within marriage which may occur due to the woman's low age at marriage if she marries a relation who is much older than herself, such as a maternal uncle; this would tend to increase fertility.

Consanguineous marriage is incorporated into the regression models estimated further on in two ways. First, we define a dummy variable for whether or not a woman had married a relation. Second, we use a statistical measure of the 'coefficient of inbreeding' (Bittles, Cobles and Appaji Rao, 1993: 111–16).

'Ideational' Influences

Ideational theories of fertility challenge the basic economic assumption of the 'new household economics', that the changing balance between the costs and benefits of childbearing reduces the demand for children and is the key to the fertility transition (Cleland and Wilson, 1987; See also Cleland, 1993: 345–52). The proponents of the ideational view argue that findings showing a relationship between education for women and declining fertility are due to changing perceptions, ideas, and aspirations rather than to changes in women's economic circumstances. They suggest also that changes in social norms and attitudes towards birth control may be the key factors which determine the timing of the fertility transition (Cleland and Wilson, 1987: 25; See also Cleland, 1993: 345–52).

Evidence for the importance of ideational theories is found in the case of historical European populations. In the case of 700 provinces in historical Europe, fertility began to decline in a short period of time, in 59 per cent of the provinces between 1890 and 1920, and in 71 per cent of the provinces between 1880 and 1930 (Cleland and Wilson, 1987). However, economic development in European countries showed no association with the date at which significant fertility declines began (Knodel and van de Walle, 1986). The practice of family limitation was largely absent (except in France, where from the 1780s family limitation was widespread), and cultural settings influenced the onset and spread of fertility declines independently of socio-economic conditions (ibid., Lesthaeghe and Wilson, 1986). As Cleland and Wilson (1987: 24) put it,

in historical Europe, just as in the developing world today, the culture of subpopulations, loosely defined by religion, language or region, appears to exert a major influence on the timing of reproductive change, independently of levels of development, education or provision of family planning services.

It is necessary to examine this theory carefully, both because of its importance to the explanation of fertility decline, and because it epitomizes the most divisive issue in demography between economics and other disciplines, namely, the way in which 'culture' affects demographic outcomes (Lesthaeghe and Surkyn, 1988: 1). Cleland and Wilson's argument that ideas and aspirations are vital in the fertility transition is interesting but measuring these ideational changes, and distinguishing them from changes in behaviour for other reasons, appears to be extremely difficult. Moreover, the debate about the causes of the fertility transition in Europe is still unresolved (Galloway, Hammel and Lee, 1994: 135–58; Ogilvie, 1997). These arguments must not be taken to imply that the present study is opposed to the ideational view of fertility.[19] Rather, it is the view of the present study that the most important aspect of the ideational theory, which has relevance for Karnataka and other parts of south India such as Tamil Nadu, is the hypothesis that ideational change about attitudes towards birth control may be important to the timing of the fertility transition.[20]

For example, it is hypothesized that one reason why contraceptive use is higher and fertility is lower in south Indian states such as Tamil Nadu is because there is greater exposure to the mass media, a much

---

[19]Economists have also explained the theory of 'ideational change' in terms of the existence of multiple equilibria and the methods by which social norms may change in a society. For more on this, see Dasgupta, 2000.

[20]This is also suggested by Knodel and van de Walle, 1986; and also by Cotts Watkins, 1990: 241–72.

higher proportion of mothers who receive antenatal care with much better use of maternal and child-health services than in north India, and the percentage of girls aged 6–14 attending school is high.[21] However, the most interesting outlier among the south Indian states is Andhra Pradesh. This state has a very high proportion of females aged 6 years and over who are illiterate (62 per cent) with only 55 per cent of females aged 6–14 years attending school. However, Andhra Pradesh has managed to achieve a total fertility rate of 2.2 births per woman mainly because 62 per cent of its households receive electricity and 75 per cent of ever-married women are exposed to the mass media (Retherford and Ramesh, 1996). This example is particularly important because it is an exception to the argument that high levels of education are a necessary precondition for achieving replacement-level fertility and may provide some empirical support for the influence of 'ideational change' on fertility.[22]

Perhaps the 'ideal' model of fertility is then one which does not depend wholly, on the one hand, on diffusion of ideas and changes in aspirations or, on the other hand, on pure economic determinants, but on some combination of socio-economic influences and changes in attitudes towards birth control influenced by 'social interactions'—the influence of personal networks of small communities (Bongaarts and Watkins, 1996: 657; Lesthaeghe and Surkyn, 1988: 1–45). The most important feature of this model is that, as opposed to a dichotomy between socio-economic theories and ideational theories, such a model sees no conflict between both operating simultaneously, but sees an important orchestrating role for social interactions, as observed in the experience of the transition to replacement levels of fertility in parts of south India.

One of the major problems with ideational change is that it is hard to observe and measure. In the econometric analysis conducted later in this chapter, the age of the woman was used as a control variable in order to take into account the fact that some women who had been interviewed

---

[21]Retherford and Ramesh, 1996: 2. However, there are also socio-economic characteristics which distinguish Tamil Nadu from north Indian states such as Uttar Pradesh (UP). First, the percentage of females aged 6–14 years attending school in Tamil Nadu is 79 per cent compared with 48 per cent in UP; the percentage of females aged 6 years who are illiterate is 44 per cent in Tamil Nadu compared with 69 per cent for UP; the percentage of ever-married women who work outside their homes is much higher (47 per cent in Tamil Nadu compared with 13 per cent in UP); more households have electricity (64 per cent in Tamil Nadu compared with 32 per cent in UP); and many more ever-married women are regularly exposed to the electronic mass media in Tamil Nadu (78 per cent in Tamil Nadu compared with 35 per cent in UP).

[22]See also evidence from Bangladesh in Koenig et al., 1992: 352–64.

had not, as yet, completed their fertility. However, once all other socio-economic factors are controlled for, if fertility is observed to rise with a woman's age, this may also be a reflection of 'ideational change' in aspirations or norms concerning fertility over time.

CHILDREN EVER BORN IN RAMANAGARAM

In Chapter 3, trends in fertility and religious differences in fertility between Hindus, Muslims, and Christians were explored for all of India, Karnataka state, and Bangalore rural district. To what extent does the Ramanagaram sample also reveal demographic differences between religious groups? Table 8.11 presents data on the number of children ever born (CEB) for each religious group. This is the dependent variable used in the regression models presented in the next section of this chapter.

A majority of the women in the sample had either 2 or 3 children, although there were 15 who had between 7 and 9 children. The modal value for the Muslims, at 4 children, was much higher than that for the Hindus and the Christians, at 2 children. The means also appeared to

TABLE 8.11: CHILDREN EVER BORN, RAMANAGARAM SAMPLE (1996)

No.	All women		Hindus		Muslims		Christians	
	No.	%	No.	%	No.	%	No.	%
0	13	7.0	8	7.8	4	5.7	1	7.1
1	27	14.4	15	14.6	10	14.3	2	14.3
2	45	24.1	29	28.2	9	12.8	7	50.0
3	38	20.3	27	26.2	10	14.3	1	7.1
4	25	13.4	12	11.7	11	15.7	2	14.3
5	18	9.6	6	5.8	11	15.7	1	7.1
6	6	3.2	1	1.0	5	7.1	0	0.0
7	11	5.9	5	4.9	6	8.6	0	0.0
8	2	1.1	0	0.0	2	2.9	0	0.0
9	2	1.1	0	0.0	2	2.9	0	0.0
10	0	0.0	0	0.0	0	0.0	0	0.0
More than 10	0	0.0	0	0.0	0	0.0	0	0.0
Total	187	100.0	103	100.0	70	100.0	14	100.0
Mean	3.04		2.66		3.73		2.29	
Median	3.00		2.50		4.00		2.00	
Mode	2.00		2.00		4.00		2.00	
Maximum	9.00		7.00		9.00		5.0	
Minimum	0.00		0.00		0.00		0.00	

differ greatly, with Muslim women having 1.07 children more on average than the Hindus and 1.41 more on average than the Christians. While the difference between Hindus and Christians was not found to be significant at the 95 per cent level, the differences in means between Hindus and Muslims and between Muslims and Christians were statistically significant. In the Ramanagaram sample, the Muslims have higher fertility than the Hindus and the Christians, and this difference is nearly one child on average.

These findings on number of children ever born essentially raise the following questions. First, what is the impact of religion on differences in the number of children ever born, once other factors are controlled for? Is a certain number of children desired for their own sake, for religious reasons, or for other considerations such as family obligations or economic benefits accruing from children? Finally, how do other factors, such as the age of the woman, which may reflect the diffusion of ideas and changes in aspirations, affect the number of children ever born?

AN ECONOMETRIC MODEL OF THE DETERMINANTS OF FERTILITY

Of all the factors discussed in the introductory section, those which emerged as appropriate for inclusion in a model of the nonproximate determinants of fertility for the women in the Ramanagaram sample were the following: the education of the woman; the education of her husband; income; the occupation of the woman; the occupation of her husband; marital consanguinity; the presence of extended family in the household; the desire for a son; provisions of water and fuel infrastructure; differences in religion and caste; and the age of the woman. These factors were chosen on a number of grounds. First, information on all of them could be obtained by means of intensive questioning of the women of Ramanagaram. Second, they are all factors which are not endogenously determined with fertility itself.[23] It is for this reason that the proximate determinants of fertility are not included here as explanatory variables. In all models estimated, the dependent variable was female fertility, measured as the total number of children ever born to the woman.

The analysis was conducted as follows. First, fourteen preliminary

[23]It is recognized that one can resolve the endogeneity of the proximate determinants issue by using simultaneous equations models to estimate fertility. However, given the range of nonproximate factors on which data was obtained, and the small size of the sample, OLS methods using the nonproximate determinants were regarded as preferable.

models (not reported here) were estimated which experimented with different measures of certain variables, in order to determine the 'best' specification of the model. Then, using this 'best' specification, an F-test was performed in order to find out whether the effect of the socio-economic and other determinants of fertility differed significantly for the sub-samples of the Hindus and the Muslims compared with the 'pooled' model of Hindus and Muslims together. Finally, interaction terms between the explanatory variables and the Hindu and Muslim religion dummies were introduced into the general model in order to estimate a final model of fertility, incorporating slope effects as well as shift effects.

Of all the preliminary models estimated, the model which emerged as the 'best' model, showed that the factors which affected fertility were female university education, husband's primary and secondary education, the position of first-born sons in the birth order, the Muslim dummy variable, the Hindu dummy variable, whether or not the woman's husband was employed in domestic industry, the woman's age, and the number of female extended family members resident in the household.

The model had several interesting features. First, though husband's primary and secondary education were significant, the signs on the two coefficients were opposite. An additional year of primary education for the husband increased fertility by 0.15 children, while an additional year of secondary education decreased fertility by 0.23 children. Both the Hindu and Muslim dummies were significant and positive, indicating that both Hindus and Muslims had, on average, more children than the Christians, who form the base category. If a woman was Muslim she had 1.31 children more, on average, than if she was Christian. If a woman was Hindu, she had 0.95 children more, on average, than if she was Christian. However, a Wald test showed that the effect on fertility of being Hindu was not significantly different to the effect of being Muslim. The position of sons in the birth order was also highly significant: controlling for other factors, if a woman had a son who was one position later in the birth order she had 0.47 more children on average. If the husband was employed in domestic industry, he had 0.86 fewer children than if he was employed in other occupations. This model also highlighted a possible 'ideational' influence in that a woman's age had a significant positive influence on her fertility (although this may simply result from her having had a larger fertile lifespan in which to have children). The model explained 57 per cent of the variation in children ever born.

The next step in the analysis was to estimate the preliminary model on sub-samples of Hindus and Muslims, and to compare these regressions with a 'pooled' model estimated for Hindus and Muslims combined. This was done by using an F-test. The sub-sample regressions on Hindus and Muslims are reported in Tables 8.12 and 8.13, and the pooled model for Hindus and Muslims in Table 8.14.

TABLE 8.12: OLS ESTIMATES OF THE DETERMINANTS OF CHILDREN EVER BORN, HINDUS ONLY (RAMANAGARAM, 1996)

Regressor	Coefficient	Standard Error	T Ratio [Prob.]
Constant (CONST)	–0.473	0.514	– 0.920 [0.360]
Woman's education			
Secondary education of woman (SEDU)	–0.107	0.068	–1.570 [0.120]
University education of woman (UEDU)	–0.085	0.131	–0.648 [0.519]
Husband's education			
Primary education of husband (PEDUSP)	0.076	0.084	0.905 [0.368]
Secondary education of husband (SEDUSP)	–0.086	0.086	–1.007 [0.317]
Husband's occupation			
Husband employed in domestic industry (DOMINDU)	–0.726	0.269	–2.697 [0.008][c]
Son-preference			
Position of first-born son in the birth order (SONPRF)	0.484	0.132	3.656 [0.000][c]
Female extended family			
Number of female extended family (FEXFAM)	–0.002	0.079	–0.022 [0.982]
Woman's age			
Woman's age (AGE)	0.090	0.013	7.008 [0.000][c]
Fuel infrastructure			
Household uses gas/kerosene for fuel (GASKERO)	–0.044	0.355	–0.123 [0.902]
$\bar{R}^2$	0.594		
Residual sum of squares	110.930		

Notes: Dependent variable is CEB: the total number of children ever born to the woman. Sample consists of 103 ever-married Hindu women.
[a]indicates significance at 0.10 level, [b]indicates significance at 0.05 level and [c]indicates significance at 0.01 level.

TABLE 8.13: OLS ESTIMATES OF THE DETERMINANTS OF CHILDREN EVER BORN,
MUSLIMS ONLY (RAMANAGARAM, 1996)

Regressor	Coefficient	Standard Error	T Ratio [Prob.]
Constant (CONST)	−0.206	0.747	−0.275 [0.784]
Woman's education			
Secondary education of woman (SEDU)	−0.042	0.090	−0.462 [0.645]
University education of woman (UEDU)	−0.421	0.182	−2.313 [0.024][b]
Husband's education			
Primary education of husband (PEDUSP)	0.315	0.097	3.247 [0.002][c]
Secondary education of husband (SEDUSP)	−0.259	0.095	−2.725 [0.008][c]
Husband's occupation			
Husband employed in domestic industry (DOMINDU)	−1.208	0.479	−2.525 [0.014][b]
Son-preference			
Position of first-born son in the birth order (SONPRF)	0.275	0.151	1.826 [0.073][a]
Female extended family			
Number of female extended family (FEXFAM)	−0.721	0.160	−4.495 [0.000][c]
Woman's age			
Woman's age (AGE)	0.098	0.016	−4.495 [0.000][c]
Fuel infrastructure			
Household uses gas/kerosene for fuel (GASKERO)	−0.789	0.445	−1.772 [0.081][a]
$\bar{R}^2$	0.656		
Residual sum of squares	125.754		

Notes: Dependent variable is CEB: the total number of children ever born to the woman.
Sample consists of 70 ever-married Muslim women.
[a]indicates significance at 0.10 level, [b]indicates significance at 0.05 level and [c]indicates significance at 0.01 level.

TABLE 8.14: OLS ESTIMATES OF THE DETERMINANTS OF CHILDREN EVER BORN, POOLED MODEL OF HINDUS AND MUSLIMS (RAMANAGARAM, 1996)

Regressor	Coefficient	Standard Error	T Ratio [Prob.]
Intercepts			
Hindu religion dummy (HINDU)	–0.197	0.380	–0.519 [0.604]
Muslim religion dummy (MUSLIM)	0.094	0.439	0.215 [0.830]
Woman's education			
Secondary education of woman (SEDU)	–0.048	0.056	–0.866 [0.388]
University education of woman (UEDU)	–0.228	0.114	–2.008 [0.046][b]
Husband's education			
Primary education of husband (PEDUSP)	0.171	0.063	2.704 [0.008][c]
Secondary education of husband (SEDUSP)	–0.195	0.064	–3.050 [0.003][c]
Husband's occupation			
Husband is employed in domestic industry (DOMINDU)	–1.037	0.250	–4.146 [0.000][c]
Son-preference			
Position of first-born son in the birth order (SONPRF)	0.394	0.010	3.956 [0.000][c]
Female extended family			
Number of female extended family (FEXFAM)	–0.220	0.077	–2.857 [0.005][c]
Woman's age			
Woman's age (AGE)	0.090	0.010	9.467 [0.000][c]
Fuel infrastructure			
Household uses gas/kerosene for fuel (GASKERO)	–0.351	0.287	–1.222 [0.224]
$\bar{R}^2$	0.592		
Residual sum of squares	279.971		

Notes: Dependent variable is CEB: the total number of children ever born to the woman. Sample consists of 173 ever-married Hindu and Muslim women.
[a]indicates significance at 0.10 level, [b]indicates significance at 0.05 level and [c]indicates significance at 0.01 level.

The F-test rejects the null hypothesis that the coefficients on the explanatory variables are equal for Hindus and Muslims.[24] This established that at least one socio-economic factor affects the number of children ever born differently for Hindus than it does for Muslims. It, therefore, seemed justified to go on to examine in detail the manner in which the various socio-economic factors exercise their influence on the fertility of Muslims, Hindus, and Christians in Ramanagaram.

This was done by introducing interaction factors (multiplicative dummy variables) into the fertility model. All the explanatory variables were interacted with the Hindu and Muslims religion dummies. The model which resulted from this estimation is reported in Table 8.15.

The first significant variable was women's university education. Higher education is postulated as influencing fertility for several reasons: it may increase the opportunity costs of women's time; it may bring into operation the 'quantity-quality' trade-off; university education encourages women to study later into their fertile lifespan which may directly delay marriage and childbearing; it may make women more effective users of family planning methods; and it may inculcate values incompatible with high fertility. University education was significant at the 0.01 level for Muslims, but not at all significant for Hindus and Christians. Neither secondary nor primary education was significant for any religious group. According to the model, a one-year increase in university education decreased Muslim women's fertility by 0.40 children. A Wald test showed that the effect of university education on fertility was significantly different for Muslims than for Hindus. Wald tests also showed that while the effect of university education on fertility for Christians was similar to that for Hindus, the effect of university education on fertility differed between Christians and Muslims.

---

[24]The null hypothesis was that the coefficients on all the explanatory variables for Hindus were equal to the coefficients on all the explanatory variables for Muslims. As in Chapter 6, the F-test is defined as:

$$F\left(k, n-2k\right) = \frac{\text{RSS}^{\text{Restricted}} - \text{RSS}^{\text{Unrestricted}} / k}{\text{RSS}^{\text{Unrestricted}} / n - 2k}$$

where:

$$F = \frac{279.9714 - 236.6835 / 12}{236.6835 / 173 - 20} = 2.332$$

As the critical value of $F(12, 153)$ is 1.83, and the calculated $F = 2.332 > 1.83$, the F-test rejects the null hypothesis.

TABLE 8.15: OLS ESTIMATES OF THE DETERMINANTS OF CHILDREN EVER BORN, ALL RELIGIONS (RAMANAGARAM, 1996)

Regressor	Coefficient		Standard Error	T Ratio [Prob.]
Intercepts				
Constant (CONST)	0.999		1.023	0.975 [0.331]
Muslim religion dummy (MUSLIM)	−0.798		1.128	−0.707 [0.481]
Hindu religion dummy (HINDU)	−1.762		1.122	−1.570 [0.118]
Woman's education				
University education of woman (UEDU)	−0.002		0.039	−0.047 [0.962]
University education of Muslim woman (MUEDU)	−0.402	c	0.084	−4.763 [0.000]
University education of Hindu woman (HUEDU)	−0.109		0.104	−1.049 [0.296]
Husband's education				
Husband's primary education (PEDUSP)	−0.161		0.168	−0.957 [0.340]
Primary education of Muslim husband (MPEDUSP)	0.488	b	0.198	2.467 [0.015]
Primary education of Hindu husband (HPEDUSP)	0.264		0.185	1.429 [0.155]
Husband's secondary education (SEDUSP)	−0.003		0.084	−0.034 [0.973]
Secondary education of Muslim husband (MSEDUSP)	−0.285	c	0.108	−2.638 [0.009]
Secondary education of Hindu husband (HSEDUSP)	−0.150		0.104	−1.439 [0.152]
Husband occupation				
Husband employed in domestic industry (DOMIND)	−0.781		0.479	−1.631 [0.105]
Muslim husband employed in domestic industry (MDOMIND)	−0.310		0.693	−0.447 [0.655]
Hindu husband employed in domestic industry (HDOMIND)	0.121		0.559	0.217 [0.828]

Regressor	Coefficient		Standard Error	T Ratio [Prob.]
Son-preference				
Position of first-born son in the birth order (SONPRF)	1.130	c	0.156	7.254 [0.000]
Position of first-born son for Muslims (MSONPRF)	−0.809	c	0.213	−3.795 [0.000]
Position of first-born son for Hindus (HSONPRF)	−0.590	c	0.204	−2.892 [0.004]
Fuel infrastructure				
Household uses gas/kerosene (GASKERO)	0.086		0.326	0.264 [0.792]
Muslim household uses gas/kerosene (MGASKERO)	−0.746	a	0.422	−1.767 [0.079]
Hindu household uses gas/kerosene (HGASKERO)	−0.307		0.443	−0.694 [0.489]
Female extended family				
Female extended family resident (FEXFAM)	−0.014		0.087	−0.165 [0.869]
Muslim female extended family resident (MFEXFAM)	−0.677	c	0.149	−4.560 [0.000]
Hindu female extended family resident (HFEXFAM)	−		−	−
Woman's age				
Woman's age (AGE)	0.013		0.025	0.521 [0.603]
Muslim woman's age (MAGE)	0.085	c	0.029	2.949 [0.004]
Hindus woman's age (HAGE)	0.082	c	0.029	2.840 [0.005]
$\bar{R}^2$	0.606			

Notes: Dependent variable is CEB: the total number of children ever born to the woman. Sample: 187 ever-married Hindu, Muslim and Christian women. Base category: Christians.
[a]indicates significance at 0.10 level, [b]indicates significance at 0.05 level and [c]indicates significance at 0.01 level.

The next significant variable was husband's primary education. If a Muslim man had an additional year of primary education, this increased his wife's fertility by 0.33 children. Husband's primary education was not significant for Hindus and Christians. A Wald test showed that there is no significant difference in the effect of husband's education on the fertility of Muslims and Hindus. Wald tests also showed that while the effect of husband's primary education on children ever born for Christians is similar to its effect for Hindus, the effect of husband's primary education on fertility differed between Christians and Muslims.

Husband's secondary education decreased fertility significantly for Muslims, but had no effect for Hindus and Christians. This may be because Muslim men who have attended secondary school prefer wives who are more educated, or they too prefer better 'quality' children to a higher 'quantity'. Wald tests showed that the effect of husband's secondary education on Hindu fertility was not significantly different from its effect on Muslim fertility; nor was it significantly different on Christian fertility compared to its effect on Hindu fertility. A Wald test showed that the effect of husband's secondary education on fertility differed significantly between Christians and Muslims.

The next significant variable was whether the husband was employed in domestic industry. Hypothesis-testing with this variable showed that its effect on fertility was not significantly different between the three religious groups.

Son-preference, measured through the position of the first-born son in the birth order, was significant for Hindus, Muslims, and Christians at the 0.05 per cent significance level, implying that son-preference may be captured in a 'pure demographic accident' variable affecting fertility. If a Hindu woman had a son who was one place later in the birth order, this raised her fertility by 0.32 children; if a Muslim woman had a son who was one place later in the birth order, this raised her fertility by 0.54 children; and if she was Christian, this raised her fertility by 1.13 children. A Wald test showed that son-preference had similar effects on Hindu and Muslim fertility. Analogous tests established that the position of the first-born son affected fertility among Christians significantly differently to its effect among Hindus and Muslims.

The next variable to affect fertility was the woman's age, which was significant for both Hindus and Muslims at the 0.01 level, but not significant for the Christians. A Wald test accepted the restriction that the effect of woman's age on children ever born was not significantly different for Hindus than for Muslims. Analogous tests established that the effect of woman's age on fertility was significantly different for Christians to its effect for either Hindus or Muslims.

The next variable to affect fertility was the presence in the household of resident female extended family. As argued earlier, one reason why this variable is used is that it is highly correlated with total household size and is used as a proxy for it.[25] This variable had no significant influence on the fertility of Hindus and Christians, but if a Muslim woman had one additional female family member, this decreased her fertility by 0.69 children, an effect significant at the 0.01 level. Though this finding may appear counter-intuitive, given that female extended family members are postulated as reducing the time-costs to parents of having children by taking over some of the child care responsibilities, this suggests perhaps the influence of other women encouraging family planning (as we saw in the qualitative evidence in Chapter 7). Alternatively, it may reflect greater monitoring of couples' observance of abstinence norms in households containing extended family members. Moreover, extended family members may substitute for children either spatially or as productive members of the family labour force. A Wald test showed that the effect of female extended family on the fertility of Muslim households was significantly different from their effect on the fertility of Hindu and Christian households.[26]

The next variable influencing fertility was the availability of fuel infrastructure. This variable was not significant for Hindus and Christians, but a Muslim household had 0.66 fewer children if it used gas or kerosene rather than firewood as a primary source for fuel. A Wald test showed that the effect of using gas or kerosene for fuel on fertility was not significantly different for Hindus and Muslims. Analogous tests established that the effect of using gas or kerosene as a primary source of fuel does not have significantly different effects on fertility between Christians and Hindus, and between Christians and Muslims.

Finally, we must consider the intercept terms. None of the intercept terms were significant. Moreover, Wald tests showed that religious affiliation alone does not exert a separate effect on the fertility of the three religious groups.[27]

[25]It may be recollected that this was done in order to facilitate interpretation of the coefficient on the total-expenditure variable, that is, it was necessary to control for the fact that some families had higher expenditure not because they were richer, but because they had more members living in the household. As total household size could not be used in the model because it is endogenously determined with total fertility, the female-extended-family variable was used instead, because it was highly correlated with total household size.

[26]It may be recollected that HFEXFAM could not be included in this model due to perfect collinearity with the other regressors. Hence, it is not possible to test the equality of MFEXFAM = HFEXFAM separately.

[27]Three hypotheses were tested: first, whether the coefficient on CONST equals the

The findings from the interaction model support the conclusion that differences in fertility among religious groups are not due to religion alone. Rather, the causes of religious differentials in fertility in India are to be found more in the background socio-economic characteristics of members of different religious groups, and in their patterns of response to changes in these characteristics, than in religion by itself.

CONCLUSIONS AND IMPLICATIONS FOR POLICY

For many decades now, in both theoretical models and empirical studies, economists, demographers, and anthropologists have been concerned with explaining fertility trends in India. For the most part, these empirical analyses of fertility have taken the form either of large sample surveys or of micro-demographic investigations in localized areas. This chapter has adopted the second approach. It has attempted to assess the influence of the nonproximate developmental factors that affect fertility, using a sample of 201 households from Ramanagaram taluk in Karnataka in south India from which information was collected on a very wide variety of variables. What light do the findings from the Ramanagaram sample shed on the various economic, social, and religious factors which have been hypothesized to influence fertility theoretically in India and elsewhere?

Let us turn our attention first to the factors which did not turn out to be significant predictors of fertility. The first factor considered is the occupation of the woman. In this study, woman's occupation was measured in three ways: whether or not the woman had a primary occupation, whether or not the woman had a skilled occupation, and whether or not the woman had a silk-related occupation. If a woman performs a silk-related occupation, her fertility may be higher because many of the silk-related processes (such as silkworm rearing, cocoon-boiling, and silk-reeling) required a continuous supply of child labour. Thus, if a woman was in a silk-related occupation, she may have had higher fertility because of the increased demand for child labour. However, even this measure of women's occupation was not significant either for Hindus, Muslims, or Christians.

One of the reasons why none of the measures of women's occupation were significant predictors of fertility may be because of the nature of

coefficient on CONST+MUSLIM; second, whether the coefficient on CONST equals the coefficient on CONST+HINDU; and third, whether the coefficient on MUSLIM equals the coefficient on HINDU. All three hypotheses were accepted.

work in the silk industry: the available work for women in Ramanagaram is still too compatible with child rearing, and in this respect varies too little across women, to exert any effect on their fertility decisions. Moreover, this characteristic of women's occupations is likely to be similar to that found in other parts of rural India.

Income is a second factor often hypothesized to affect fertility. The argument usually goes that as income rises, initially it increases fertility and then later reduces it. In the present study, income was measured in three different ways: as total expenditure, as total foodgrains expenditure, and through an index of the ownership of items of consumer equipment. In no model was any of the income measures a significant determinant of fertility. This suggests either that income does not exercise an impact on fertility, or that a pure 'income effect' on fertility is completely outweighed by various other 'substitution effects' in our models. This finding is surprising in the light of other fertility studies, and given the wide range of variation in income in the Ramanagaram sample.

The next factor that was found to exert no influence on fertility was marital consanguinity. Theoretically, it has been postulated that fertility should be higher in consanguineous marriages than in marriages where partners are unrelated, mainly because of the large age differences between spouses in consanguineous unions. On the other hand, consanguineous marriages may lead to lower fertility because of greater female autonomy arising from the fact that wives stay near their families of origin. In the present study, consanguinity was measured using a dummy variable and the coefficient of inbreeding. The theoretical expectation of higher fertility in consanguineous unions was not confirmed in the interaction model.

The next factor which was not significant related to some measures of husband's occupation. Some occupations for men are supposed to increase a couple's fertility (farming, domestic industry), others to decrease it (skilled occupations). In the models presented here, neither skilled nor farming occupations for husbands significantly affected fertility. The fact that the farming-occupation variable was insignificant implies that fertility was not affected specifically by an increased demand for child labour in agriculture, probably because many occupations in cottage or small-scale industry in Ramanagaram also used child labour. The insignificance of the skilled-occupation variable may be because this variable is highly correlated with men's secondary education, which (as we shall see later) exerted a negative effect on fertility. Husband's employment in domestic industry does affect fertility overall, and in a negative direction, but it is difficult econometrically to isolate its effect on fertility for individual religious groups. Hypothesis-testing showed that the effect of domestic industry on fertility was not significantly different between Hindus, Muslims, and Christians.

Let us now turn our attention to those factors which emerged as significant determinants of fertility. The first factor is the education of the woman. Theoretically, this variable is hypothesized to lower fertility because it may delay marriage, because women acquire better knowledge of contraception, and because women with education have healthier babies with lower child mortality. Education is also very important from the perspective of population policy because recent studies have argued that in other developing countries, such as in Kenya, the apparent success of the country's population policy can be largely attributed to the success of its education policy in increasing primary and secondary school enrolment, particularly for girls (Ajayi and Kekovole, 1998: 113–56). However, girls' schooling can only lead to lower fertility when class, community, and gender politics are changed in order to make female empowerment possible. Education alone may not lead to decreased fertility, unless the structural contexts in which women find themselves are also taken into account (Jeffery and Jeffery, 1997: 255–56).

The relationship between more education and lower fertility is particularly supposed to hold for secondary and university education. In the models presented here, female university education emerged as one of the most important variables influencing fertility, at least for Muslim women. Its importance suggests that in Ramanagaram, education affects women's abilities to make decisions about fertility only at higher educational levels. It may be that higher education significantly influences women's status in the household, by enabling them to make independent decisions, such as decisions about contraception. Higher education may also be increasing the opportunity costs of women's time, and motivating and enabling mothers to produce fewer but better 'quality' children, because each child is now more costly to raise. Or it may be the case that the aspirations and values which education can convey, which are incompatible with high fertility, are only transmitted in high school and university.

While university education decreased the fertility of Muslims, it had no significant effect on the fertility of the Hindus and the Christians. Moreover, there was a difference in the effect of husband's university education on Muslim fertility compared to Hindu fertility; and also between Muslim fertility and Christian fertility. One reason why Muslims in Ramanagaram may be so much more susceptible to university education than the Hindus and the Christians may be that Muslim women were the least likely of all the three religious groups to go on to university.

Hence, at the margin, an additional year of university education may affect them more. Another reason may be that there was only one Arts College in the town which women of all religions attended. However, at the level of school, while Muslim girls mainly attended the Urdu schools, Christian and Hindu girls attended the Anganwadi and other primary state schools, where information about family planning, at least at the secondary school level, was regularly imparted. Hence, perhaps Muslim girls were more affected by an additional year of university education because the interaction with women of all religions at university had a larger impact on their own views about fertility and small family norms. It should also be remarked that no measure of women's education appears to affect the fertility of Hindus and Christians, which is a very surprising finding, especially given the importance of this variable in so many studies of fertility in other societies. One possible reason for this is, given that women's education and husband's education are highly correlated, for Hindus and Christians husband's secondary education is picking up the effect of education on fertility (as discussed further on).

Husband's education is also postulated to influence fertility, either in a negative or in a positive direction, depending upon the level of the income of the husband, and the relative difference between husband's income and wife's income. If the husband has greater education, this is hypothesized to increase the opportunity cost of women's time, resulting in the desire for fewer, but better-'quality' children. On the other hand, if a husband who is highly educated prefers a wife who is also highly educated or has a skilled job, then this would reduce fertility. An alternative view is that husband's education increases fertility if the husband is educated and employed and believes that he can afford to support a wife and family. This may then give rise to higher fertility by lowering both women and men's age at marriage.

In the models estimated for Ramanagaram, husband's primary education exercised a significant positive influence on fertility only for Muslims. This variable was not significant for Hindus and Christians. However, Wald tests established that the effect of husband's primary education was not significantly different for Muslims compared with Hindus, even though it was significantly different from its effect for the Christians. The fact that for Muslims, husband's primary education exercises a *positive* role on fertility implies that at least for this religious community, a few years of education alone do not reduce men's demand for children, nor does it necessarily mean that Muslim men marry 'likes' in the marriage market. Nor, perhaps, does education influence Muslim men's ideas about using contraception. A few years of education do not also make Muslim men want to favour child-quality over child-quantity. However, if a Muslim man is educated beyond this level (as explored further on), his education does exercise the expected negative effect on fertility, as it does for Hindu and Christian men likewise.

For all three religions, husband's secondary education exercised a significant and negative influence on fertility. This suggests that an increase in husband's secondary education may be increasing the opportunity costs of both parents' time, resulting in fewer, but better-quality children, or that educated husbands marry 'likes' and that, therefore, both husband and wife hold low-fertility norms. Further, while husband's secondary education does affect fertility, it affects it significantly more for Muslims than for Christians. Perhaps one reason for this finding is that Christian women in Ramanagaram had greater autonomy than Muslim women. Hence, the influence of Christian men on couples' decisions is not as great as in Muslim households, where the men's decisons about fertility may be very important and even override those of the women. This difference in autonomy may well be what is being expressed in the greater significance of the husband's-secondary-education variable for Muslim households.

The next factor we consider is the position of the first-born son in the birth order. This variable in essence measured whether a pure demographic 'accident'—how long it took to have a son—could have an impact on total fertility. This factor was very significant and positive for all three religious groups. We can conclude, therefore, that how soon the couple succeeds in having a son strongly influences total children ever born in Ramanagaram, after controlling for the influence of other possible determinants. This is consistent with other evidence, both from the Ramanagaram questionnaire and from India more generally, that parents expect to derive considerable benefits from sons in the form of old age care, and possibly also in the form of contributions to family income earlier in life. Even though the position of the son in the birth order was significant for all three religious groups, this effect was different between Hindus and Christians and between Muslims and Christians, though not between Hindus and Muslims. The difference was expressed mainly in the value of the coefficient on the son-preference variable, which was much higher for Christians than for Muslims and Hindus. Though it is not possible to make generalizations because the sample size of Christians is small, greater son-preference among the Christians may be because the Christian community in Ramanagaram are originally migrants from Tamil Nadu, and their minority status in Karnataka relative to both Hindus and Muslims (since they make up only 2 per cent of the population in the taluk) may make them depend more on sons for insurance cover.

The next significant variable was the presence of extended family members in the household. This variable was used for two reasons. First, it was used as a proxy for total household size with which it is highly correlated. This was done so as to control for those households which had higher total expenditure not because they are richer, but because they have more members. Second, it is often hypothesized that the presence of extended family significantly reduces the costs of child rearing for parents, increasing fertility because parents only bear a portion of the costs of childbearing. Alternatively, extended family may reduce fertility if there is a lack of privacy, and if traditional taboos on sexual intercourse are observed at certain times due to strict monitoring by the extended family.

What was particularly interesting about this variable in the interaction model was that (counter to theory) it had a negative coefficient, at least for Muslims. That is, if a Muslim household had an extra female family member, this reduced the number of children ever born. This counters the existing theories about the effects of the extended family system increasing fertility. Instead, among Ramanagaram Muslims resident family seems to reduce fertility. There are several possible reasons for this. First, the presence of extended family may lead to residential crowding, reducing living space for new offspring. Second, the direction of causation may in fact be the opposite: exogenous reproductive problems may have resulted in reduced fertility, creating more living space and labour demand, thereby encouraging co-resident extended family. Third, the presence of the extended family may result in surveillance of the couple's sex lives, particularly in the case of post-partum taboos leading to reduced fertility. Fourth, exogenous availability of extended family may have increased household labour supply, substituting for children and contributing to lower fertility. Fifth, it may be that because the concept of a child-centred nuclear family is replacing the notion of the extended family, this results in lower fertility. Finally, female extended family may be directly encouraging lower fertility through the mechanism discussed in Chapter 7 where qualitative information from the Ramanagaram interviews showed that women consulted with female extended family members on issues which related to contraception, and mothers-in-law positively encouraged daughters-in-law to have sterilization operations after a certain number of children had been born. Examining differences by religion, the effect of female extended family for Muslim households was significantly different from the effects on Hindu and Christian households, for whom this variable was not significant. Perhaps one reason why female extended family resident was more important for Muslim households was because of purdah restrictions, which limited Muslim women's mobility, resulting in their greater dependence on extended family and consequently, greater monitoring of Muslim women's fertility behaviour.

The age of the woman was included in the model for two reasons. The first was that it acted as a control variable, because many younger women may not have completed their fertility at the time of survey. Second, it acted as a measure of 'ideational change' over time, based on the hypothesis that the social equilibrium with regard to fertility depends on 'strategic complementarities' in decision-making by individuals, and the history of the social system. The effect of woman's age on fertility was very significant. Although this was probably because the older women in the sample had had more time to have more children, it may also be reflecting the same set of influences we observed with the negative relationship between woman's age and her age at marriage, that is, of changes over time in norms and ideas about fertility. Examining differences by religion, this variable was significant for Hindus and Muslims, but not for Christians; the size of the effect did not differ significantly between Hindus and Muslims. Perhaps one reason why this variable did not affect the Christians as much as the Hindus and Muslims was because older Christian women in Ramanagaram have greater autonomy and have experienced a change in norms with respect to lower fertility within their community earlier than women of the other two religious groups, whether through the influence of radio and television or through the influence of the meetings on women's issues which took place at their local church on Sundays.

The next factor we consider is water and fuel infrastructure. It has been hypothesized that a major reason for rural households to have many children is to help with collecting water and fuel. In the interaction model, if the household used gas or kerosene for fuel, this had a significant and negative effect on fertility, although only for Muslim households. One reason for this finding may be that Muslim households did not use daughters at all for collecting fuel because of purdah restrictions, but did use sons. This may have increased the demand for sons, and hence fertility, for those Muslim households which were dependent on firewood for fuel, and consequently decreased fertility for those Muslim households which used alternative sources of fuel such as gas or kerosene. However, the fact that this variable was significant for one religious group only, and that Wald tests showed this result not to be significantly different between religions, casts some doubt on its importance. One explanation may be that parents are simultaneously making decisions about a number of matters, such as the number of children to have and/or whether to use firewood or kerosene for fuel, and in these models we only observe the outcome. Another possible explanation is that access to piped water or gas may be highly correlated with other regressors such as educational status, occupations of both men and women, and income, and these regressors may be picking up the effect of some of the infrastructure variables.

Finally, we consider whether the religion of the respondent affects fertility independently of any differences in socio-economic character-istics across religious groups. Theoretically, adherence to some set of religious beliefs is hypothesized to affect fertility either directly (in terms of its normative precepts) or indirectly (in terms of other characteristics associated with it). In Chapter 3, we explored the theories postulating an impact of religion on fertility in considerable detail. In the analysis of fertility in Ramanagaram, religion was measured in terms of Hindu and Muslim dummy variables and an index of piety. In the interaction model the effect of religion on fertility is *not* significantly different between Hindus, Muslims, and Christians, as evidenced in the acceptance of the hypotheses that the intercept terms for the three religious groups were not significantly different from each other. The demographic differences between religious groups in Ramanagaram are expressed more in terms of significant differences in the effects of various socio-economic factors which influence fertility in this society, not in religious affiliation by itself.

In summary, what can we say about Hindu–Muslim fertility in Ramanagaram? Both Hindus and Muslims have high fertility when com-pared with the Christians. The difference however of one child in the mean level of fertility between Hindus and Muslims disappears once we have controlled for the influence of other socio-economic factors. The results from the interaction model suggest that rather than religion, demographic divergence was actually related to other socio-economic characteristics such as education, age, infrastructure, son-preference, female extended family, and differences in how members of different religions respond demographically to these socio-economic influences. This finding is consistent with the more general theoretical observation made in Chapter 3 that there is little theological difference between Hinduism and Islam with regard to matters relating to demographic behaviour, except in their positions on birth control. These findings are also consistent with the analyses of age at marriage and contraceptive use presented in Chapters 6 and 7, which also found that religion does not exert a pure 'theological' impact after controlling for other socio-economic factors, at least between Hindus and Muslims.

However, this conclusion may have to be qualified by taking into account that the Muslim community in Ramanagaram *taluk* is economically richer and more urbanized than Muslim communities elsewhere in India. This might explain the closeness of Hindu and Muslim demographic characteristics in this region. This caveat however does lend strong support to the more general issue raised by the present study, namely that as socio-economic factors are targeted more strongly, fertility among religious groups in India will tend to converge.

This has obvious implications for population policy at the state and taluk levels. In post-Independence India, Karnataka is one of the four states in the south which are collectively considered to have performed well on demographic indicators, as compared with national trends and in comparison with other states in north India. However, what this analysis has shown is that even if state averages are considered good, there are still likely to be significant demographic differences between groups within states. Such differences require further research and may be important in formulating government policy.

The main policy implications of these findings are as follows. First, it is important to target religious leaders because of the influence they wield. These leaders would be particularly important in influencing opinion about the timing of marriage and in encouraging information and communication about health services. Second, it is important to target ideas about religion and to clarify the theological position of religion on the family. Third, since community has a profound influence on fertility, it is necessary to involve communities collectively, for example, by community education initiatives that provide information about religion or other aspects of social life that may influence demographic behaviour. Finally, it is important to target the socio-economic factors that affect population and development more widely. For lowering fertility, these socio-economic factors include targeting women's education, husband's education, ideas about (and the economic pressures underlying) son-preference, the provision of infrastructure, influence of female extended family, and changes in social norms. However, the findings from Ramanagaram also support the more important policy conclusion that it might be important to target different religious groups in different ways. The policy measures which would specifically affect Hindu and Christian fertility are those which relate to changing perceptions about the importance of sons as a means of insurance cover, and using the media to further influence changes in social norms about fertility. For Muslims, possible policy measures include increased state support for education for both Muslim women and their husbands; encouraging the influence of female extended family who appear to have a positive effect on Muslim women's fertility; and finally, public provision of gas or kerosene oil as alternatives to firewood collection.

What would the individual women of Ramanagaram have to say about attempts to reduce their fertility? We conclude this chapter by returning to their views. At the end of the questionnaire, the 201 women were asked to reflect on what they felt about the growth of population in the towns and villages of Ramanagaram *taluk*. Their responses to this question are presented in Table 8.16.

The Ramanagaram women appeared overwhelmingly to believe that the population in their town and villages was growing too fast. Of the women in the sample, 86 per cent believed that population growth was too fast, and the percentage was high among all religions—at 81 per cent of Hindus, 89 per cent of Muslims, and 100 per cent of Christians. This may suggest that attempts to formulate government policy to reduce fertility will have active support at the grass-roots level. However, the other findings of the study show that individual fertility is still quite high, and that this is because of socio-economic factors which will need to change before the collective demographic aspirations of these Indian women can be realized. It is only by recognizing that socio-economic factors influence different religious groups in different ways that we may be able to devise policy measures which can address the patterns of demographic response found in Ramanagaram and elsewhere in India.

TABLE 8.16: REACTIONS TO THE GROWTH OF POPULATION IN THE TOWN/VILLAGE, RAMANAGARAM SAMPLE (1996)

Response	All women		Hindus		Muslims		Christians	
	No.	%	No.	%	No.	%	No.	%
Growing too fast	172	85.5	90	81.1	67	89.3	15	100.0
Growth is about right	11	5.5	9	8.1	2	2.6	0	0.0
Don't know	18	8.9	12	10.8	6	8.3	0	0.0
Total	201	100.0	111	100.0	75	100.0	15	100.0

chapter nine

Conclusion
Religion and a Reorientation

You are a small girl, not yet five and I wonder in what kind of
India you will grow up and in what kind of India you will serve.
... You were hardly two years when you had a little sister. I was
immensely pleased that it was also a girl. I know girls are not
wanted—especially in our custom-ridden and conservative
country, but I feel that it is only women who can make the world
a happy place. ... Once you decide to fortify yourself with
knowledge and offer your services to help humanity, nothing
can come in your path. I know you may marry, but remember
this, that once you decide to marry, you must not forget your
country ... and our suffering fellow-beings.[1]

S hakuntala's vision for her daughter in 1946 seems as relevant to
Indian women today as it was over half a century ago. In keeping
with that vision, the present study was motivated by the desire to
serve the concerns of a small community of Hindu, Muslim, and Christian
women in the taluk of Ramanagaram in the south Indian state of
Karnataka via a micro-demographic exploration of the socio-economic
and religious determinants of their age at marriage, their contraceptive
choices, and their fertility. This was done in order to fulfil the more
general aim of this study, which was to explore the relationship between
the socio-economic and religious determinants of fertility, in order to
understand their consequence for socio-economic and population
policies in India.

[1]Extracts from a letter, written in English, from a south Indian mother, Shakuntala Rao
(aged 26 years), to her daughter, Srilata (aged 4 years), Madras, India, 23 December 1946.

The history of India in the post-colonial era, and more particularly in the 1980s and 1990s, has seen the pervasive expansion of 'communalism'. This phenomenon uses religion for political gains or economic rent-seeking. Within this spirituality-with-competition nexus, confrontations between religious groups, particularly between Hindus and Muslims, have involved both large-scale communal rioting with great destruction of life and property, and less violent, but equally volatile, debates about the numerical preponderance of one group relative to another, with specific focus on the impact of religion on fertility behaviour. In this debate, more often than not exacerbated by prejudice, the distinction between the sacred and the secular becomes blurred. The present study contributes to this debate with an academic examination of the theoretical and empirical links between religion and reproduction in India today.

This study originally set out to answer four questions. First, can the observed higher fertility of some religious communities relative to others in India be attributed to socio-economic characteristics or to theological beliefs?[2] Does the intensity of religious observance influence fertility? How does women's status vary across religions and is this significant for fertility? Finally, might 'convergence' in the demographic behaviour of different religious groups (as in the case of Catholic and non-Catholic fertility in the 1970s in the USA) occur in any society?

There are four hypotheses about how religion can affect demographic outcomes (Chamie, 1977: 365–82). The first is the 'pure religion effect': that the theological content of a religion exercises an independent effect on decision-making about fertility. The present study examined the theological content of Islam and Hinduism concerning marriage, children, birth control, and the position of women. It concluded that the theological content of Hinduism and Islam concerning demographic decisions is very similar. From a purely theological perspective, both religions would tend to encourage high fertility, with little difference between the two.

The second hypothesis is that religious differentials in fertility are due not so much to theology, but to differences in the socio-economic characteristics of individual members of different religions. These include not only economic characteristics such as education, income, or occupation, but also societal and household characteristics such as resident female extended family or access to infrastructure as well as community characteristics such as caste.

[2]For example, in an early analysis of fertility differentials by religion in India, Mandelbaum argued that differences in fertility by religion are more to do with differences in income and education than with differences in religion. See Mandelbaum, 1974: 46.

A third hypothesis of how religion may affect fertility is minority group status, but this study has treated this not as a separate hypothesis, but as one more characteristic of the population.

A fourth effect of religion on fertility is an interaction, possibly with religion as the cause, between religious affiliation and the level of different socio-economic characteristics. This is an illustration of the 'discrimination' hypothesis, that different religious groups may have differential access to socio-economic factors, such as to health and family planning services. For example, it is possible that Muslims may exhibit higher fertility than other religious groups because the family planning programme is dominated overwhelmingly by sterilization as the most common means of birth control. If this is a method of birth control that local Islamic religious leaders are less likely to be inclined towards favourably, then this may result in higher fertility among Muslims because of discrimination in the access to reversible means of birth control. This example illustrates the way in which socio-economic factors interact with religious beliefs, and provides guidance for a directed policy intervention in the form of better access to reversible means of birth control, particularly in regions where minority communities predominate.

This study investigated in detail only the first two hypotheses since explaining differences in all socio-economic characteristics that might affect fertility was far beyond the purview of this fieldwork. It was then examined, using both quantitative and qualitative evidence, if either of these hypotheses explained religious differentials in fertility within a sample of 201 rural women in the taluk of Ramanagaram in the south Indian state of Karnataka.

It is important to emphasize that any conclusion derived from the Ramanagaram sample cannot be representative of all of India. First, compared with some other parts of India, levels of living in Karnataka are relatively good. The rural women from whom the Ramanagaram sample was selected are relatively prosperous compared to their counterparts in some parts of north India. Second, the small size of the sample means that the conclusions drawn, particularly for sub-groups of the population, must not be taken to be representative of all of India's Hindus, Muslims, and Christians. There may well be demographic differences by religion in other parts of India which are different from those in Ramanagaram, and have different determinants. Notwithstanding these caveats, the present study contributes to the debate on religion and fertility in India and regards it as valuable to investigate if there are demographic differentials by religion in a population which is broadly homogenous, faces a similar set of factor prices, and has uniform access to family planning.

From just looking at the monovariate descriptive statistics before taking into account differences in any other characteristic, in the Ramanagaram sample Muslim marriage age is higher than Hindu marriage age; contraceptive use among Muslims is less than among Hindus and Christians; and Muslims had one child more than Hindus. This last finding is similar to that made in other studies of Karnataka, and in other studies of India. Almost all statements about religious differentials in demographic behaviour in India tend to stop with such monovariate descriptive statistics. The present study sought to investigate whether these religious differentials were upheld even after taking into account differences in other socio-economic attributes.

The age at which a woman marries is hypothesized to be an important proximate determinant of fertility. Over the last century or so, the age at marriage has been steadily rising in India. This has been attributed to many causes, including, among others, increasing education for girls, ideational change wrought by changing perceptions about the 'proper' time to marry and the decline in the incidence of child marriage. The present study examined trends in marriage age in Ramanagaram, both quantitatively and qualitatively. Mean marriage age among Hindus was lower than among Muslims and Christians, at least before controlling for the influence of other factors. The study also found that for the Ramanagaram women, the age at marriage had been rising over time, more so after 1978 with the imposition of the Child Marriage Restraint Act, as was the gap between the age at menarche and the age at marriage. There was also qualitative evidence supporting the hypothesis of a 'marriage squeeze' and a 'rising price of husbands' because dowry payments were ordering a market characterized by hypergamy.

An econometric investigation of the age at marriage showed that the factors tending to increase age at marriage for the women covered in the sample were more years of education, particularly secondary education, a later age at menarche, higher income, whether the woman's husband performed a skilled occupation and a later year of marriage. Of all of these socio-economic factors, the role of education in increasing marriage age must be emphasized. Whether through government schools or through the Anganwadi movement, encouraging girls to be sent to school, at least up to the SSLC level, seems to be particularly crucial in order to increase their marriage age. Another very interesting finding of the econometric analysis was the significant and positive 'year of marriage' variable, which may indicate 'ideational change' over time in the norms surrounding age at marriage in Karnataka. Perhaps the most telling confirmation of this emerges from qualitative evidence:

when the Ramanagaram women were asked at what age they wished their unmarried daughters to be married in the future, the average of their responses was 18.9 years, which was higher than the mean of their own marriage age (17.3 years).

This study also focused on whether religion exercised a significantly different effect on marriage age for Hindus, Muslims, and Christians covered in the sample. The study found that the effect of religion on marriage age was not significantly different between Hindus and Muslims, but was significantly different between Hindus and Christians, and between Muslims and Christians. The interaction model also showed that the effect of different socio-economic factors on the age at marriage of Hindus and Muslims was not significantly different between them either. However, the Christians were different from the Hindus and from the Muslims, and this difference was expressed in terms of the effect of some socio-economic factors such as women's secondary education, total expenditure, and the year of marriage. Thus, a combination of socio-economic factors such as education and some change in social norms about marriage appear to account for the patterns of rising marriage age in Ramanagaram. These findings have important policy implications for state-level population policies in India. First, it is important to enforce better the Child Marriage Restraint Act of 1976. This is one of the aims of the National Population Policy of 2000 as well. In addition to this, the present study also recommends that educational infrastructure and the media be used more strongly to influence social norms about the 'proper' age to marry. This is also one area in which religious leaders could work closely with village panchayats in order to exert a positive influence on delaying marriage as the influence of the community on social norms concerning marriage are important, a finding that emerged both from the quantitative and qualitative evidence.

A second major proximate influence on fertility is the use of contraception. Access to family planning in Karnataka, as indeed in some other Indian states, is very widespread. This was reflected in the qualitative questioning of the Ramanagaram women, most of whom had easy access to contraception, either through the system of doorstep delivery of contraceptives, or through the public-sector provision of the tubal ligation method. Most women had access to at least one method of contraception, though Muslim women appeared to use the system of doorstep delivery of contraceptives less than Hindus or Christians. In the Ramanagaram sample, less than half the women had used a method of contraception. Of these methods, sterilization operations using the tubal ligation method were by far the most popular. Given the easy availability of contraception in Ramanagaram, the main determinants of contraceptive use there were factors influencing contraceptive *acceptability*.

Moreover, a close look at 'unwanted' fertility and fertility preferences in Ramanagaram suggests that while these measures are very useful as an indication of desires about fertility, all too often women's stated preferences and revealed preferences differ; questionnaire surveys have to be carefully formulated in order to obtain accurate estimates of 'unwanted' fertility. This is because women's responses are influenced by whether they are asked for a general positive statement or a concrete normative one, by their existing number of children, and by other qualitative factors.

According to the perceptions of the women in the Ramanagaram sample, religion did influence the acceptability of contraception. The most interesting qualitative finding was that most Muslim women thought their religion did disapprove of contraception and over one-quarter of them disagreed with this perceived position of their religion on contraception. Even though a number of scholars have argued that Islam does not oppose contraception, the Muslim women of Ramanagaram think that such prohibitions do exist. From a policy perspective, this suggests immediately a role for local religious leaders, who can attempt to clarify the theological position of religion on the decision to use contraception, and to promote a small family norm in order to influence fertility preferences.

Turning to whether religion actually did influence contraceptive choice, the study found that the factors affecting the probability of contraceptive use in Ramanagaram were woman's education, husband's education, ease of access to contraception, female extended family resident, and the woman's age. Religion did not have an impact on contraceptive use either for the Hindus or for the Muslims, after controlling for the effect of other socio-economic factors. Moreover, there was also little difference between Hindus and Muslims in the socio-economic characteristics which affected their contraceptive practice, although there were differences between both of them and the Christians. Interestingly, for a constant level of any one characteristic, it exerts different effects for different religious groups. For example, if we take a single socio-economic characteristic such as women's education, the effect of this on the probability of contraceptive use for all women is positive. However, the impact of women's education on the decision to use contraception for Christians is greater than that for either Hindus or Muslims. This finding has important implications for state-level education policy in India. Consequently, education policy towards the Christians, who were already better educated, may need to be different from that towards Hindus and

Muslims. For Hindus and Muslims, education may need to be targeted more strongly. The most important policy implication of this analysis, however, is that population policy in developing countries may have to *target different religious groups in different ways*, in order to increase contraceptive use.

Having considered the two important proximate fertility determinants, age at marriage and contraceptive choice, the determinants of fertility in Ramanagaram were explored. The econometric analysis found that the factors affecting children ever born in Ramanagaram were women's university education, husband's primary education, husband's secondary education, position of first-born sons in the birth order, female extended family members resident, woman's age, and whether the household used gas/kerosene in lieu of firewood for fuel.

Looking at differences across religions prior to controlling for other variables, the mean number of children ever born for Muslims was one child higher than for Hindus. However, after taking into account the effects of other factors, there was no statistically significant difference in the intercept terms for Hindus and Muslims, suggesting that religion is not exercising a direct effect on fertility levels. Interestingly, though, there were differences in the slopes of the regression lines for the three religious groups, indicating that the set of socio-economic factors affecting fertility differ across religions, and that some socio-economic attributes affect the fertility of different religions in different ways. Thus, Hindu fertility is influenced mainly by the woman's age and the position of first-born sons in the birth order, while Muslim fertility is affected by those two variables plus woman's university education, husband's primary and secondary education, whether the household used gas or kerosene as a source of fuel, and the number of female extended family resident. This implies that any fertility policy undertaken in Ramanagaram—and possibly other religiously diverse societies—needs to target different religious groups differently. For Muslims, policies focusing on education and infrastructure would be strongly indicated. For Hindus, by contrast, policies focusing on 'ideational' change such as messages conveyed through the mass media would seem to be more important, insofar as woman's age reflects changing norms, and son-preference arises from norms rather than from considerations of insurance. For both groups, however, insofar as son-preference arises from insurance considerations, the Ramanagaram findings provide support for policies directed at providing old age pensions or access to micro-credit by women (as has been successful in Bangladesh) in order to reduce women's dependence on surviving sons (Steele, Amin and Naved, 1998).

The findings from Ramanagaram show clearly, however, that it is not religious affiliation or religious observance which affects fertility, but rather the manner in which religion is interpreted by individuals. This was evidenced in the fact that the index of piety created as a measure of religious observance was not significant in any of the regression models.

The implications of these findings of the effect of religion on fertility for Indian politics and policy-makers are simple but important. First, they provide no empirical support for views which ascribe demographic differentials to differences in theology, or which indulge in stereotyping the behaviour of one religious group relative to another. Rather, they suggest that it is necessary to focus on how the content of a religion is *interpreted* by individual members of that religion and the corresponding impact on their lives. Therefore, community and religious leaders may need to be targeted because of the influence they may wield. For example, one of the key qualitative findings from Ramanagaram was that Muslim women *think* that their religion prohibits contraception, even though theologically (as we saw in Chapter 3) this point is highly debated. In this case, the actual theological content of Islam is irrelevant to decision-making about fertility by Muslim women in Ramanagaram.

The findings from this study suggest directions for a possible re-orientation of population policy, and development policy in India. These findings provide us with a set of policy recommendations that would enable religion to be integrated more closely into population policy, education policy, and development policy.

The role of religion in demographic decision-making is not woven explicitly into the New Population Policy of 2000. While the policy emphasizes the role that can be exerted by religious leaders to promote the small family norm, and suggests that the government will actively enlist their support in various ways, it however, does not elaborate on this in detail. The findings from the present study, however, provide the basis for more detailed recommendations of exactly how religious leaders and others can influence popular opinion, and upon the manner in which their support is likely to be enlisted, to influence demographic outcomes in India.

There are four ways in which religious leaders may be integrated into population policy. First, religious leaders might work in tandem with local governments at the level of the village panchayat, in order to provide information about maternal and child health services. It is important that religious leaders work with governments at this level; the continuous interaction of religious leaders with elected women members of the panchayat would be particularly important for dealing with women's issues at the level of the village.

Second, small community initiatives such as those organized by religious organizations could be useful in order to provide information about family planning and birth-spacing, or infant and child care. The use of religious organizations in this unconventional way would be particularly relevant to the policy's avowed aim 'to increase innovative social marketing schemes for affordable products' (GOI, 2000: 7).

Third, religious groups and religious leaders could have a particularly important role in educating adolescent populations, as they are likely both to command a considerable amount of respect from the young, and to exert an important influence on their behaviour. This is one way in which under-served population groups such as adolescents might be targeted, particularly because adolescent marriage and pregnancy are particularly widespread in rural areas.

Fourth, religious groups and leaders may have a major role to play in providing 'information, education, and communication'—religious leaders who speak in local dialects and who are familiar with the local context in which couples make reproductive decisions, can be very effective if they convey messages such as information about encouraging the use of maternal and child health services. Religious leaders, for example, could also urge families to enforce strictly the Child Marriage Restraint Act of 1976. This measure alone would exert a tremendous impact on delaying the age at marriage, particularly in the rural areas, and consequently on total fertility.

The second key finding of the present study was that socio-economic factors, especially women's and men's education, need more emphasis. Numerous studies of the relationship between education and fertility have found this relationship to be vital to fertility declines and the findings from Ramanagaram substantiate this.[3] The mean number of years of education for married women in the Ramanagaram sample was only 5.5 years. This is very low and is definitely one area which government policy needs to target. More importantly, even if schooling is provided, more research needs to be done on the quality of schooling provided, on how to make mothers send their daughters to school, and on why they might prefer alternatives such as Anganwadi schools, as observed in Ramanagaram. More research should also be devoted to enquiring about what it *is* in education (for both men and women), be it the acquisition of skills or the learning of values, that reduces their fertility.

---

[3]Kishor argues that female enrolment in literacy classes and in primary school is one of the major factors behind small families in Tamil Nadu. See Kishor, 1994: 65-100. See also Drèze and Murthi, 2001.

Education policy in particular would benefit from explicitly taking into account religion in the following ways. First, the provision of education, particularly for women, must be increased. Second, the incentives to make women send their children to school should be increased. One possible incentive is extending the mid-day meal scheme, which has been used with great success in Tamil Nadu, to other states. This has the added benefit of addressing issues of nutrition as well as education.

Thirdly, the provision of schooling infrastructure needs to be targeted explicitly. Recent research on the quality of schooling provided suggests that this is important particularly in the context of education for women (Lloyd, Mensch and Clark, 1998). Another method which is relevant particularly in the context of minority populations, and which has been undertaken successfully in Kerala, is where teachers are sent to teach students in specific villages, or are provided with district-funded mobile libraries. Given the finding of the present study that some religious groups may need to be targeted more strongly than others, this method could be used to educate children, and particularly girls from minority communities, in their accustomed environment.

A related issue is that of women's status. Religious leaders can use their influence to encourage literacy. This is a role that has been played by film stars, politicians, and other opinion makers particularly in south India, but there is little reason to believe that this role cannot also be played by religious leaders.

Finally, the role of non-formal education, as exemplified in the role of the Anganwadi movement, should be extended. This is particularly important in the context of religion, where purdah restrictions might prevent mothers from sending daughters to school. The National Policy on Education outlined in 1986 planned to target this issue strongly, but evidence suggests that this needs to be implemented better, in order particularly to increase the demand for schooling.

The third key finding of this study is that the analysis of fertility behaviour in Ramanagaram shows that different religious groups may need to be targeted in different ways if it is thought desirable to try to influence people's fertility. For example, in Ramanagaram, Muslim husbands' education needs more targeting in order to affect women's fertility, while for Hindus, women's own education and changing attitudes toward son-preference may be the key to lower fertility. One way in which different religious groups may be targeted in different ways is through local government institutions such as village panchayats, who may be more familiar both with local contexts, and with the history of local policies to foster regional economic development. This knowledge could be used to assess the possibility of targeting the specific needs of different religious groups, and to address them accordingly.

Other policy measures which could have a direct impact on reducing fertility in India more widely are further education about family planning, instituting systems of social security to reduce the dependence on children for insurance reasons, further attention to laws which would deal with gender relations, and further action on enforcing property rights, particularly those of women (Egerö, 1994: 26–7).

This study has also generated findings which indicate the need for further research in a number of areas. There are variables which affect demographic outcomes in south India, such as the role of the female extended family in influencing demographic decision-making, which need to be explored more deeply. Although the econometric results of this study confirm the traditional role of the extended family acting negatively on contraceptive use and fertility, qualitative evidence from Ramanagaram indicated that this role may be changing, with the female extended family (especially mothers and mothers-in-law) becoming increasingly proactive in encouraging younger women family members to undertake family planning. The importance of these female social networks in influencing fertility change needs more thorough empirical investigation.

Secondly, the role of marital consanguinity on age at marriage and contraceptive choice in south India more generally, and Karnataka in particular, needs more research. Marital consanguinity is a distinctive feature of social organization and marriage practice in Karnataka and has been widely postulated as increasing fertility. However, even though measures of consanguinity were included in models of marriage age, contraceptive choice, and fertility for Ramanagaram, this variable was not shown to exercise a significant effect. It was argued earlier that consanguinity may be popular in Karnataka because of the need to reduce dowry payments in marriage, and as a means of diversifying risk. Consanguinity also has positive consequences for female autonomy in that it is argued that if women are closer to their natal homes, they have greater mobility and autonomy. Although this relationship was not explored fully, this is another area requiring further research, especially given the emphasis placed upon it in the demographic and anthropological literature.

The age at menarche as a determinant of the age at marriage is another variable which needs further explanation. Although this variable has been quite thoroughly researched in the field of medicine, the present study has shown that it also belongs in the field of economic demography. It was postulated here that the positive relationship observed between the age at menarche and the age at marriage arose because of underlying nutritional and health-related variables which led both to early menarche and to advantages in a competitive marriage market. This hypothesis would benefit from deeper theoretical and empirical explanation. For developing countries, its importance is further emphasized because of its relation to changes in women's nutritional status, and investments in their health capital.

In the Indian context, another relationship which this study suggests needs further exploration is that between caste and demographic behaviour. There were several indications that among the Ramanagaram Hindus, caste was an important determinant of demographic patterns. Though there was not enough information in the Ramanagaram data set to test the empirical relationships between caste and fertility more fully, it would be possible to conduct a similar type of analysis to that which has been conducted for religion in this study, by focusing on caste instead.[4] Given Indian political concerns to improve the position of the more disadvantaged castes, exploring the sources of caste differences in fertility is an important undertaking.

Another relationship deserving further empirical research is the link between infrastructure provision and fertility. The Ramanagaram study found that all members of the household, but particularly women and children, were responsible for water and fuel-collection tasks. This may have been one reason for higher fertility. Certainly, in the case of Muslims, those families who used gas and kerosene and did not rely primarily on firewood had lower fertility than others, even after controlling for socio-economic variables. This is one area which government policy can target. For power, the government can implement the proposals advocated for Ramanagaram by the 1995 infrastructure consultants: these included installing a sub-station, increasing power supply to 40 MW, phasing out power cuts, and stabilizing voltage fluctuations. For water, the infra-structure report recommended the digging of additional borewells, the establishment of reservoirs for water storage, the implementation of the Cauvery water supply scheme, efficient recovery of water taxes imposed by the state government, and streamlining of the administrative set-up that deals with water supply and distribution issues. Some of these proposals are applicable not only to Ramanagaram, but also to other

---

[4]The importance of combining quantitative and anthropological methods in order to investigate the effects on fertility of inter- and intra-jati relations has also been argued by Lipton, 1992: 1543-4.

states in India more widely. Until such proposals are implemented effectively, as observed both from the analysis of water and fuel provision in Ramanagaram in Chapter 4 and the comments of the women themselves, irregular water supply and collecting firewood imply that as many hands as possible are required in order to collect the household's daily water and fuel requirements. Moreover, there is little doubt that in all of India, water and fuel collection will go on constituting a disincentive to send children (particularly daughters) to school.

This study found that while there were no differences between Hindus and Muslims in terms of the determinants of their age at marriage and in terms of the determinants of their contraceptive use, there were differences between them in the socio-economic determinants of their fertility. Given the 'proximate determinants' framework which was adopted to study fertility behaviour in Ramanagaram, these findings suggest that the nonproximate influences on fertility are acting on Hindus and Muslims differently—not via differences in their age at marriage nor via differences in their adoption of contraception, but through some other proximate determinant, such as natural fertility, length of breastfeeding, duration of couple separation during the fertile period (as affected by divorce or migration), or differences in their practice of abortion. For example, as argued elsewhere in this study, early studies of fertility in the Mysore region did argue that Hindu religious prescriptions on the length of couple separation just after childbirth and prohibiting sexual intercourse during certain religious festivals were responsible for lower Hindu than Muslim fertility in the early part of this century. While the Ramanagaram data set was limited in that it did not collect detailed information on all of these other proximate determinants, these findings do suggest that more research would be desirable, particularly on the determinants of abortion practices and couple separation.

It must be recognized that this study is essentially one which revolves around socio-economic determinants of fertility. Although this kind of analysis is very useful, an even more broadly-based study, which tried to measure 'ideational change' in a more detailed way, such as by evaluating the relative contributions of socio-economic and diffusion factors on the decision to use contraception, would be valuable. Although some attempt was made to measure ideational change in the models of marriage age, contraceptive choice, and fertility, using the 'year of marriage' and 'woman's age' variables, it must be recognized that the lack of data which measured ideational change in detail limited an in-depth exploration of the influence of social norms on fertility.

Although this study has concentrated particularly on religion and fertility, it has also been more generally a study of women and their status in Indian society. As discussed earlier, one of the key issues with which this study was concerned was how women's status varies across religions and whether this is significant for fertility. Women's status is broadly perceived to be better in south India than in north India. Indeed, this has been attributed to the nature of social organization and marriage practices in south India, better autonomy and mobility, female education, and largely proactive regional governments who have taken a keen interest in promoting a small family ideal and literacy, and who have recognized these two avenues as a key potential for growth. However, while the quantitative and qualitative findings from Ramanagaram substantiate all of these hypotheses, the data collected do indicate that there is room for even more improvement and change in the status of women in south India, particularly with regard to the relationship between men and women. This conviction emerges not merely from the quantitative findings, but more vitally, from the opinions of the Ramanagaram women themselves.

At the end of the questionnaire, the women were asked to reflect on five questions, as a way of assessing their perceptions about the changes around them in Ramanagaram town or their village over the previous five-year period. They were asked to rate on a scale of 'better, same, or worse' their own economic position, the relations between religious groups, violence between men, violence between men and women and the position of women five years previously, compared to the point at which they were interviewed.

Of the women in the sample, 44 per cent said that their economic position had improved over five years: 50 per cent of Hindus, 33 per cent of Muslims, and 47 per cent of Christians. Twenty-four per cent of women said that their economic position had become worse: 18 per cent of Hindus, 36 per cent of Muslims, and 7 per cent of Christians. Very clearly, of all the three groups, the Muslim women believed most that their economic position had worsened over time.

The women were also asked if they thought that communal relations between religious groups had become better, stayed the same, or become worse over five years. There were major communal riots in Ramanagaram in 1989-90, and as an observer in the area, my impression was that the relations between religious groups were somewhat tense. The women of Ramanagaram confirmed this impression in their responses to this question. Of the women in the sample, 54 per cent said that relations between religious groups had become worse compared to that five years before, 31 per cent said that relations had stayed the same, and only 15 per cent that they had improved. This was fairly uniform across religious groups, with 53 per cent of Hindus, 53 per cent of Muslims, and 60 per cent of Christians saying that relations between religious groups had become worse over the five-year period.

The women were asked if the degree of violence among men, and between men and women, in the town or village had increased, decreased, or remained at the same level. In the whole sample, 61 per cent of women said that violence among men had become worse, 35 per cent that said it had stayed the same, and only 4 per cent said that it had decreased. There were 61 per cent of Hindus, 63 per cent of Muslims, and 53 per cent of Christians who said that violence among men had become worse. Interestingly, the percentages are higher among Hindus and Muslims, relative to the Christians, possibly because the main conflict between religious groups in Ramanagaram taluk in recent years has been between Hindus and Muslims. An even larger proportion of women believed that domestic violence between men and women had increased (63 per cent), while only 4 per cent thought it had decreased. There were 61 per cent of Hindus, 65 per cent of Muslims, and 60 per cent of Christians who thought domestic violence had become worse over five years. One possible explanation for this, to which many of the Ramanagaram women alluded, either directly or indirectly, was the increasing incidence of alcohol-related abuse by their husbands.

Finally, the women of Ramanagaram did not think that their position in their town or village was improving. The query on any change in their position over the past five years drew rather pessimistic comments from them. Of the women in the sample, 71 per cent believed that their position had remained the same, 21 per cent felt it had got worse and only 10 per cent thought that it had improved. There were 63 per cent of Hindus, 64 per cent of Muslims, and 87 per cent of Christians who thought that their position had stayed the same. However, while only 7 per cent of Christians thought that their position was worse than before, there were as many as 29 per cent of Hindus and 27 per cent of Muslims who thought that their position was worse than before.

Thus, the majority of women in the sample interviewed in Ramanagaram taluk believed that their family's economic position had somewhat bettered, that the relations between religious groups, the level of violence between men, and the level of violence between men and women had become worse, while their own position as women in the taluk had remained at about the same level as five years before. Muslim and Hindu women believed more that they were worse off, particularly with regard to their economic position and with regard to their own position as women resident in the town or village, compared with the Christians. Such qualitative evidence indicates that even in south India, there is still room for improvement in women's status, and areas in which public policy can play a more effective role.

In examining if women's status varies across religions, the most significant finding was that on most indicators, be it education, income, or occupation, Christian women emerged as much better off than their Hindu and Muslim counterparts. Though the main focus of this study was not Christian fertility in Ramanagaram, comparisons with the Christians made for useful insights. The higher status of women among the Christian community, as reflected in their access to education and greater independence in decision-making abilities, was noteworthy. Moreover, whether or not it had anything to do with the Church of South India, the example of the Christians illustrates the influence of female education on demographic outcomes. Given the recent emergence of some communal violence against Indian Christians, these findings have somewhat disturbing implications (Sarkar, 1999).

In summary, this study has tried to undertake an assessment of India's population policy as it stands in relation to religion, particularly in the context of the New Population Policy of 2000. This chapter has outlined the manner in which the substance of the research undertaken in Karnataka provides a set of recommendations that has relevance both to population policy in India and to development policy more widely. Given the extremely sensitive nature of the issue of the role of religion in fertility behaviour, it is important to understand that incorporating religion into population policy directly needs to integrate multiple levels of government decision-making, religious groups and their leaders, and the existing infrastructure that caters for family planning, maternal and child health, and education. Such a task is extremely complex and difficult, but the findings from this research hope to have indicated the direction for a possible reorientation of India's population policy, and to have suggested the mechanisms through which such policy guidance may be translated into positive demographic outcomes.

Finally, the last question on which it is important to reflect is whether convergence in Hindu, Muslim, and Christian fertility in India is possible. I believe that it is, if government policy were to target different religious groups in different ways that affect their fertility, but in a sensitive manner which works in tandem with religious leaders. Having established that community influences on fertility were more significant than individual religious observance, the present study suggests the importance of a multi-pronged approach to studying religious differentials in fertility within a country. However, the most important conclusion of the present study is that religious differentials in fertility are the observed outcome of a complex set of factors derived from differences across religious groups in both socio-economic characteristics and the effect of these characteristics on demographic decision-making. This has far-reaching implications for both policy and politics in a religiously pluralistic society such as India. Until public policy moves in such directions, attaining Shakuntala's vision for Indian women, and Indian people in general, seems some distance away.

References

Agarwal, B. (1994), *A Field of One's Own: Gender and Land Rights in South Asia*, Cambridge, Mass.: Cambridge University Press.

Agnihotri, S. B. (2000), *Sex Ratio Patterns in the Indian Population: A Fresh Exploration*, New Dehi: Sage Publications.

Ahmad, I. (1984), 'Political Economy of Communalism in Contemporary India', Economic and Political Weekly, vol. XIX, nos 22 & 23, June 2-9.

Ainsworth, M., Beegle, K. and Nyamate, A. (1996),'The Impact of Women's Schooling on Fertility and Contraceptive Use: A Study of Fourteen Sub-Saharan African Countries', *World Bank Economic Review*, vol. 10, no. 1, January, pp. 85-122.

Ajayi, A. and Kekovole, J. (1998), 'Kenya's Population Policy: From Apathy to Effectivenes', in A. Jain, ed., *Do Population Policies Matter? Fertility and Politics in Egypt, India, Kenya and Mexico*, New York: Population Council, pp. 113-56.

Aldrich, J. H. and Nelson, F. D. (1984), *Linear Probability, Logit and Probit Models*, London: Sage Publications.

Allen, D. (1993), *Religion and Political Conflict in South Asia: India, Pakistan, and Sri Lanka*, Delhi: Oxford University Press.

Aly, H. Y. and Shields, M. P. (1991), 'Son-preference and Contraception in Egypt'. *Economic Development and Cultural Change*, vol. 39, no. 2, pp. 353-70.

Amin, S., Diamond I. and Steele, F. (1996), 'Contraception and Religious Practice in Bangladesh', Policy Research Division Working Paper, no. 83, New York: Population Council.

Anand, S. and Harris, C. (1989), 'Food and Standard of Living: An Analysis Based on Sri Lankan Data', University of Oxford Applied Economics Discussion Paper Series, no. 84.

Anderson, K. H., Hill, M. A. and Butler, J. S. (1987), 'Age at Marriage in Malaysia: A Hazard Model of Marriage Timing', *Journal of Developmental Economics*, vol. 26, no. 2, pp. 223-34.

Appleton, S. (1996), 'How Does Female Education Affect Fertility? A Structural Model for Côte d'Ivoire', *Oxford Bulletin of Economics and Statistics*, vol. 58, no. 1, pp. 139–166.

Arends-Kuenning M. (1997), 'The Equity and Efficiency of Doorstep Delivery of Contraceptives in Bangladesh', Policy Research Division Working Paper, no. 101, New York: Population Council.

Bachchan, H. R. (1998), *In the Afternoon of Time*, An Autobiography of Harivansh Rai Bachchan, edited and translated from Hindi by Rupert Snell, Delhi: Viking, pp. 163–4.

Bagchi, A.K. (1970), 'European and Indian Entrepreneurship in India 1900–30', in Leach and Mukherjee, ed., *Elites in South Asia*, Cambridge: Cambridge University Press.

——— (1991), 'Predatory Commercialization and Communalism in India', in S. Gopal (ed.), *Anatomy of a Confrontation: The Babri Masjid–Ramjanmabhoomi Issue*, Delhi: Penguin, pp. 193–218.

Balagopal, K. (1992), 'Why Did December 6, 1992 Happen?' *Economic and Political Weekly*, vol. XXVIII, no. 17, 24 April, pp. 790–5.

Balk, D. (1994), 'Individual and Community Aspects of Women's Status and Fertility in Rural Bangladesh', *Population Studies*, vol. 48, no. 1, pp. 21–45.

Basu, A. M. (1992), *Culture, the Status of Women and Demographic Behaviour*, Oxford: Clarendon Press.

——— (1993), 'Cultural Influences on the Timing of First Births in India: Large Differences that Add Up to Little Difference', *Population Studies*, vol. 47, no. 1, pp. 85–95.

——— (1997), 'The "Politicisation" of Fertility to Achieve Non-Demographic Objectives', *Population Studies*, vol. 51, no. 1, pp. 5–18.

Basu, A. M. and Amin, S. (2000), 'Some Preconditions for Fertility Decline in Bengal: History, Language Identity, and an Openess to Innovations', Policy Research Division Working Paper, no. 142, New York: Population Council.

Batliwala, S., Anitha, B. K., Gurumurthy, A. and Wali, C. S. (1998), *Status of Rural Women in Karnataka*, Bangalore: National Institute of Advanced Studies.

Bayly, C. A. (1983), *Rulers, Townsmen and Bazaars: North Indian Society in the Age of British Expansion 1770–1870*, Cambridge UK: Cambridge University Press.

Beck, L. and Keddie, N. eds (1978), *Women in the Muslim World*, Cambridge Mass.: Harvard University Press.

Becker, G. S. (1973), 'A Theory of Marriage: Part I', *Journal of Political Economy*, vol. 81, no. 4, pp. 813–46.

——— (1974a), 'A Theory of Marriage: Part II', *Journal of Political Economy*, vol. 82, no. 2: pt. 2, pp. S11–S26.

——— (1974b), 'A Theory of Marriage', in T.W. Schultz, ed., *Economics of the Family: Marriage, Children and Human Capital*, Chicago: NBER, pp. 299–344.

——— (1981), *A Treatise on the Family*, Cambridge Mass.: Harvard University Press.

——— (1991), *A Treatise on the Family: Enlarged Edition*, Cambridge Mass.: Harvard University Press.

Becker, G. S. and Lewis, H. G. (1973), 'On the Interaction Between the Quantity and Quality of Children', *Journal of Political Economy*, vol. 81, no. 2, Part II, pp. S279–S288.

Biddlecom, A. E., Casterline J. B. and Perez, A. E. (1996), 'Men's and Women's Views of Contraception', *Policy Research Division Working Paper*, no. 92, New York: Population Council.

Birdsall, N. M. (1976), 'Women and Population Studies', *Signs*, vol. 1, no. 3, pp. 699–712.

—— (1989), 'Economic Analyses of Rapid Population Growth', *World Bank Research Observer*, vol. 4, no. 1, pp. 23–50.

Birdsall, N. M. and Griffin, C. G. (1988), 'Fertility and Poverty in Developing Countries', *Journal of Policy Modelling*, vol. 10, no. 1, pp. 29–55.

Bittles, A. H. (1994), 'The Role and Significance of Consanguinity as a Demographic Variable', *Population and Development Review*, vol. 20, no. 3, March, pp. 561–84.

Bittles, A. H., Cobles, J. M. and Appaji Rao, N. (1993), 'Trends in Consanguineous Marriage in Karnataka, South India, 1980–1989', *Journal of Biosocial Science*, vol. 25, no. 1, pp. 111–16.

Blake, J. (1984), 'Catholicism and Fertility: On Attitudes of Young Americans', *Population and Development Review*, vol. 10, pp. 329–40.

Blundell, R. W., Browning M. A. and Meghir, C. (1989), 'A Microeconometric Model of Intertemporal Substitution and Consumer Demand', UCL Economic Discussion Paper, pp. 89–110.

Blundell, R. W. and Preston, I. (1992), 'The Distinction between Income and Consumption in Measuring the Distribution of Household Welfare', UCL Discussion Paper, London, pp. 92–101.

—— (1994), 'Income or Consumption in the Measurement of Inequality and Poverty?' Institute for Fiscal Studies Working Paper, vol. 94/12, London, pp. 1–17.

Blundell, R. W., Preston I. and Walker, I., eds (1994), *The Measurement of Household Welfare*, Cambridge UK: Cambridge University Press.

Bodmer, W. F. and Cavalli-Sforza, L. L. (1976), *Genetics, Evolution, and Man*, San Francisco: W. H. Freeman.

Boldsen, J. L. (1992), 'Season of Birth and Recalled Age at Menarche', *Journal of Biosocial Science*, vol. 24, no, 2, pp. 167–73.

Bongaarts, J. (1978), 'A Framework for Analysing the Proximate Determinants of Fertility', *Population and Development Review*, vol. 4, no. 1, pp. 105–32.

—— (1991), 'The KAP-Gap and the Unmet Need for Contraception', *Population and Development Review*, vol. 17, no. 2, pp. 293–313.

—— (1993), 'The Supply–Demand Framework for the Determinants of Fertility: An Alternative Implementation', *Population Studies*, vol. 47, no. 3, pp. 437–56.

—— (1997a), 'Trends in Unwanted Childbearing in the Developing World', Policy Research Division Working Paper, no. 98, New York: Population Council.

—— (1997b), 'The Role of Family Planning Programmes in Contemporary

Fertility Transitions', in G. W. Jones, et al., eds, *The Continuing Demographic Transition*, Oxford: Clarendon Press, pp. 422–43.

Bongaarts, J. and Bruce, J. (1995), 'The Causes of Unmet Need for Contraception and the Social Content of Services', *Studies in Family Planning*, vol. 26, no. 2, pp. 57–75.

Bongaarts, J. and Watkins, S. C. (1996), 'Social Interactions and Contemporary Fertility Transitions', *Population and Development Review*, vol. 22, no. 4, pp. 639–82.

Borooah, V. (2001), 'Differences in Demographic Outcomes between Hindus, Muslims and Scheduled Castes/Tribes in India', mimeo, School of Economics and Politics, University of Ulster.

Bose, A. (1991), *Demographic Diversity of India: 1991 Census, State and District Level Data: A Reference Book*, Delhi: B. R. Publishing.

Boulier, L. and Rosenzweig, M. (1978), 'Age, Biological Factors and Socio-Economic Determinants of Fertility', *Demography*, vol. 15, pp. 487–97.

Bourgeois-Pichat, J. (1967), 'Social and Biological Determinants of Human Fertility in Nonindustrial Societies', *Proceedings of the American Philosophical Society*, vol. 3, pp. 160–3.

Brian Arthur, W. (1981), Book Review of G. S. Becker's 'A Treatise on the Family', *Population and Development Review*, vol. 8, no. 2, pp. 393–7.

Brien, M. J. and Lillard, L.A. (1994), 'Education, Marriage and First Conception in Malaysia', *Journal of Human Resources*, vol. XXIX, no. 4, pp. 1167–204.

Bulatao, R. A. and Lee, R. D. (1983), Determinants of Fertility in Developing Countries, New York: Academic Press.

Cain, M. (1977), 'The Economic Activities of Children in a Village in Bangladesh', *Population and Development Review*, vol. 3, no. 3, pp. 201–27.

—— (1978), 'The Household Life Cycle and Economic Mobility in Rural Bangladesh', *Population and Development Review*, vol. 4, no. 3, pp. 421–38.

—— (1981), 'Risk and Insurance: Perspectives on Fertility and Agrarian Change in India and Bangladesh', *Population and Development Review*, vol. 7, no. 3, pp. 435–74.

—— (1984), 'Women's Status and Fertility in Developing Countries: Son Preference and Economic Security', *World Bank Staff Working Papers*, no. 682, Washington, D. C: World Bank.

Cain, M., Khanam, S. R. and Nahar, S. (1979), 'Class, Patriarchy and Women's Work in Bangladesh', *Population and Development Review*, vol. 5, no. 3, pp. 405–38.

Caldwell, J. C. (1980), 'Mass Education as a Determinant of the Timing of Fertility Decline', *Population and Development Review*, vol. 6, no. 2, pp. 225–55.

—— (1986), 'Routes to Low Mortality in Poor Countries', *Population and Development Review*, vol. 12, no. 2, pp. 171–220.

—— (1996), 'Demography and Social Science', *Population Studies*, vol. 50, no. 3, pp. 305–33.

Caldwell, J. C. and Caldwell, P. (1990), 'Cultural Forces Tending to Sustain High Fertility', in G. T. Acsadi, G. Johnson-Acsadi and R. A. Bulatao, eds *Population*

Growth and Reproduction in Sub-Saharan Africa: Technical Analyses of Fertility and Its Consequences, Washington D. C.: World Bank, pp. 199–214.

—— (1997), 'Population Growth, Physical Resources and Human Resources in Sub-Saharan Africa', in P. Dasgupta, K. Mäler and A. Vercelli, eds *The Economics of Transnational Commons*, Oxford: Clarendon Press, pp. 118–40.

Caldwell, J. C., Caldwell, P. and Orubuloye, I. O. (1992), 'Fertility Decline in Africa: A New Type of Transition?' *Population and Development Review*, vol. 18, no. 2, pp. 211–42.

Caldwell, J. C., Reddy, P. H. and Caldwell, P. (1983), 'The Causes of Marriage Change in South India.' *Population Studies*, vol. 37, no. 3, pp. 343–61.

—— (1985), 'Educational Transition in Rural South India', *Population and Development Review*, vol. 11, no. 1, pp. 29–51.

Carlson, E. (1979), 'Family Background, School and Early Marriage', *Journal of Marriage and the Family*, vol. 41, no. 2, pp. 341–53.

Cassen, R. H. (1976), 'Population and Development: A Summary', *World Development*, vol. 4, no. 10 &11, pp. 785–830.

Cassen, R. H. et al. (1994), *Population and Development: Old Debates, New Conclusions*, US Third World Policy Perspectives, vol. 19, New Brunswick: Transaction Publishers.

Castro Martin, T. (1995), 'Women's Education and Fertility: Results from Twenty Demographic and Health Surveys', *Studies in Family Planning*, vol. 26, no. 4, pp. 187–202.

Centerwall, W. R. and Centerwall, S. A. (1966), 'Consanguinity and Congenital Anomalies in South India: A Pilot Study', *Indian Journal of Medical Research*, vol. 54, pp. 1160–7.

Chamie, J. (1977), 'Religious Differentials in Fertility: Lebanon, 1971', *Population Studies*, vol. 31, no. 2, pp. 365–82.

Chandra, B. (1984), *Communalism in Modern India*, New Delhi: Vikas Publishers.

Chandra, S. (1993), 'Of Communal Consciousness and Communal Violence', *Economic and Political Weekly*, vol. XXVIII, no. 36, 4 September, pp. 1883–7.

Chandrasekaran, C. (1952), 'Cultural Patterns in Relation to Family Planning in India', in *Report of the Proceedings of the Third International Conference on Planned Parenthood*, Mumbai: Family Planning Association of India.

Chaudhuri, S. and Ravallion, M. (1994), 'How Well do Static Indicators Identify the Chronically Poor?' *Journal of Public Economics*, vol. 53, no. 3, pp. 367–94.

Chen, J. A., Hicks, W. L., Johnson, S. R. and Rodriguez, R. C. (1990), 'Economic Development, Contraception and Fertility Decline in Mexico', *Journal of Development Studies*, vol. 26, no. 3, pp. 408–24.

Chen, L. C., Huq, E. and D'Souza, S. (1981), 'Sex Bias in the Family Allocation of Food and Health Care in Rural Bangladesh', *Population and Development Review*, vol. 7, no. 1, pp. 55–70.

Cleland, J. (1993), 'Equity, Security and Fertility: A Reaction to Thomas', *Population Studies*, vol. 47, pp. no. 2, 345–52.

Cleland, J. and Wilson, C. (1987), 'Demand Theories of the Fertility Transition: An Iconoclastic View', *Population Studies*, vol. 41, no. 1, pp. 5–30.

Christensen, G. (1992), 'Sensitive Information: Collecting Information on Livestock and Informal Credit,' in S. Devereux and J. Hoddinott, eds *Fieldwork in Developing Countries*, London: Harvester Wheatsheaf, pp. 124–37.

Cochrane, S. H. (1975), 'Children as By-Products, Investment Goods and Consumer Goods: A Review of Some Micro-Economic Models of Fertility', *Population Studies*, vol. 29, no. 3, pp. 373–90.

—— (1979), 'Fertility and Education: What Do We Really Know?' *World Bank Staff Occasional Papers*, no. 1379, Washington, D. C. World Bank.

—— (1983), 'Effects of Education and Urbanisation on Fertility', in R. A. Bulatao and R. D. Lee, eds *Determinants of Fertility in Developing Countries*, New York: Academic Press, pp. 992–1026.

Cochrane, S. and Farid, S. (1990), 'Socioeconomic Differentials in Fertility and their Explanation', in G. Acsadi, G. Johnson-Acsadi and R. A. Bulatao, eds *Population Growth and Reproduction in Sub-Saharan Africa: Technical Analysis of Fertility and its Consequences*, Washington D. C.: World Bank, pp. 144–54.

Cochrane, S. and Guilkey, D. K. (1995), 'The Effects of Fertility Intentions and Access to Services on Contraceptive Use in Tunisia', *Economic Development and Cultural Change*, vol. 43, no. 4, pp. 779–804.

Conklin, G. H. (1973), 'Urbanisation, Cross-Cousin Marriage and Power for Women: A Sample from Dharwar', *Contributions to Indian Sociology*, New Series, vol. 7, pp. 53–63.

Cotts Watkins, S. (1990), 'From Local to National Communities: The Transformation of Demographic Regions in Western Europe 1870–1960', *Population and Development Review*, vol. 16, no. 2, pp. 241–72.

Coulson, N. and Hinchcliffe, D. (1978), 'Women and Law Reform in Contemporary Islam', in L. Beck and N. Keddie, eds *Women in the Muslim World*, Cambridge Mass.: Harvard University Press, pp. 37–49.

Cramer, J. S. (1991), *The Logit Model: An Introduction for Economists*, London: Edward Arnold.

Das Gupta, M. (1994), 'What Motivates Fertility Decline? A Case Study from Punjab, India', in B. Egerö and M. Hammarskjöld, eds *Understanding Reproductive Change: Kenya, Tamil Nadu, Punjab, Costa Rica*, Lund: Lund University Press, pp. 101–33.

Das Gupta, M., Chen, L. C. and Krishnan, T. N., eds (1995), *Women's Health in India: Risk and Vulnerability*, Mumbai: Oxford University Press.

Dasgupta, P. (1993a), *An Inquiry into Well-Being and Destitution*, Oxford: Clarendon Press, pp. 343–70.

—— (1993b), 'Poverty, Resources and Fertility: The Household as a Reproductive Partnership', in A. B. Atkinson, ed. *Alternatives to Capitalism*, New York: St. Martin's Press, pp. 207–43.

—— (1995a), 'The Population Problem: Theory and Evidence', *Journal of Economic Literature*, vol. 33, no. 4, pp. 1879–902.

—— (1995b), 'Population, Poverty and the Local Environment', *Scientific American*, vol. 272, no. 2, February, pp. 26–31.

—— (2000), 'Population and Resources: An Exploration of Reproductive and

Environmental Externalities', *Population and Development Review*, vol. 26, no. 4, pp. 643–89.

Day, L. H. (1968), 'Natality and Ethnocentrism: Some Relationships Suggested by a Study of Catholic–Protestant Differentials', *Population Studies*, vol. 22, no. 1, pp. 27–50.

Deshpande, C. R. (1978), *Transmission of the Mahabharata Tradition. Vyasa and Vyasids*, Simla: Institute of Advanced Study.

Devereux, S and Hoddinott, J., eds (1992), *Fieldwork in Developing Countries*, London: Harvester Wheatsheaf.

Dharmalingam, A. and Philip Morgan, S. (1996), 'Women's Work, Autonomy and Birth Control: Evidence from Two South Indian Villages', *Population Studies*, vol. 50: no. 2, pp. 187–201.

Drèze, J. and Murthi, M. (2001), 'Fertility, Education and Development: Evidence from India', *Population and Development Review*, 27: 1, pp. 33–63.

Drèze, J. and Sen, A. (1995), *India: Economic Development and Social Opportunity*, Oxford: Clarendon Press.

Duraisamy, P. (1988), 'An Econometric Analysis of Fertility, Child Schooling and Labour Force Participation of Women in Rural Indian Households', *Journal of Quantitative Economics*, vol. 4, no. 2, pp. 293–316.

Dyson, T. and Crook, N., eds (1984), *India's Demography: Essays on the Contemporary Population*, New Delhi: South Asian Publishers.

Dyson, T. and Moore, M. (1983), 'On Kinship Structure, Female Autonomy and Demographic Behaviour in India', *Population and Development Review*, vol. 9, no. 1, pp. 35–60.

Easterlin, R. A. (1975), 'An Economic Framework for Fertility Analysis', *Studies in Family Planning*, vol. 6, pp. 54–63.

——— (1978), 'The Economics and Sociology of Fertility: A Synthesis', in C. Tilly, ed. *Historical Studies of Changing Fertility*, Princeton : Princeton University Press, pp. 57–134.

Economist (1994), 3 September, pp. 21–3.

Egerö, B. (1994), 'Reproductive Change is a Social Process', in B. Egerö and M. Hammarskjöld, eds *Understanding Reproductive Change: Kenya, Tamil Nadu, Punjab, Costa Rica*, Lund: Lund University Press, pp. 9–30.

Egerö, B. and Hammarskjöld, M., eds (1994), *Understanding Reproductive Change: Kenya, Tamil Nadu, Punjab, Costa Rica*, Lund: Lund University Press.

Engineer, A. A. (1984a), 'Understanding Communalism', *Economic and Political Weekly*, vol. XIX, no. 18, 5 May, pp. 752–6.

——— (1984b), 'Bombay-Bhiwandi Riots in National Political Perspective,' *Economic and Political Weekly*, vol. XIX, no. 29, 21 July pp. 1134–6.

——— (1986), 'Maharashtra: Engulfed in Communal Fire', *Economic and Political Weekly*, vol. XXI, no. 23, 7 June, pp. 994–7.

——— (1991), 'Making of the Hyderabad Riots', *Economic and Political Weekly*, vol. XXVI, no. 6, 9 February, pp. 271–4.

——— (1993a), 'Surat: Bastion of Communal Amity Crumbles', *Economic and Political Weekly*, vol. XXVIII, no.7, 13 February, pp. 262–4.

_____ (1993b), 'Bombay Shames India', *Economic and Political Weekly*, vol. XXVIII, nos 3 and 4, 16–23 January, pp. 81–5.

_____ (1994), 'In the Shadow of Communalism', *Seminar*, vol. 413, January, pp. 64–70.

_____ (1997), 'Women in Islam: Valiant Warriors and Able Rulers', *The Times of India*, 22 January.

Epstein, T. S. (1973), *South India: Yesterday, Today and Tomorrow: Mysore Villages Revisited*, London: Macmillan Press.

Ermisch, J. F. (1981), 'Economic Opportunities, Marriage Squeezes and the Propensity to Marry: An Economic Analysis of Period Marriage Rates in England and Wales', *Population Studies*, vol. 3, no. 3, pp. 347–56.

Farid, S. (1987), 'A Review of the Fertility Situation in the Arab Countries of Western Asia and North Africa', in *Fertility Behaviour in the Context of Development: Evidence from the World Fertility Survey*, New York: UN Department of International Economic and Social Affairs, Population Studies no. 100.

Federici, N., Mason, K. O. and Sogner, S., eds (1993), *Women's Position and Demographic Change*, Oxford: Clarendon Press.

Folbre, N. (1992), '"The Improper Arts" Sex in Classical Political Economy', *Population and Development Review*, vol. 18, no. 1, pp. 105–21.

Frank, O. and McNicoll, G. (1987), 'An Interpretation of Fertility and Population Policy in Kenya', *Population and Development Review*, vol. 13, no. 2, pp. 209–43.

Frisbie, P. (1986), 'Variation in Patterns of Marital Instability among Hispanics', *Journal of Marriage and the Family*, vol. 48, no. 1, pp. 99–106.

Frisch, R. E. (1982), 'Evidence for a Secular Trend in the Age at Menarche', *New England Journal of Medicine*, vol. 306, pp. 1033–5.

Gallagher, E., and Searle, M. (1983), 'Women's Health Care: A Study of Islamic Society', in J. H. Morgan, ed. *Third World Medicine and Social Change*, Lanham: University Press of America, pp. 85–96.

Galloway, P. R., Hammel, E. A. and Lee, R. D. (1994), 'Fertility Decline in Prussia, 1875–1910: A Pooled Cross-Section Time Series Analysis', *Population Studies*, vol. 48, no. 1, pp. 135–58.

Gellner, E. (1981), *Muslim Society*, Cambridge, UK: Cambridge University Press.

Ghallab, M. (1984), 'Population Theory and Policies in the Islamic Model', in J. Clarke, ed. *Geography and Population: Approaches and Applications*, Oxford: Pergamon, pp. 232–41.

Golde, G. (1975), *Catholics and Protestants: Agricultural Modernization in Two German Villages*, New York: Academic Press.

Goldstone, J. A. (1986), 'The Demographic Revolution in England: A Re-Examination', *Population Studies*, vol. 49, no. 1, pp. 5–33.

Gopal, S. (1991), *Anatomy of a Confrontation: The Ramjanmabhoomi–Babri Masjid Issue*, Delhi: Penguin.

_____ (1989), *Radhakrishnan: A Biography*, Delhi: Oxford University Press.

Goulet, D. (1980), 'Development Experts: The One-Eyed Giants', *World Development*, vol. 8, no. 7/8, pp. 481–9.

Government of India, (2000), *National Population Policy*, Delhi.

Government of Karnataka (1995a), *Karnataka Urban Infrastructure Development Report*, Finance Ministry, GHK/MRM International Limited.
____ (1995b), *Outline Structure Plan for Ramanagaram: Final Report*, Bangalore.
____ (1999), *Human Development in Karnataka 1999*, Bangalore: Planning Department, Government of Karnataka.
Govinda Reddy, P. (1988), 'Consanguineous Marriages and Marriage Payment: A Study among Three South Indian Caste Groups', *Annals of Human Biology*, vol. 15, no. 4, pp. 263–8.
Goyal, R. P. (1975), *'Shifts in Age at Marriage in India and Different States during 1961–71'*, Delhi: Institute of Economic Growth, mimeographed.
____ (1990), *'Differential Fertility by Religion in India'*. Delhi: Population Research Centre, Institute of Economic Growth, mimeographed.
Graff, H. J. (1979), 'Literacy, Education and Fertility, Past and Present: A Critical Review', *Population and Development Review*, vol. 5, no. 1, March, pp. 105–40.
Greene, W. H. (1997), *Econometric Analysis*, 3rd edition, London: Prentice-Hall International.
Guilkey, D. K. and Jayne, S. (1997), 'Fertility Transition in Zimbabwe: Determinants of Contraceptive Use and Method Choice', *Population Studies*, vol. 51, no. 2, pp. 173–89.
Gulati, S. (1992), 'Developmental Determinants of Demographic Variables in India: A District Level Analysis', *Journal of Quantitative Economics*, vol. 8, no. 1, pp. 157–72.
Hajnal, J. (1982), 'Two Kinds of Preindustrial Household System', *Population and Development Review*, vol. 8, no. 3, pp. 449–94.
Hammel, E. A. (1990), 'A Theory of Culture in Demography', *Population and Development Review*, vol. 16, no. 3, pp. 455–85.
Harriss, B. (1990), 'The Intra-Family Distribution of Hunger', in J. Drèze and A. Sen, eds *The Political Economy of Hunger*, Oxford: Clarendon Press, pp. 351–424.
Hasan, M., ed. (1981), *Communal and Pan-Islamic Trends in Colonial India*, Delhi: Manohar Publishers.
Heer, D. M. (1966), 'Economic Development and Fertility', *Demography*, vol. 3, no. 2, pp. 423–44.
Heer, D. M. and Turner, E. (1965), 'Aerial Differences in Latin America's Fertility', *Population Studies*, vol. 18, no. 3, pp. 279–92.
Heer, D. M. and Youssef, N. (1977), 'Female Status among Soviet Central Asian Nationalities: The Melding of Islam and Marxism and its Implications for Population Increase', *Population Studies*, vol. 3, no. 1, pp. 155–73.
Herbert, J. (1965), *An Introduction to Asia*, translated by Manu Banerji, London: George Allen and Unwin.
Hern, W. M. (1992), 'Polygyny and Fertility among the Shipibo of the Peruvian Amazon', *Population Studies*, vol. 46, no. 1, pp. 53–64.
Hill, P. (1982), *Dry Grain Farming Families: Hausaland (Nigeria) and Karnataka (India) Compared*, Cambridge UK: Cambridge University Press.
Hinde, R. A. (1999), *Why Gods Persist*, London and New York: Routledge.

Hirschman, C. (1985), 'Premarital Socio-Economic Roles and the Timing of Family Formation: A Comparative Study of Five Asian Societies', *Demography*, vol. 22, no. 1, pp. 35–59.

Ibrahim, S. E. and Ibrahim, B. L. (1998), 'Egypt's Population Policy: The Long March of State and Civil Society', in A. Jain, ed., *Do Population Policies Matter? Fertility and Politics in Egypt, India, Kenya and Mexico*, New York: Population Council, pp. 19–52.

Indian National Social Action Forum (1997), Chapter 4 on 'Population of Minorities', Bombay: Indian National Social Action Forum, Chennai, India.

Indian Statutory Commission Report, 1930, vol. IV, Part I: 97–107.

International Institute of Population Sciences (1995), *National Family Health Survey 1992–93: Karnataka*, Mumbai: IIPS.

Irudaya Rajan, S. (1987), 'Family Planning Programme in India: An Economic Evaluation', *The Indian Economic Journal*, vol. 34: no. 4, pp. 79–86.

Irudaya Rajan, S., Mishra, U. S. and Vimala, T. K. (1996), 'Choosing a Permanent Contraceptive: Does Son Preference Matter?' *Economic and Political Weekly*, vol. XXXI, no. 29, 20 July, pp. 1980–4.

Iyer, S. (1994), *Demographic and Economic Explanations for the Resurgence of Communalism in India since 1984*, Working Paper, Centre for History and Economics, Cambridge.

—— (2000), *Religion and the Economics of Fertility in South India*, Ph.D. dissertation, Faculty of Economics and Politics, University of Cambridge.

Jaffe, A. J. and Azumi, K. (1960), 'The Birth Rate and Cottage Industries in Underdeveloped Countries', *Economic Development and Cultural Change*, vol. IX: 1, Part 1, pp. 52–63.

Jain, A. (1998), *Do Population Policies Matter? Fertility and Politics in Egypt, India, Kenya and Mexico*, New York: Population Council.

Janakarajan, S., Olsen, N. and Seabright, P. (1996), 'The Determinants of Marriage Payments in Rural South India', mimeo, Cambridge.

Janakarajan, S. and Seabright, P. (1996), 'Subjective and Objective Indicators of Welfare Change Over Time: Evidence from a Resurvey', mimeo, Cambridge.

Janssen, S. G. and Hauser, R. M. (1981), 'Religion, Socialisation and Fertility of Married Couples', *Demography*, vol. 18, no.4, pp. 511–28.

Jeffery, R. and Basu, A. M., eds (1996), *Girls' Schooling, Women's Autonomy, and Fertility Change in South Asia*, New Delhi: Sage Publications.

Jeffery, R. and Jeffery, P. (1997), *Population, Gender and Politics: Demographic Change in Rural North India*, Cambridge UK: Cambridge University Press.

—— (2000), 'Religion and Fertility in India', *Economic and Political Weekly*, vol. XXXV, nos 35 and 36, 26 August–2 September 2, pp. 325–9.

Jejeebhoy, S. (1992), 'Women's Education, Fertility and the Proximate Determinants of Fertility', Paper for the Expert Group Meeting on Population and Women, Gaborone, Botswana, 22–6 June, International Conference on Population and Development 1994, UNFPA, Document ESD/P/ICPD.1994/EG.III/13.

Kabeer, N. (1997), 'Women, Wages and Intra-Household Power Relations in Urban Bangladesh', *Development and Change*, vol. 28, no. 2, April, pp. 261–302.

Käsler, D. (1988), *Max Weber: An Introduction to his Life and Work*, translated by P. Hurd., Cambridge: Polity Press.

Kay, J. A., Keen, M. J. and Morris, C. N. (1984), 'Estimating Consumption from Expenditure Data', *Journal of Public Economics*, vol. 23, no. 1–2, pp. 169–81.

Keeley, M. C. (1977), 'The Economics of Family-Formation', *Economic Inquiry*, vol. 15, no. 2, pp. 238–50.

Kennedy, E. and Haddad, L. (1994), 'Are Pre-Schoolers from Female-headed Households Less Malnourished? Results from Ghana and Kenya', *Journal of Development Studies*, vol. 30, no. 3, April, pp. 680–95.

Kennedy, E. and Peters, P. (1992), 'Household Food Security and Child Nutrition: The Interaction of Income and Gender of Household Head', *World Development*, vol. 20, no. 8, August, pp. 1077–85.

Kelley, A. C. (1988), 'Economic Consequences of Population Change in the Third World', *Journal of Economic Literature*, vol. 26: no. 4, pp. 1685–728.

Ketkar, S. L. (1979), 'Determinants of Fertility in a Developing Society: The Case of Sierra Leone', *Population Studies*, vol. 33, no. 3, pp. 479–88.

Kishor, S. (1994), 'Fertility Decline in Tamil Nadu', in B. Egerö and M. Hammarskjöld, eds *Understanding Reproductive Change: Kenya, Tamil Nadu, Punjab, Costa Rica*, Lund: Lund University Press, pp. 65–100.

Knodel, J. E. and van de Walle, E. (1986), 'Lessons from the Past: Policy Implications of Historical Fertility Studies', in A. J. Coale and S. C. Watkins, eds *The Decline of Fertility in Europe*, Princeton: Princeton University Press, pp. 390–419.

Koenig, M. A., Rob, U., Ali Khan, M., Chakraborty, J. and Fauveau, V. (1992), 'Contraceptive Use in Matlab, Bangladesh in 1990: Levels, Trends and Explanations', *Studies in Family Planning*, vol. 23, no. 6, pp. 352–64.

Kraft, J. M. and Coverdill, J. E. (1994), 'Employment and the Use of Birth Control by Sexually Active Single Hispanic, Black and White Women', *Demography*, vol. 31, no. 4, pp. 593–602.

Kriedte, P., Medick, H. and Schlumbohm, J. (1981), *Industrialization before Industrialization: Rural Industry in the Genesis of Capitalism*, Cambridge UK: Cambridge University Press.

Krishna, G. (1985), 'Communal Violence in India', *Economic and Political Weekly*, vol. XX, no. 2, 12 January, pp. 61–74.

Landau, R. (1958), *Islam and the Arabs*, London: George Allen and Unwin.

Landes, D. S. (1998), *The Wealth and Poverty of Nations*, London: Little, Brown and Company.

Laslett, P. (1988), 'The European Family and Early Industrialisation', in J. Baechler, J. A. Hall and M. Mann, eds *Europe and the Rise of Capitalism*, Cambridge: Cambridge University Press, pp. 234–41.

—— (1983), 'Family and Household as Work Group and Kin Group: Areas of

Traditional Europe Compared', in R. Wall, J. Robin and P. Laslett, eds *Family Forms in Historic Europe*, Cambridge UK : Cambridge University Press, pp. 513–63.

Lee, R. D. and Miller, T. (1991), 'Population Growth, Externalities to Childbearing, and Fertility Policy in Developing Countries', *Proceedings of the World Bank Conference on Development Economics 1990*, Fisher, S., de-Tray, D and Shah, S., eds (1991). Washington D.C.: World Bank, pp. 275–304.

Le Mee, J., translated (1975), *Hymns from the Rig Veda*, London: Jonathan Cape, verse 8.71.9: 147.

Lesthaeghe, R. and Surkyn, J. (1988), 'Cultural Dynamics and Economic Theories of Fertility Change', *Population and Development Review*, vol. 14, no. 1, March, pp. 1–45.

Lesthaeghe, R. and Wilson, C. (1986), 'Modes of Production, Secularization and the Pace of Fertility Decline in Western Europe 1870–1930', in A. J. Coale and S. C. Watkins, eds *The Decline of Fertility in Europe*, Princeton: Princeton University Press, pp. 261–92.

Ling, T. (1980), 'Buddhist Values and Development Problems: A Case Study of Sri Lanka', *World Development*, vol. 8, no. 7/8, pp. 577–86.

Lipton, M. (1992), 'Economics and Anthropology: Grounding Models in Relationships', *World Development*, vol. 20, no. 10, October, pp. 1541–6.

—— (1997), 'Editorial: Poverty—Are There Holes in the Consensus?' *World Development*, vol. 25, no. 7, July, pp. 1003–7.

Lipton and Ravallion, M. (1995), 'Poverty and Policy', in *Handbook of Development Economics*, J. Behrman and T. N. Srinivasa, eds vol. 3B, Handbooks in Economics, vol. 9, Amsterdam, New York and Oxford: Elsevier Science, North Holland, pp. 2551–657.

Lipton, M. and Moore, M. (1972), 'The Methodology of Village Studies in Less Developed Countries', *Institute of Development Studies Discussion Paper*, no. 10.

Livson, N. and McNeill, D. (1962), 'The Accuracy of Recalled Age at Menarche', *Human Biology*, vol. 34, no. 3, pp. 218–21.

Lloyd, C. B., Mensch, B. S. and Clark, W. H. (1998), 'The Effects of Primary School Quality on the Educational Participation and Attainment of Kenyan Girls and Boys', Policy Research Division Working Paper, no. 116, New York: Population Council.

Lutz, W. (1983), 'Culture, Religion and Fertility: A Global View', *Genus*, vol. 43, no. 3–4, pp. 15–35.

Malhotra, A., Vanneman, R. and Kishor, S. (1995), 'Fertility Dimensions of Patriarchy and Development in India', *Population and Development Review*, vol. 21, no. 2, pp. 281–305.

Malthus, T. R. (1817), *An Essay on the Principle of Population*, fifth edition, vol. III, London: John Murray.

Mamdani, M. (1972), *The Myth of Population Control*, New York: Monthly Review Press.

Mandelbaum, D. G. (1974), *Human Fertility in India: Social Components and Policy Perspectives*, California: Berkeley Press.

Madras Communications Institute (1994), *India Population Data Sheet*, Chennai.

Mason, K. O. (1993), 'The Impact of Women's Position on Demographic Change during the Course of Development', in N. Federici, K. O. Mason and S. Sogner, eds *Women's Position and Demographic Change*, Oxford: Clarendon Press, pp. 19–42.

Mason, K. M. and Taj, A. M. (1987), 'Differences between Women's and Men's Reproductive Goals in Developing Countries', *Population and Development Review*, vol. 13, no. 4, pp. 611–38.

May, D. A. and Heer, D. M. (1968), 'Son Survivorship Motivation and Family Size in India: A Computer Simulation', *Population Studies*, vol. 22, no.2, pp. 199–210.

——— (1984), 'Consequences of Rapid Population Growth: An Overview and Assessment', *Population and Development Review*, vol. 10:, no. 2, pp. 177–240.

McNicoll, G. (1980), 'Institutional Determinants of Fertility', *Population and Development Review*, vol. 6, no. 3,pp. 441–62.

Mcquillon, K. (1989), 'Economic Structure, Religion and Age at Marriage: Some Evidence from Alsace', *Journal of Family History*, vol. 14, no. 4, pp. 331–46.

Michael, M. and Tuma, N. (1985), 'Entry into Marriage and Parenthood by Young Men and Women: The Influence of Family Background', *Demography*, vol. 22, no. 4, pp. 515–44.

Miller, P. W. (1988), 'Economic Models of Fertility Behaviour in Australia', *Australian Economic Papers*, vol. 27, no. 50, pp. 65–79.

Morgan, S.P. and Niraula, B.B. (1995), 'Gender Inequality and Fertility in Two Nepali Villages', *Population and Development Review*, vol. 21, no. 3, pp. 541–61.

Mosher, W. D. and Hendershot, G. E. (1984a), 'Religion and Fertility: A Replication', *Demography*, vol. 21, no. 2, pp. 185–91.

——— (1984b), 'Religious Affiliation and Fertility of Married Couples', *Journal of Marriage and the Family*, vol. 46, no. 3, pp. 671–7.

Mosher, W. D., Johnson, D. P. and Horn, H. C. (1986), 'Religion and Fertility in the United States: The Importance of Marriage Patterns and Hispanic Origin', *Demography*, vol. 23, pp. 367–79.

Moulasha, K and Rama Rao, G. R. (1999), 'Religion-Specific Differentials in Fertility and Family Planning', *Economic and Political Weekly*, vol. 34, no. 42, pp. 3047–51.

Muhuri, P. K. and Menken, J. (1997), 'Adverse Effects of Next Birth, Gender and Family Composition on Child Survival in Rural Bangladesh', *Population Studies*, vol. 51, no. 3, pp. 279–94.

Murthi, M., Guio, A. C. and Drèze, J. (1995), 'Mortality, Fertility and Gender Bias in India: A District-Level Analysis', *Population and Development Review*, pp. 745–82.

Nag, M. (1983), 'The Impact of Sociocultural Factors on Breastfeeding and Sexual Behaviour', in R. A. Bulatao and R. D. Lee, eds *Determinants of Fertility in Developing Countries*, New York: Academic Press, pp. 163–98.

——— (1984), 'Some Cultural Factors Affecting the Costs of Fertility Regulation', *Population Bulletin of the United Nations*, vol. 17, pp. 17–38.

Nag, M. and Kak, N. (1984), 'Demographic Transition in a Punjab Village', *Population and Development Review*, vol. 10: no. 4, pp. 661–78.

Nagi, M. (1984), 'Trends and Differentials in Moslem fertility', *Journal of Biosocial Science*, vol. 16, pp. 189–204.

Narasimaiah, C. V. (1994), *N for Nobody*, Delhi: Oxford University Press.

Nash, M. (1980), 'Islam in Iran: Turmoil, Transformation or Transcendence?' *World Development*, vol. 8, pp. 555–61.

Nehru J. (1946), *The Discovery of India*, London: Meridian.

——— (1936), *An Autobiography*, London: Bodley Head.

Niraula, B. B. and Morgan, S. P. (1996), 'Marriage Formation, Post-Marital Contact with Natal Kin and Autonomy of Women: Evidence from Two Nepali Settings', *Population Studies*, vol. 50, no. 1, pp. 35–50.

Notestein, F. W. (1953), 'The Economics of Population and Food Supplies', in *Proceedings of the Eighth International Conference of Agricultural Economists*, London: Oxford University Press, pp. 13–31.

Obermeyer, C. M. (1992, 'Islam, Women and Politics: The Demography of Arab Countries', *Population and Development Review*, vol. 18, no. 1, pp. 33–60.

Office of the Registrar-General, Demography Division (1988), *Census of India 1981: Fertility in India. An Analysis of 1981 Census Data*, V. S. Verma, Series 1, India: Occasional Paper 13 of 1988, Delhi: Controller of Publications.

——— (1991), *Census of India 1991: Provisional Population Totals*, A. R. Nanda, Series 1, India, Paper 1 of 1991, New Delhi: Registrar General.

——— (1995), *Census of India 1991: Paper 1 on Religion*, New Delhi: Registrar General.

Office of the Registrar General and Census Commissioner, *Census of India 1991*, Part II-B, vol. I: Primary Census Abstract General Population, pp. V for Tbl 3.27.

Ogilvie, S. C. (1997), *State Corporatism and Proto-Industry: The Württemberg Black Forest 1580–1797*, Cambridge UK: Cambridge University Press.

Ogilvie, S. C. and Cerman, M., eds (1996), *European Proto-Industrialization*, Cambridge UK: Cambridge University Press.

Olsen, R. J. (1987), 'Cross-Sectional Methods for Estimating the Replacement of Infant Deaths', in T. P. Schultz, ed. *Research in Population Economics*, vol. 6, A Research Annual Greenwich, Connecticut and London: JAI Press, 1988; pp. 111–36.

Omondi-Odhiambo, M. (1997), 'Men's Participation in Family Planning Decisions in Kenya', *Population Studies*, pp. 29–40.

Omran, A. (1980), *Population in the Arab World: Problems and Prospects*, London: Croom Helm.

Oppong, C. (1983),'Women's Roles, Opportunity Costs, and Fertility', in R. A. Bulatao and R. D. Lee, eds *Determinants of Fertility in Developing Countries*, New York: Academic Press, pp. 547–89.

Ostersehlt, D. and Dankerhopfe, H. (1991), 'Changes in Age at Menarche in Germany: Evidence for a Continuing Decline', *American Journal of Human Biology*, vol. 3, no. 6, pp. 647–54.

Pandey, G. (1990), *The Construction of Communalism in Colonial North India*, Delhi: Oxford University Press.

_____ (1991), 'In Defence of the Fragment: Writing about Hindu–Muslim Riots in India Today', *Economic and Political Weekly*, vol. XXVI, nos. 11 and 12, Annual Number, pp. 559–72.

Parker Mauldin, W. (1993) 'Population Programs and Fertility Regulation', in R. A. Bulatao and R. D. Lee, eds *Determinants of Fertility in Developing Countries*, vol. 2, New York: Academic Press, pp. 267–94.

Philip Morgan, S. and Niraula, B. B. (1995), 'Gender Inequality and Fertility in Two Nepali Villages', *Population and Development Review*, vol. 21:, no. 3, pp. 541–61.

Preston, S. H. and Mari Bhat, P. N. (1984), 'New Evidence on Fertility and Mortality Trends in India', *Population and Development Review*, vol. 10, no. 3, pp. 481–503.

Pritchett, L. H. (1994), 'Desired Fertility and the Impact of Population Policies', *Population and Development Review*, vol. 20, no. 1, pp. 1–55.

Puri, B. (1993), 'Indian Muslims Since Partition', *Economic and Political Weekly*, vol. XXVIII, no. 40, 2 October, pp. 2141–9.

Qureshi, S. (1980), 'Islam and Development: The Zia Regime in Pakistan', *World Development*, vol. 8, no. 7/8, pp. 563–75.

Radhakrishnan, S. (1927), *The Hindu View of Life*, London: George Allen and Unwin.

_____ (1939), *Eastern Religions and Western Thought*, Oxford: Clarendon Press.

_____ (1947), *Religion and Society*, London: George Allen and Unwin.

Ragab, I. A. (1980), 'Islam and Development', *World Development*, vol. 8, no. 7/8, pp. 513–21.

Ramaswamy, T. N. (1962), *Kautilya's Arthasastra: Essentials of Indian Statecraft*, London: Asia Publishing House.

Rao, P. S. S. and Inbaraj, S. G. (1977), 'Inbreeding in Tamil Nadu, South India', *Social Biology*, vol. 24, pp. 281–8.

Rao, P. S. S., Inbaraj, S. G. and Jesudian, G. (1972), 'Rural–Urban Differentials in Consanguinity', *Journal of Medical Genetics*, vol. 9, pp. 174–8.

Rao, V. (1993), 'The Rising Price of Husbands: A Hedonic Analysis of Dowry Increases in Rural India', *Journal of Political Economy*, vol. 101, no. 4, pp. 666–77.

Retherford, R. D. and Ramesh, B. M. (1996), 'Fertility and Contraceptive Use in Tamil Nadu, Andhra Pradesh and Uttar Pradesh', *National Family Health Survey Bulletin*, vol. 4, no. 3, ISSN 1083–8678.

Riccio, J. A. (1979), 'Religious Affiliation and Socioeconomic Achievement', in R. Wuthnow, ed. *The Religious Dimension: New Directions in Quantitative Research*, New York: Academic Press, pp. 199–228.

Rodrigues, M. (1986), 'Bhiwandi: Will the Peace Hold?' *Economic and Political Weekly*, vol. XXI, no. 24, 14 June, pp. 1049–50.

Rosenzweig, M. R. and Schultz, T. P. (1985), 'The Demand for and Supply of Births: Fertility and its Life Cycle Consequences', *American Economic Review*, vol. 75, no. 5, pp. 992–1015.

_____ (1982), 'Market Opportunities, Genetic Endowments, and Intrafamily

Resource Distribution: Child Survival in Rural India', *American Economic Review*, vol. 72, no. 4, pp. 803–15.

——— (1989), 'Schooling, Information and Nonmarket Productivity: Contraceptive Use and its Effectiveness', *International Economic Review*, vol. 30: no. 2, pp. 457–77.

Rosenzweig, M. R. and Stark, O. (1989), 'Consumption Smoothing, Migration and Marriage: Evidence from Rural India', *Journal of Political Economy*, vol. 97, no. 4, pp. 905–26.

Sander, W. (1995), *The Catholic Family*, Boulder: Westview Press.

Sarkar, T. (1981), 'Communal Riots in Bengal', in M. Hasan, ed. *Communal and Pan-Islamic Trends in Colonial India*, Delhi: Manohar, pp. 284–301.

Sarkar, S. (1999), 'Coversion and Politics of the Hindu Right', *Economic and Political Weekly*, vol. XXXIV, no. 26, 26 June, pp. 1691–700.

Sathar, Z. A. and Casterline, J. B. (1998), 'The Onset of Fertility Transition in Pakistan', *Policy Research Division Working Paper*, no. 112, New York: Population Council.

Sen, A. K. (1976), 'Poverty: An Ordinal Approach to Measurement', *Econometrica*, vol. 44, no. 2, pp. 219–31.

——— (1994), 'Population: Delusion and Reality', *The New York Review of Books*, vol. XLI, no. 15, 22 September, pp. 62–9.

Schuler, S. R., Hashemi, S. M. and Riley, A. P. (1997), 'The Influence of Women's Changing Roles and Status in Bangladesh's Fertility Transition: Evidence from a Study of Credit Programmes and Contraceptive Use', *World Development*, vol. 25, no. 4, pp. 563–75.

Schull, W. J., Yanase, T. and Nemoto, H. (1966), 'Kuroshima: The Impact of Religion on an Island's Genetic Heritage', *Human Biology*, vol. 34, no. 4, pp. 271–98.

Schultz, T. P. (1982), 'Family Composition and Income Inequality', *Population and Development Review, Supplement*, pp. 137–50.

——— (1990), 'Testing the Neo-Classical Model of Family Labour Supply and Fertility', *Journal of Human Resources*, vol. 25, no. 4, pp. 599–634.

Scrimshaw, S. C. M. (1978), 'Infant Mortality and Behaviour in the Regulation of Family Size', *Population and Development Review*, vol. 4, no. 3, pp. 383–403.

Shamasastry, R. (1951), Translation into English of Kautilya's *Arthasastra*, Mysore: Sri Raghuveer Printing Press.

Shapiro, D. (1996), 'Fertility Decline in Kinshasa', *Population Studies*, vol. 50, no. 1, pp. 89–103.

Shapiro, D. and Tambashe, O. (1997), 'Education, Employment and Fertility in Kinshasa and Prospects for Changes in Reproductive Behaviour', *Population Research and Policy Review*, Penn State Department of Economics Working Paper, Pennsylvania State University, vol. 16, no. 3, pp. 259–87.

Shariff, A. (1993), *Some Socio-Economic and Demographic Aspects of Population According to Religion in India*, mimeo Mumbai: Centre for the Study of Society and Secularism.

——— (1999), *India Human Development Report: A Profile of Indian States in the 1990s*, Oxford: Oxford University Press.

Singer, M. (1966), 'Religion and Social Change in India: The Max Weber Thesis, Phase Three', *Economic Development and Cultural Change*, pp. 497–505.

Singh, M. (1992), 'Changes in Age at Marriage of Women in Rural North India', *Journal of Biosocial Science*, vol. 24: no. 1, pp. 123–30.

Singh, S., Casterline, B. and Cleland, J. G. (1985), 'The Proximate Determinants of Fertility: Sub-National Variations', *Population Studies*, vol. 39: no. 1, pp. 113–35.

Sopher, D. E., ed. (1980), *An Exploration of India: Geographic Perspectives on Society and Culture*, London: Longman chapter 10, pp. 289–327.

Srinivas, M. N. (1965), 'The Cult of the *Okka*', in *Religion and Society Among the Coorgs of South India*, Oxford: Oxford University Press.

—— (1989), 'Culture and Human Fertility in India', in *The Cohesive Role of Sanskritisation and Other Essays*, Oxford: Oxford University Press, pp. 123–44.

—— (1976), *The Remembered Village*, Berkeley: University of California Press.

—— (1994), *The Dominant Caste and Other Essays*, revised and enlarged edition, Oxford: Oxford University Press.

Srinivasan, K. (1995), 'Recent Fertility Trends and Prospects in India', *Current Science*, vol. 69, no. 7, 10 October, pp. 577–86.

—— (1998), *Basic Demographic Techniques and Applications*, Delhi: Sage Publications.

Srinivasan, K. and Jejeebhoy, S. (1981), in *Dynamics of Population and Family Welfare*, K. Srinivasan and S. Mukherji, eds Chennai: Popular Prakashan, pp. 91–117.

Standing, G. (1983), 'Women's Work Activity and Fertility', in R. A. Bulatao and R. D. Lee, eds *Determinants of Fertility in Developing Countries*, New York: Academic Press, pp. 517–46.

Stark, O. (1981), 'The Asset Demand for Children During Agricultural Modernisation', *Population and Development Review*, vol. 7, no. 4, pp. 671–75.

Steele, F., Amin, S. and Naved, R. T. (1998), 'The Impact of an Integrated Micro-Credit Program on Women's Empowerment and Fertility Behaviour in Rural Bangladesh', *Policy Research Division Working Paper*, no. 115, New York: Population Council.

Stigler, G. J. (1993), 'Economic Competition and Political Competition', in C. K. Rowley, ed. *Public Choice Theory*, Aldershot: Elgar, pp. 258–73.

Stinner, W. F. and Mader, P. D. (1975), 'Government Policy and Personal Family Planning Approval in Conflict Settings: The Case of the Muslim Minority in Southern Philippines', *Population Studies*, vol. 29, no. 1, pp. 53–9.

Subbamma, M. (1988), *Islam and Women*, translated by M. V. Ramamurthy, New Delhi: Stirling Publishers.

Summers, L. H. (1994), 'Investing in All the People', EDI Seminar Paper, no. 45, Washington, D. C.: World Bank.

Suryanarayana Murthy, C. (2000), *Sri Lalita Sahasranama with Introduction and Commentary*, Mumbai: Bharatiya Vidya Bhavan Publications.

Taft Morris, C. and Adelman, I. (1980), 'The Religious Factor in Economic Development', *World Development*, vol. 8, no. 7/8, pp. 491–501.

Tambiah, S. J. (1973), 'Dowry and Bridewealth, and the Property Rights of Women in South Asia', in J. Goody and S. J. Tambiah, eds *Bridewealth and Dowry*, Cambridge UK: Cambridge University Press, pp. 100–10.

Tanner, M. J. (1973), 'Trend toward Earlier Menarche in London, Oslo, Copenhagen, the Netherlands and Hungary', *Nature*, vol. 243, pp. 95–6.

Tey N. P., Tan, P. C., Ng, S. T., Kuppusamy, S. and Wan Sabri, W. H. (1995), 'Contraceptive Choices in the Rural Areas of Peninsular Malaysia: Determinants and Change', mimeo, University of Malaya.

Thapa, M. (1993), 'Women's Concerns in Relation to Contraceptive Methods Currently Used in the SAARC Region', Resource Paper No. WG III/2, SAARC Ministerial Conference on Women and Family Health, 21–3 November, Kathmandu, Nepal.

Thimmaiah, G. (1977), 'Inequality of Income and Poverty in Karnataka (A Socioeconomic Profile)', *The Indian Economic Journal*, vol. 25: no. 2, pp. 119–29.

Thomas, N. (1993), 'Economic Security, Culture and Fertility: A Reply to Cleland', *Population Studies*, vol. 47, no. 2, pp. 353–9.

Thorner, D., Kerblay, B. and Smith, R. E. F., ed. (1986), *A. V. Chayanov on the Theory of Peasant Economy*, Manchester: Manchester University Press.

Thornton, A. (1979), 'Religion and Fertility: The Case of Mormonism', *Journal of Marriage and the Family*, vol. 41, no. 1, pp. 131–42.

UN (1961), *Mysore Population Study*, UN Department of Social and Economic Affairs, New York.

Uppal, J. S. (1986), 'Hinduism and Economic Development in South Asia', *International Journal of Social Economics*, vol. 13, no. 3, pp. 20–30.

Van de Kaa, D. J. (1996), 'Anchored Narratives: The Story and Findings of Half a Century of Research Into the Determinants of Fertility', *Population Studies*, vol. 50, no. 3, pp. 389–432.

Van Heek, F. (1966), 'Roman Catholicism and Fertility in the Netherlands: Demographic Aspects of Minority Status', *Population Studies*, vol. 20, pp. 125–38.

Vanaik, A. (1991), 'Examining the Ayodhya Conflict', *Economic and Political Weekly*, vol. XXVI, no. 17, 27 April, pp. 1099–101.

Vedantam, V. (1999), 'Privilege and Resentment: Religious Conflict in India', in *Christian Century*, 14 April, the Christian Century Foundation.

Visaria, L., Jijeebhoy, S. and Merick, T. (1999), 'From Family Planning to Reproductive Health: Challenges Facing India', *International Family Planning Respectives*, vol. 25, Issue Supplement (January), S44–S49.

Visaria, P. and Chari, V. (1998), 'India's Population Policy and Family Planning Program: Yesterday, Today and Tomorrow', in A. Jain, ed. *Do Population Policies Matter? Fertility and Politics in Egypt, India, Kenya and Mexico*, New York: Population Council, pp. 53–112.

Visaria, P., Visaria, L. and Jain, A. (1995), *Contraceptive Use and Fertility in India: A Case Study of Gujarat*, New Delhi: Sage Publications.

Vlassoff, C. (1992), 'Progress and Stagnation: Changes in Fertility and Women's Position in an Indian Village', *Population Studies*, vol. 46, no. 2, pp. 195–212.

Vlassoff, M. (1979), 'Labour Demand and Economic Utility of Children: A Case Study in Rural India', *Population Studies*, vol. 33: no. 3, pp. 487–99.

—— (1982), 'Economic Utility of Children and Fertility in Rural India', *Population Studies*, vol. 36: no. 1, pp. 45–59.

Vlassoff, M. and Vlassoff, C. (1980), 'Old-Age Security and the Utility of Children in Rural India', *Population Studies*, vol. 34, no. 3, pp. 487–99.

Weber, M. (1992), *The Protestant Ethic and the Spirit of Capitalism*, translated by T. Parsons, introduced by A. Giddens, London: Unwin.

—— (1979), 'The Blending of Catholic Reproductive Behaviour', in R. Wuthnow, ed. *The Religious Dimension: New Directions in Quantitative Research*, New York: Academic Press, pp. 231–40.

Westoff, C. F. (1988), 'Is the KAP-Gap Real?' *Population and Development Review*, vol. 14, no. 2, pp. 225–32.

Westoff, C. F. and Jones, E. F. (1979), 'The End of "Catholic Fertility"', *Demography*, vol. 16, no. 2, pp. 209–17.

Westoff, C. F. and Ryder, N. B. (1977a), *The Contraceptive Revolution*, Princeton: Princeton University Press.

—— (1977b), 'The Predictive Validity of Reproductive Intentions', *Demography*, vol. 14, no.4, pp. 431–53.

Wilber, C. K. and Jameson, K. P. (1980), 'Religious Values and Social Limits to Development', *World Development*, vol. 8, no. 7/8, pp. 467–79.

White, E. (1978), 'Legal Reforms as an Indicator of Women's Status in Muslim Nations', in L. Beck and N. Keddie, eds *Women in the Muslim World*, Cambridge Mass.: Harvard University Press, pp. 52–68.

World Bank (1991), *Social Indicators of Development*, Washington, D. C.: World Bank.

Wrigley, E. A. and Schofield, R. S. (1981), *The Population History of England 1541–1871: A Reconstruction*, Cambridge: Edward Arnold.

Wyon, J. B. and Gordon, J. E. (1971), *The Khanna Study: Population Problems in Rural Punjab*, Cambridge, Mass.: Harvard University Press.

Youssef, N. H. (1978), 'The Status and Fertility Patterns of Muslim Women', in L. Beck and N. Keddie, eds *Women in the Muslim World*, Cambridge Mass.: Harvard University Press, pp. 69–99.

Glossary

a.ˈngan	Central courtyard of a home (Hindi)
Anganwadi	Primary school level teaching by a woman trained for the purpose, in the courtyard of her home
aarti	Hindu act of worship which involves lighting an oil lamp or camphor flame (Sanskrit)
aasé	Love (Kannada)
aasrama	Four stages of life in Hindu philosophy (Sanskrit)
aasti	Bequest, usually of landed property (Kannada)
aatman	Infinite real self (Sanskrit)
Advaita Vedanta	Hindu philosophical text (Sanskrit)
agarbatti	Incense-stick (Hindi)
amma	mother (Kannada)
ardhanarisvara	Another name for the Hindu god Shiva, depicted in this form as half-man and half-woman (Sanskrit)
artha	Interest (Sanskrit)
Arthasastra	Hindu text which sets out the laws of government (Sanskrit)
beedi	Hand-rolled cigarette (Hindi and Tamil)
Bhagavad Gita	Hindu holy book (Sanskrit)
bhakti	Belief or faith (Sanskrit)
bindge	Pot of water, approximately equal to half a bucket (Kannada)
bindi	Red circular mark worn on forehead by Hindu women (Hindi)
Brahmanda Purana	Hindu philosophical text which describes the Kalpa and Manvantara age; geography, geneologies, and the Hindu goddess Lalita (Sanskrit)

brahmachari	Celibate (Sanskrit)
brahmin	Man of learning (Sanskrit)
chandrika	Circular trays with concentric partitions in which silkworms are reared (Kannada)
charkha	Hand-operated instrument for silk-reeling (Kannada)
coolie	Unskilled worker (Kannada)
dargha	Burial sites of saints or seers (Urdu)
dharma	Ethical living or the 'path of righteousness' (Sanskrit)
Dharma sastra	Hindu philosophical text (Sanskrit)
fatwa	Religious injunctions (Arabic)
fiqh	Jurisprudence (Arabic)
gadi	Vehicle or cart (Kannada and Hindi)
grihastha	Householder (Sanskrit)
grihasthaasrama	Stage of the householder in the fourfold division of life in Hindu philosophy (Sanskrit)
guna	Finite or empirical body (Sanskrit)
hobli	Sub-division of a taluk, consisting of 20–30 villages (Kannada)
hottu	Sawdust and coconut husks used for fuel (Kannada)
idda	Period of waiting before divorce under Islamic law (Arabic)
ijtihad	Interpretations of the Koran, which provide rules for novel situations (Arabic)
jati	Sub-caste (Sanskrit)
jumka	Long gold earrings, usually worn by brides (Hindi and Kannada)
kama	Desire and enjoyment (Sanskrit)
karma	Actions in present and past births (Sanskrit)
keerti	Prestige (Sanskrit)
kohl	Black cream used for eye make-up (Hindi)
Koran (or Quran)	Holy book of Islam (Arabic)
kshatriya	Man of power (Sanskrit)
kumari bharya	A woman who is pregnant but not legally married (Sanskrit)
lokasamgraha	To discover the world's potential for virtue and to derive happiness therefrom (Sanskrit)
lakh	A hundred thousand (Hindi)
madrasa	School for religious teaching (Urdu)
Mahabharata	Hindu epic poem about the 'great war' between two sets of

cousins, the Pandavas and the Kauravas of Hastinapura (Sanskrit)

mahr	Dower paid to the bride under the Islamic marriage contract (Arabic)
mana	Unit of measurement for firewood (Kannada)
mandi	Market or group of stalls/shops (Hindi and Kannada)
maulana	Man learned in religious scriptures (Arabic and Urdu)
moksha	Salvation or spiritual freedom (Sanskrit)
mufti	Jurist (Arabic)
mullah	Man learned in religious scriptures (Arabic and Urdu)
nallah	Small drain for flowing water (Hindi)
Nitimanjari	Hindu philosophical text (Sanskrit)
panchayat	Village council of five members (Hindi)
panchayati-raj	Local self-government institutions (Hindi) Rule of governance of the panchayat (Hindi)
puja	Hindu ritual for religious worship (Sanskrit)
pundit	Hindu learned man (Sanskrit)
purdah	Seclusion and observing the veil in public (Arabic and Urdu)
purusartha	Fourfold objects of life in Hindu philosophy (Sanskrit)
qazi	Judge (Arabic)
ragi	Green finger millet, a coarse grain grown in southern Karnataka (Kannada)
rath yatra	Chariot procession (Hindi)
Ramayana	Hindu epic poem about the life of the Hindu king Rama of Ayodhya, believed to be a reincarnation of the Hindu god Vishnu (Sanskrit)
Rg Veda	The first and oldest of the four Vedas or Hindu holy books (Sanskrit)
rishi	Sage or learned man (Sanskrit)
sadaq	Dower paid to the bride's guardian under the Islamic marriage contract (Arabic)
sahadharmini	Concept in Indian philosophy which views the woman's earthly role as mainly to be a helpmate to her husband in his pursuit of the 'path of truth and righteousness' (Sanskrit)
Sarvodaya	Religious movement in Sri Lanka
saññyasin	Free suprasocial man (Sanskrit)
Sharia	Islamic law (Arabic)

shilanyas	Foundation-laying ceremony (Sanskrit)
sloka	Couplet or verse (Sanskrit)
sraddha	Hindu rituals performed to honour deceased ancestors (Sanskrit)
sudra	Man of service (Sanskrit)
Sunna	Prophet Mohammad's interpretations of the Koran and its application to various situations (Arabic)
talaq	Divorce (Arabic)
talaq-al-bida	The 'divorce of innovation' under the Islamic marriage contract (Arabic)
taluk	Revenue sub-division, consisting of 100–300 villages (Kannada and Hindi)
tapahpradhanya	Self-control or self-denial (Sanskrit)
ulema	Learned men (Arabic and Urdu)
Upanishads	Hindu religious scriptures (Sanskrit)
vaisya	Man of skilled productivity (Sanskrit)
vanaprastha	Forest recluse (Sanskrit)
vargeeti	A woman's husband's brother's wife (Kannada)
varna	Fourfold organization of society in Hindu philosophy (Sanskrit)
Vedas	Hindu religious scriptures (Sanskrit)
vidya	Learning (Sanskrit)
vriddhashram	Old-age home (Kannada and Hindi)
yajñapradhanya	Worldly pursuits (Sanskrit)

Index

Dattak putri yojana 25
daughters-in-law 142, 183, 209
demand for children 129, 131–2, 134,
    175, 190
demand-side determinants of contra-
    ception 131
demography and demographers 191,
    204
demographic
    accident 183, 202, 208
    indices by religion 46–51
    phenomena, misrepresentations of
    168
dependent variables
    average values 87, 89
    characteristics 87–90
    distribution of age at marriage 87–
    8
    distribution of children-ever-born
    89–90
    standard deviations 87, 89
desired family size 71, 151, 153–6
desired fertility 131, 151–2
development policy 127, 221, 229; see
    also population policy and
    education policy
dialects 28, 222
diffusion 131
    effects 165, 167, 191
discrimination
    against the girl child 149, 183
    hypothesis 31, 216
discriminating interventionism 17
divorce
    and costs 97
    and Hinduism 38–9
    and Islam 33–4
doctors' views 144
domestic industry 102, 123, 133, 162,
    175, 195, 202, 205–06
domestic violence 72
doorstep delivery of contraceptives
    145, 218
dower (or dowry)
    and age at marriage 96–7, 110–11,
    217

and consanguinity 105, 122
    in Islam 33
Dravidian culture 177 n

Easterlin 131
ecological effects 9
education
    and age at marriage 93–5, 117, 122,
    123–4, 126, 128
    and contraception 132–3, 138,
    157, 159–60, 161, 164, 168
    and fertility 172–3, 19–2, 194–5,
    199–202, 206–7, 211–2, 215,
    222–3, 229
    of the husband 111, 122, 156, 194,
    207–8
    infrastructure 64, 167
    by religion 76–7, 206
    and school attendance 192
    policy 206, 220–1, 223
    primary, secondary, and university
    level 94–5, 117
    structural context of 206
    of women 111–2, 123–4, 156, 194
educational background of respondents
    71, 76–7, 95; see also literacy
electricity 63–4, 192
employment for women 95–6, 97, 168,
    173–4
empowerment, female 206
environmental degradation 177
ethnic differences and marriage 100–1
Europe
    economic development and fertility
    191
    family limitation 191
    and menarche 102
    pre-industrial 96, 106–07, 122,
    183–4
    historical fertility declines 191
expenditure 71
    composition of 85
    and contraception 133–4
    and fertility 205
    and marriage 98–9, 111–2, 118, 121,
    124–5

QUESTIONNAIRE

Date and time of interview: Respondent number:
Language the interview was conducted in: Kannada/Hindi/Tamil/Telugu/English

I. Census information

1. Name:
2. Town/village: Village A/B/C/D/E/Ramanagaram town
3. Caste and *jati*:
4. Age:
5. Religion: Hindu/Muslim/Christian/Other
6. What is your primary language of communication?
   Kannada/Hindi/Urdu/Tamil/Telugu/English/Other
7. Can you read and/or write your primary language of communication?   Y/N
8. Can you read and/or write any other language(s)?   Y/N
9. If yes, which language(s): Kannada/Hindi/Urdu/Tamil/Telugu/English/ Other
10. Years of education: Primary/Secondary/University
11. Occupation: Primary/Secondary/Any other
12. Marital status: Single/Widowed/Divorced/Deserted (Married, spouse absent)/Married/
    Remarried
13. How old were you at menarche?
14. How old were you when you first married?
15. How old were you when you married the man you are currently married to?
16. How old were you when you started living with your first husband?
17. How old were you when you started living with your current husband?
18. Details of husband:
    Age; Years of education (Primary/Secondary/University); Occupation (Primary/Secondary/
    any other)
19. Before you got married, was your husband related to you in any way? Y/N
20. If yes, what type of relationship was it?
    First cousin on father's side/First cousin on mother's side/Second cousin on mother's side/
    Second cousin on fathers' side/Maternal uncle/Brother-in-law/Other blood relation/Other
    non-blood relation
21. How many children do you have?
22. How old were you at the birth of your first child?
23. Details of children:
    Name; Sex; Age; Schooling; Years of education; residence
24. Details of other resident members of the household:
    Name; Sex; Age, Relationship to household head; Years of education; Occupations
25. How much land does your family/husband have?
26. Is it self-owned or leased-in? self-owned/leased-in/other
27. Average monthly consumer expenditure:
    Rent; Foodgrains; Fruits/vegetables; Meat/fish; Milk; Alcoholic beverages; Tobacco/betel;
    Cinema/entertainment; Food for children; Clothing for children; Education for children;
    Miscellaneous (eg. talcum powder, cream, kumkum etc.)
28. Do you own any of the following?
    Transistor or radio/Bicycle/Fan/Cot/Moped or scooter/Watch/Television/Chair or bench

II. Structure of/and decision-making within the family

29. Name five people with whom you have the closest contact.
30. Who decides who goes to school? Woman alone/Husband/Father-in-law/Parents/Parents-
    in-law/Male relative/Female relative/Joint family/Husband and wife together/Woman and
    other relatives/Other
31. Who decides who performs housework? Woman alone/Husband/Father-in-law/Parents/

Parents-in-law/Male relative/Female relative/Joint family/Husband and wife together/
Woman and other relatives/Other

32. Who decides who performs income-earning work? Woman alone/Husband/Father-in-law/
Parents/Parents-in-law/Male relative/Female relative/Joint family/Husband and wife
together/Woman and other relatives/Other

33. Who decides how to spend money? Woman alone/Husband/Father-in-law/Parents/Parents-
in-law/Male relative/Female relative/Joint family/Husband and wife together/Woman and
other relatives/Other

34. To what extent does 'custom' decide these matters? Custom is important/Custom is
unimportant/Do not know

35. Does your daughter help in the cooking?   Y/N

36. What age did your daughters get married?

37. What age will your unmarried daughters be married?

38. Would you/did you allow your daughters to continue schooling after
puberty?   Y/N

III. Economic value of children—benefits and costs

39. How many hours a day (approximately) do children spend doing tasks such as:
Grazing/Helping mother/Working in other employment (e.g. silk-reeling units)

40. What is your main source of water? Collected by hand in water pots either from the river
or public tap/Pipe/Tap/Other

41. If collected by hand, which family member(s) collects water? Woman/Husband/Sons/
Daughters/Sisters-in-law/Father-in-law/Mother-in-law/Brothers-in-law/Daughters-in-law/
Sons-in-law/Servants/Other

42. How many hours a day do you or any family member spend collecting water?

43. What is your main source of fuel? Firewood/Gas/Kerosene/Firewood delivered home/
Other

44. If firewood, which family member(s) collect the wood?
Woman/Husband/Son/Daughters/Sisters-in-law/Father-in-law/Mother-in-law/Brothers-
in-law/Daughters-in-law/Sons-in-law/Servants/Others

45. How many hours a day do you or any family member spend collecting firewood for fuel?

46. When you get old (above 60 years), who would you live with?
Son/Daughter/Husband/Alone/Old-age home/Other

47. What do you do about income if something unforeseen happens (e.g. someone
is ill)? The children leave school/Son or daughter in the city sends you more money/Use
savings/Borrow from neighbours/Pawn jewellery/Other

Direct and opportunity costs of children

48. Are boys more expensive than girls?   Y/N/Do not know

49. Why/why not?

50. If there is not enough food, do boys get: more/less/the same as girls?

51. If a girl is ill, would you spend: more/same/less/on medical expenses as compared to a boy?

52. Do you ever save aside money for your daughters?

53. Have you saved gold/jewellery for her?

54. Who looks after the children in the home when you are not here?
Husband/Mother/Father/Mother-in-law/Sister/Brother/Father-in-law/Sister-in-law/
Daughter-in-law/Brother-in-law/Other relation/Friend(s)/Neighbour/Servant/No one—they
stay on their own

IV. Reproduction, contraception and health-care
Fertility

55. Do you wish to have another child? Yes/No/Not sure/Do not know

56. If yes, would you prefer a boy or a girl? Boy/Girl/Either/Do not know

57. Why?

58. Is the birth of a boy better news/worse news/same as the birth of a girl?
59. Does your husband want another child? Yes/No/Not sure/Do not know
60. Have your children been planned?   Y/N
61. Do you have a desired number of children?   Y/N
62. If yes, what is it?
63. Would you have wanted less children? Yes/No/Not sure/Do not know
64. Why?
65. Do you think large families are better than small ones? Yes/No/Not sure/Do not know
66. Did you breastfeed your children?   Y/N

Contraception and health

67. Do you talk about contraception with your husband? Yes/No/Never/Other comment
68. Have you ever used any birth control techniques? Pills (mala d.)/Intra-uterine device (copper-t)/Condom (nirodh)/Sterilization operation/Any other method/Never used any method
69. Between you and your husband, who makes the decisions about birth control? Wife/Husband/Husband and wife together/Not applicable
70. Apart from your spouse, which female family member would you discuss family planning with? Mother/Sister/Sister-in-law/Mother-in-law/Friend/Neighbour/Other
71. How often do you see your family planning officer or go to the health centre/hospital? Often/Not often/Only in illness/Not at all
72. How easy is it for you to get access to contraception? Easy/Not easy/From the nurse who visits the locality
73. What are the sleeping arrangements for couples/ architecture of the house?
74. Does your religion permit contraception/abortion? Yes/No/Do not know/Not sure/Other comment
75. Do you have any personal views about the position of your religion on contraception/abortion? Yes/No/Do not know/Not sure/Other comment
76. What do you feel about the growth of population in your town/village? Too fast/about right/Too slow/Do not know/Not sure/Other comment

V. Religion and women's status

Religion

Please rate on a scale of 1 to 5: 1. Not at all   2. Not very much   3. Medium   4. Quite a bit   5. Very much

77. How faithfully do you practice your religion?
78. How much does it matter to you what the local priests think of you?
79. Would you ask advice from your priest about aspects of your life?
80. How often do you go to the temple/mosque/church?
81. Do you interact with neighbours who do not belong to your religion?
82. Are your children religious too and do they go to the temple/mosque/church/worship at home?
83. Do they practise religion to your satisfaction?

Women's status

84. Do you feel that women's views are represented through the municipality? Yes/No/Do not know/Other comment
85. Is this important to you? Yes/No/Do not know/Other comment
86. Over the past five years, what do you feel about:
  a. Your own economic position: Better/Same/Worse
  b. Relations between different religious groups in the village/town: Better/Same/Worse
  c. Level of violence between men: Better/Same/Worse
  d. Level of violence between men and women: Better/Same/Worse
  e. Position of women in your village/ town: Better/Same/Worse